H. W. Tilman

ADVENTURES UNDER SAIL

Selected writings of H. W. Tilman

Edited and with an Introduction

by

LIBBY PURVES

LONDON

VICTOR GOLLANCZ LTD

1982

Introduction, commentary and compilation © Libby Purves 1982

Extracts from H. W. Tilman's books:
Mischief in Patagonia © H. W. Tilman 1957
Mischief Among the Penguins © H. W. Tilman 1961
Mischief in Greenland © H. W. Tilman 1964
Mostly Mischief © H. W. Tilman 1966
Mischief Goes South © H. W. Tilman 1968
In Mischief's Wake © H. W. Tilman 1971
Ice With Everything © H. W. Tilman 1974
Triumph and Tribulation © H. W. Tilman 1977

British Library Cataloguing in Publication Data

Tilman, H. W.
    Adventures under sail.
    1. Voyages and travels—1951-
    2. Sailboats
    I. Title   II. Purves, Libby
    910.4'5   G540

ISBN 0-575-03159-X

Photoset in Great Britain by
Rowland Phototypesetting Ltd, Bury St Edmunds, Suffolk
and printed by St Edmundsbury Press,
Bury St Edmunds, Suffolk

I cannot rest from travel: I will drink
Life to the lees. . .
                            Come, my friends,
'Tis not too late to seek a newer world.
Push off, and sitting well in order smite
The sounding furrows; for my purpose holds
To sail beyond the sunset, and the baths
Of all the western stars, until I die. . .

                        Tennyson, *Ulysses*

Acknowledgements

The idea for this book was first proposed by Jeremy Burnett, proprietor of West Country Chandlers, Falmouth. H. W. Tilman's niece, Pam Davis, and her husband, Derek, provided invaluable help, as did Michael Richey of the Royal Institute of Navigation. Original editions of Tilman's work were generously lent by Pam and Derek Davis, Michael Richey and the Alpine Club library.

All the photographs come from H. W. Tilman's personal collection in his home at Bod Owen and, except for that used for the frontispiece and two others, there is no indication of the individual photographers. They are reproduced by kind permission of Pam Davis, and, in two cases, W. G. Lee. Valuable help in cataloguing and selecting these photographs has been given by John Mead of HTV Cardiff and Fuzzy Toyne.

Contents

List of Illustrations

Frontispiece H. W. Tilman

MAPS

DIAGRAM

Introduction

WHEN A MOUNTAINEER reaches his mid-fifties, and begins to find his ceiling at 20,000 feet, it seems inevitable that he should modify his ambitions and turn to less rigorous pursuits. Harold William Tilman found another solution: he took to the sea, and sailed a series of boats almost as old as himself, in search of the unclimbed peaks and glaciers at the uttermost edges of the world. They might be lower than those he had mastered in his Everest days, but the adventure and the difficulty of getting to them under sail more than made up the balance. Over the next quarter of a century, the last third of his life, he sailed over 140,000 miles to Arctic and Antarctic waters; when he was finally lost at sea, close to his eightieth birthday, he left us eight volumes about those travels. They are some of the freshest, sparest, most inspiring sailing literature in the language. From these books—out of print now, rare and hard to find—the present one is a selection.

To know Tilman the man and the mountaineer, one may read J. R. L. Anderson's comprehensive biography *High Mountains and Cold Seas*. To summarize, though, a remarkably active career: born in 1898, he fought in both wars—in his eighteenth year he was a subaltern on the Western Front, and in his forty-sixth was parachuted behind enemy lines to fight with the Albanian partisans. He was, with his companion Eric Shipton, one of the most famous climbers of the years between the wars: when they climbed Nanda Devi in the Himalaya in 1936, with minimal equipment, it was the highest peak then achieved by man. Tilman the traveller crossed Africa alone by bicycle, largely on a diet of bananas, and traced Marco Polo's footsteps across Central Asia. Yet when in 1954, at the age of fifty-six, he bought the Bristol Channel Pilot Cutter *Mischief* and fitted her out for his first expedition to cross the Patagonian ice-cap, it was the beginning of the most remarkable, and most controversial, phase of Tilman's life.

In the sea he had found something new; writing of the similarities of sailing and climbing, he pinpointed the difference:

> The sea's most powerful spell is romance; that romance which, in the course of time, has gathered around the ships and men who from the beginning have sailed upon it—the strange coasts and their discoveries, the storms and the hardships, the fighting and trading, and all the strange things which have happened and still do happen to those who venture upon it. With the mountains there is no romance. Man's association with them is relatively recent and perhaps artificial. With the sea it is as old as himself, natural and inescapable.

Bristol Channel Pilot Cutters are a fine example of a past generation of working sail: heavy, seaworthy boats, designed to race for the custom of arriving ships, to accommodate the pilots comfortably below decks, and yet be handled on the homeward journey by a man and a boy. You may see a few still, preserved by traditionally-minded yachtsmen around the coast. They are not, however, boats that the modern mind would associate readily with voyages to the icebound fjords of Greenland, or the freezing channels of the Magellan Strait. Yet Tilman chose *Mischief*, built in 1906, as a boat he could understand and could afford, and he cherished her old timbers through ten voyages and 114,000 miles. When she was lost, he replaced her with the nearest he could find: pilot cutters *Sea Breeze* and *Baroque*, which took him on his last eight Arctic voyages.

To man these boats he needed crew. These he would find through chance, through hearsay, and through curtly worded advertisements in *The Times*: *Hands wanted for long voyage in small boat; no pay, no prospects, not much pleasure* or *Cook for a cold voyage; five mouths to feed for two months*. Some of his crews

adapted to his austere notions of voyaging, attuned themselves
to his wry sense of humour, and shared his insatiable curiosity
and wonder at strange coasts; others hated every minute, and
have contributed to an unfortunate Tilman legend which still
survives, and will reappear in half-informed rags and tatters
until a new generation has read his writings and considered
the extraordinary scale of his achievements under sail. It is the
legend of the desperate old man in "terrible, unseaworthy"
boats, the "chap who kept wrecking Pilot Cutters in the ice".
A reputable yachting magazine lately saw fit to repeat the
rumour—which a glance at the record of the books would
disprove—that only one of his crews ever sailed with him
more than once, and that despite his professed scorn for
life-saving apparatus, he was "only too glad to leap into a
liferaft". It would be unkind to suggest that many of those
who joined in the sneering chorus about Tilman's voyages are
yachtsmen who themselves make a tremendous drama out of a
crossing from Brighton to Deauville in a middling swell; but it
is certainly worth countering these tales for the benefit of any
who have picked up this book in the hope of laughing at,
rather than with, Tilman.

In fact, several crews sailed with him more than once, and
others, unable to afford the time, came back to help with
fitting-out. Charles Marriott, a contemporary, put up with
many ailments and aches of middle-age aboard *Mischief*, and
came back twice for more; of his young crews, Simon
Richardson regarded the old man so highly that he invited him
on his own Antarctic expedition—tragically lost; just as earlier, Warwick Deacock asked him to skipper the schooner
Panatela to Heard Island in the Southern Ocean.

Some young crews, it is true, speak harshly of him as he did
of them—there is no lack, in the pages which follow, of
examples of tension aboard ship—but out of eighteen
voyages, only three seem to have been lastingly unhappy, and
it is perhaps salutary to remember that at these young men's
age, and younger, Tilman himself had been in the trenches of
the Western Front, watching his contemporaries die. Later
experience in the high Himalaya, at Dunkirk and Alamein, did
not teach him to expect or court luxury; the voyages of

Mischief and *Sea Breeze* were to him pure pleasure and adventure, and he met complaints about damp bunks, cold curry for breakfast or awkward winches only with impatience. He was not running a yachtsmen's course or a Youth Adventure programme; he was exploring.

As to the seaworthiness of the boats and the seamanship of the skipper, I think the record must speak. It was only after 114,000 safe sea-miles that *Mischief* was lost, under tow in an attempt at salvage. *Sea Breeze* struck a rock; the whole crew were saved and brought home. *Baroque* is afloat and sailing to this day. In twenty-four years only one crewman was lost, in the kind of freak calm-weather accident at night which could, and does, happen on the most modern of yachts; the breakages his boats suffered were no greater, considering their record of distance covered, than one might reasonably expect. He thought nothing, in any case, of sailing 600 miles home with a broken boom and the mainsail set loose-footed.

But this is a digression, forced on the editor by a careless calumny on a private hero's name. This selection of Tilman's writing about sail is, above all, a book about pleasure. Hard-won, dangerous, austere pleasure at times; but nonetheless, pure and pristine self-indulgence by a man who loved strange waters and frozen coastlines, and rejoiced in the traditions of the sea. As he put it:

> Quite apart from the pleasures of sailing a boat, the sight and sound of the sea, the adventure of achieving some distant port aided only by the wind and one's own energy and skill, there are the unspiritual attractions of a life of comfort and security in a pleasant open-air prison, with a minimum of shaving and washing, and without the trouble of undressing at night.

In making this selection, I have had to leave out much; I have not been able, perhaps, fairly to represent Tilman's faithful practice of acknowledging earlier travellers and climbers in the waters he frequented, nor his conscientious reproduction of the technical advice of the pilot books. I have regretfully curtailed much climbing detail, in the hopes that a full anthology of Tilman's mountaineering works may one day accompany this; I have tried to represent, or mention, each of his voyages in their chronological order. I have tried to represent the languorous pleasures of the long, warm, dolphin-haunted Trade Wind passages, the tension of tight pilotage in ice, the moments of danger and disaster, the delights of cooking treacle duff in a bucket and the bleak doubts of the nightwatches before a landfall. You will find Tilman's humour, some of his scholarship, and his inveterate habit of quotation, whether from Sir Francis Drake, obscure Arab proverbs, or Tallulah Bankhead ("there is less in this than meets the eye"). You will find much of the spirit of determined improvisation that inspired his most famous reply, when a young man asked him "Sir, how do I get on an expedition?"—Tilman said, "Put on your boots and go". You will find, in short, a man who even in his late seventies was always game to put on his boots, and go. A very private man, not fond of publicity or glory, who slipped quietly back into Lymington each time with less fuss than is now fashionable; who spoke little, but wrote like the proverbial angel. You will find, I hope, also, something of a tribute to Tilman's many young crews; those who worked like heroes to free the grounded *Baroque* in Spitzbergen, who helped the skipper to nurse *Mischief* through Atlantic gales; who leaped from *Sea Breeze*'s bowsprit to hack out ice bollards and moor her to giant wallowing bergs.

I cannot hope [wrote Tilman once] that anyone who reads of these voyages will partake of the pleasure of those who made them, or even of the pleasure that I have had in thus reliving them. Possibly the book may be dismissed as a picture of an elderly escapist in full flight. I do not think that label applies. . . . Each voyage had a purpose, frivolous though to many that purpose might seem. Rather than escaping from anything we were facing up to reality. As Belloc said "Everywhere the sea is a teacher of truth. I am not sure that the best thing I find in sailing is not this salt of reality. . . There, sailing the sea, we play every part of life; control, direction, effort, fate; and there can we test ourselves and know our state."

ADVENTURES UNDER SAIL

I

Introducing Mischief

In the Bristol Channel Pilot Cutter Mischief *Tilman sailed some 114,000 miles over fourteen years. She gave her name to two mountains—Mont du Mischief in the French Crozet Islands, and Mount Mischief on Baffin Island—and to a Cape, Cap Mischief on Kerguelen in the Southern Ocean. His subsequent boats were chosen for their family resemblance to* Mischief. *Here Tilman introduces his first, and best-loved boat:*

"DAMN DESCRIPTION", said Byron, "it is always disgusting." However that may be, many novelists devote more space to description than to action and the writers of crime stories usually invite us to study in detail the lay-out of the house or the library where the murder took place. On these grounds, though no one on board was murdered, I think a description of *Mischief*'s lay-out is permissible. Starting from forward below deck there is the forepeak with the chain-locker holding 45 fathoms of ⅝-inch chain on the port side and a rack for sails on the other. Stowed there also are a 60-lb. CQR anchor, a small kedge anchor, grapnel, navigation lamps, and lead-lines.

Aft of the forepeak bulkhead is the galley. It is unfortunate that the place upon which the well-being of the crew so largely depends is in the fore part of the boat where the motion is most felt and where the amount of ventilation that can be obtained depends upon the prevailing weather. The fore-hatch is the only source of ventilation and if the boat is on the wind this has to be kept closed. Air in moderation is all to the good but the man working in the galley naturally prefers it unmixed with salt water. Three gimballed Primus stoves and the sink are on the port side with a number of lockers underneath, and on the other side are more lockers and a large open bin in which the spare mainsail is generally stowed. Over this bin is a canvas pipe-cot. No one ever sleeps there and it is used for stowing sails which are passed down from the foredeck through the hatch. The movable ladder leading up to the hatch comes in handy as a chock for the cook's back when he is attending to

Bristol Channel Pilot Cutter: hull and rigging plan
(drawing by Roger Finch from *Sailing Craft of the British Isles*
Collins, 1976)

the stoves. On the bulkhead between the galley and the cabin is a hand wash-basin with a mirror above so that in the rare event of anyone wanting to shave or wash while at sea the facilities are there. Water for the galley is drawn from the main tank under the cabin table by means of a pump and there is also a pump for pumping dirty water out of the sink and the wash-basin. Thus, except that there is no way for the cook to draw the sea-water he requires but by a bucket over the side, the galley arrangements are almost on a par with the most modern kitchen. Sea-water is used whenever possible for cooking and always for washing-up. A pump for drawing it would mean yet another hole in the ship's side and such holes should be kept to a minimum.

There used to be a door in the bulkhead between galley and cabin but this has long since been abolished as an unnecessary nuisance. It might have served a purpose in shutting out smells but personally I think a good sniff of what is brewing in the galley is no bad thing, even if it is only a warning of things to come. And with no barrier between them the crew can partake of the feelings of the cook, hear him cursing vehemently if he and his pots are being thrown about, or singing cheerfully if things are going well. In the fore part of the cabin there are three bunks. Of the two on the port side, one above the other, the upper has the advantage of a deck-light which allows enough light for reading. Against that it is farther to fall if one is thrown out. The proprietors of the port-side bunks have around them ample stowage space for their gear, while the man in the starboard bunk has a part share in a narrow though elegant chest of drawers standing against the bulkhead. All three occupants of these bunks are really in clover because this is the warm part of the cabin. Just abaft the foot of the mast is a small stove which burns diesel oil. It is convenient not to have to carry coal, coke or such like fuel for heating and even in a seaway the stove burns reasonably well. It is safe enough if care is used, though on one occasion when I was on board alone at Lymington the stove touched off a holocaust in the cabin. It was my fault for not noticing the thing was leaking and that the drip-tray beneath was half full of oil. A fire extinguisher from the galley, when brought into play, merely fed the flames and filled the cabin with noxious fumes. I got out in time, grabbing another extinguisher from the engine-room as I fled, and this one, when brought into action through the cabin skylight, saved the day. Still, he who would have eggs must bear with cackling; a man can't expect to enjoy warmth without experiencing the occasional rubs that its generation may entail.

As I have said, the occupants of the three forward berths are pretty snug when the stove is lit, whereas those in the three berths in the after part of the cabin, of which mine is one, derive far less benefit from it. I see no way of remedying this. Here also there are two bunks on the port side and one, the skipper's, to starboard. This is the beamiest part of the boat. The centre space is occupied by the main water tank holding 100 gallons and between the tank and the bunks on each side there is room for a wide settee. No cushions are provided for these but some sybarites bring their own. The table fitted with fiddles sits on top of the water tank. Thus, when the crew are gathered round the table three a side, their knees and feet are more or less in contact with the water tank which in cold weather is the equivalent of a block of ice. Possibly the sort of jacket one fits round hot-water tanks to keep the heat in would in this case be equally effective in preventing the cold from getting out. The table is immediately under the raised skylight, which admits to the cabin plenty of light and sometimes plenty of water. There is headroom immediately under the skylight, elsewhere in the cabin the head must be carried bent. On the bulkhead at the after end of the cabin are lockers and shelves, one of the latter holding the small wireless receiving set and the other a barograph where it can be seen by the skipper reclining in his bunk. Beneath bunks and settees there is more stowage space for stores. There is no space for stores under the cabin sole where the inside ballast, four tons or more of iron pigs, lies tightly wedged. Even so we can carry enough stores for three or four months. About the middle of the cabin there is on each side a locker containing a 30-gallon water tank; these are filled from on deck. The total water capacity of 200 gallons is made up by a 40-gallon tank on deck above the after part of the cabin; a pipe from it leads from the deck into the cabin.

A sliding door at the after end of the cabin opens to a narrow passage which gives access to the companion-way up to the cockpit and the deck. The main engine and charging engine are on the port side of the passage and on the other is the "heads". Here, besides the lavatory, there is the 70-gallon fuel tank, hanging space for oilskins, a rack for boots, and a big locker where the Aldis lamp, hand-bearing compass, safety belts, and several other things live. The engine is boxed in and, since it is seldom in use at sea, the top of the box serves as a chart table. As well as the engines there is room on the port side for yet another 30-gallon tank and shelves for tools, bos'n's stores, blocks, shackles, cordage and small stuff. This tank was used originally for water but we now use it for paraffin. I still cherish the hope that on some future voyage, perhaps to the Islands of the Blest, it will be filled with wine. Lurking under the companion-way ladder are the two twelve-volt batteries, one for the wireless and an electric lighting system which is not much used, and the other for starting the main engine. This cannot be started by hand; if the battery is flat the engine has, so to speak, had it. Aft of the batteries is a dark cavern, the space beneath the cockpit floor and the counter, which is used for stowing warps, spare rope, and odd bits of wood.

The well of the bilge lies at the forward end of the engine-room passage-way where it is conveniently sited for catching pencils, dividers, india-rubbers, pipes, and even stop-watches, when they fall off the chart table. Having dropped two stop-watches into this well, thereby stopping them for good, I have long since given up using them. For counting the minutes or seconds that elapse between the taking of a sight and going below to read Greenwich time on the chronometer watch one can either count in one's head or use a wrist-watch. No less than three pumps can suck at this well. The main stand-by is an old-fashioned barrel-pump on deck by the cockpit which does the job handsomely with a minimum of effort. There is a rotary pump inside the "heads" which is hard to turn, often out of order, and has a nasty trick of siphoning back. More than once, having emptied the bilge with this pump, we have been startled to find it full to overflowing a few minutes later. The third is a pump worked off the charging engine, fitted by me in a misguided moment. It can deliver only a piddle at best, and the futility of fitting such a pump is evident when one considers that at sea charging engines are fickle things, and in conditions when an extra pump might be badly needed, with a lot of water coming below, the charging engine would almost certainly have been put out of action. What a lot of money owners of small boats waste on mechanical devices that cannot always be depended upon and which anyway save only a few minutes' labour!

So much for *Mischief* below deck. From the stemhead on deck the bowsprit sticks out about 12 feet and there are some 8 feet of it inboard reaching back to the bitts. Slung between the bowsprit shrouds which support it laterally is a rope net, useful for arresting sails or crew on their way into the sea. In calm weather it has been used as a hammock. The jib goes out along the bowsprit on a traveller and is set flying. The only time a man, or sometimes two men, have to go out on the bowsprit is for hanking the big reaching jib to the stay. It is therefore wise to get this sail in early if the wind freshens. The anchor chain leads out on the port side of the stem, passing first through a chain-stopper, the anchor winch being set back level with the bitts. These are two massive pieces of oak standing 3 feet above the deck. The fisherman-type anchor weighing about 100 lbs is lashed on deck near the winch, and on the other side of the foredeck, near the bitts, is carried a 9-foot dinghy. This is launched by hoisting it over the rail by means of the jib halyards. There used to be three ventilators let into the foredeck, but their copper cowls have been demolished so frequently either by the sea or rough usage that we have now plugged up the holes. Ventilators on the deck of a small boat are bound to let in as much water as air unless they are high, cumbersome affairs with water-traps, or can be mounted above the deck on the coach-house roof.

The mast is stepped well forward, about one-third of the overall length of the boat (45 feet) from the stem. Mounted on it are two winches for setting up the last bit of the throat and peak halyards. As I have said earlier, the mast has been thought hardly man enough for the job. It is a solid spar only 7½ inches in diameter and may well be the original mast. All the other

spars that were in the boat when I took her over in 1954 have at
one time or another been renewed. The only time I have
misgivings about the mast, when the possibility that it may be
precarious and not very permanent looks menacing, is in a
rough sea with insufficient wind to keep the gaff from swinging about. In those circumstances the upper part of the mast
looks as if it were being wrung or twisted like a dishcloth. But
one should speak well of the bridge that carries one over; what
bends will not break; and judging by the number of modern
masts that are broken every summer round our coasts I
believe it is not as frail as it looks.

By the bulwarks at the foot of the shrouds are two wood
kevels each holding half a dozen iron belaying pins. The pins
are fitted with a home-made device consisting of a wooden
roller round which ropes render easily when swigged on. The
wooden rollers are kinder to rope than are iron pins and cause
less wear. About five feet up the shrouds the screens for the
navigation lights are wired on; and just below the screens a
sheer-pole, too, is fixed to the shrouds, having attached to it a
couple of long pegs for holding the coiled halyards. Between
the mast and the cabin skylight there is space for a small deck
locker used for stowing the numerous short lengths of rope
required frequently for lashings, as well as the handles for both
the reefing gear and the mast winches. The reefing gear is the
Appledore type and is probably the original fitting. The cabin
stove-pipe emerges inside this locker so the lid has to be
trimmed to the wind as if it were a ventilator cowl.

The cabin skylight, mounted on a foot-high coaming, is
offset from centre so that the port-side deck is at this point
wider by a couple of feet than the starboard. The reason for
this is that when she was a pilot-cutter, the punt, as the pilots
called the dinghy, used to be carried on the port side. By means
of a tackle on the mast with its fall led to the cockpit, the man at
the helm could raise the punt clear of the bulwarks for his mate
to launch her off. The six panes of the skylight, by the way, are
of ½-inch plate glass; even so we once had one of these broken
by a wave, in the Red Sea of all places.

The twin staysail booms, dinghy oars, boathooks, and
harpoon are lashed on one side of the skylight, and on the

other, when it is not set up, the topmast. This would come in useful as a spare spar in case of accidents, and it has been used as a sheet-leg when through mischance or mismanagement we have gone aground on a falling tide—as may happen at times to the most prudent mariners.

Aft of the skylight is the 40-gallon water tank covered by a wood grating and on this is lashed an oak water-breaker holding about 6 gallons and a box for holding chafing gear. This consists of rags, bits of canvas, and ropeyarn to make up the "scotsmen" to wrap round ropes where they are liable to chafe. Rags may be scarce at the start of a voyage but as it progresses discarded shirts and trousers become increasingly available. Aft of the water tank is the sliding hatch covering the companion-way and between the two is space to lash jerry-cans of petrol for the charging engine and a 5-gallon drum of fish-oil for calming troubled waters. The staysail sheet winches are on deck alongside the cockpit coaming.

Inside the 9-inch-high coaming the cockpit is roomy enough, measuring about 5 feet by 6 feet by 2 feet deep. It has seats on both sides, their main use being to provide a stepping-stone to the deck. If the weather is fine enough the crew prefer to spend their leisure hours lying about the deck rather than sitting in the cockpit. The helmsman, too, manages best by standing up as he can thus see farther and has more control of the long brass tiller. Usually there is one among the crew who insists on sitting down throughout his watch, or even lying stretched out on one of the benches, a position from which he can see nothing but the sky and can barely watch the compass. This is mounted on a small binnacle in the middle of the cockpit floor and can be illuminated at night by a wandering lead from the chart-room. Often in the course of a voyage, owing to trouble with the charging engine or shortage of petrol, we have to forgo this lighting and rely upon the self-luminous compass card.

All round the inside of the cockpit are capacious lockers, one reserved for paint and the others for spare sheets, bos'n's chair, handy-billy, and the weather-boards for closing the entrance to the companion-way. The cockpit is self-draining in so far as it has two outlet pipes. They are of small bore, full of bends, easily blocked and difficult to clear; and the amounts of débris that collects under the cockpit grating and finds its way into the pipes is really astonishing—matches, blanket fluff, broken biscuit, sweet and chocolate wrappings, and so on. But no hairpins! The pipes drain slowly even when clear, but should the cockpit happen to be half-full of water this rapidly drains into the lockers, thence into the engine-room, and so to the bilge where it can be easily cleared.

Abaft the cockpit stands the gallows for the boom to rest on when the mainsail is down; it is a piece of 6 inches by 6 inches oak resting on substantial iron stanchions. The boom is a massive spar some 26 feet long and nearly as thick as the mast so that it is heavy enough by itself; when resting on the gallows it has on top of it the gaff and the mainsail, the canvas probably soaking wet and double its normal weight. Altogether, there-fore, when the boom is lashed down to the gallows and the boat is rolling, the stanchions are under a heavy strain. On one voyage we began to fear that they would be torn out of the deck, so that now I have had two iron cross-stays fitted as braces to keep the whole thing rigid.

Finally, between the gallows and the taffrail is the iron horse and buffer for the big main-sheet block, the single-ended mainsheet being made fast to one of two massive samson posts, one on each side of the cockpit. Bulwarks about a foot high enclose the whole of the deck and two feet above the bulwarks a wire guard rail is supported by iron stanchions. I am told that when she was a working boat there was no guardrail as this would have hindered the launching of the punt and the hoisting of it on board. Wide though the decks are, I should say that without a guard-rail it would be easy enough to lose a man overboard. Without it the crew would feel naked and unprotected, and for my part, if there were any sort of sea running, I should be inclined to go about the deck on all fours. The rail comes in handy, too, for leaning against when taking sights at times when, perhaps, owing to the sails being in the way, one cannot see the sun from the safest and steadiest position—braced against the gallows with one leg curled lovingly round a stanchion.

Mischief's dimensions, by the way, are 45 feet long, over-all,

13-foot beam, and she draws about 7 feet 6 inches aft. Her
T.M. tonnage is 29 tons, and deadweight about 35 tons. She
was built at Cardiff in 1906.

II

1955: *Voyage to Patagonia*

Mischief*'s first voyage was an ambitious one. Tilman's objective was to cross the Patagonian ice-cap, whence the great glaciers flow down to the sea on the Chilean coast. Much of the region was marked "unexplored" on the map; the ice-cap had never been crossed from the Pacific side. After a false start with an unhappy crew from the Mediterranean, Tilman brought* Mischief *to her new home port, Lymington in Hampshire; and assembled a fresh crew: W. A. Procter, an experienced yachtsman; Lieutenant M. R. Grove of the Royal Artillery; Charles Marriott, another gunner; and a dairy farmer from Sussex, John Van Tromp, who sold his farm in order to go, and who took on the task of cooking. Their route was to take them to Las Palmas in the Canaries; then "the long haul", 4,600 miles to Montevideo, and through the Straits of Magellan to the remote Peel Inlet on the Chilean coast. The voyage began on the 6th July 1955, with a departure from Falmouth. Tilman quoted Sir Francis Drake, as he approvingly noted that few who saw them sail, knew whither they were bound:*

"It is not the beginning but the continuing of the same until it be thoroughly finished that yieldeth the true glory."

THE FIRST LEG:
LYMINGTON TO LAS PALMAS

> Where lies the land to which the ship would go
> Far, far ahead, is all her seamen know
> —*Clough*

ALTHOUGH IT SMACKS of seamanlike efficiency, to say that we got our anchor and sailed out is not strictly accurate. It leaves much unsaid. In fact we had two anchors down and their cables were so lovingly entwined that for some time the foredeck was the scene of a fearful struggle and resounded with unseamanlike oaths. We passed Black Rock, and the sentiments appropriate to watching from the deck of a small ship, outward bound on a long voyage, the receding shores of one's native land, had barely found expression when the shores ceased to recede. The wind, which had hitherto been light, now failed altogether and for two hours we drifted off the headland of St Anthony viewing its not remarkable features from many different angles.

After lunching on deck, for it was a warm day for England, we got a breeze from the south-west, hoisted the Genoa and streamed the log in the hope that the voyage had really begun. By evening we had caught many mackerel. To add to our pleasure the wind went round to north-west so that we were able to lay the course for Ushant; or rather 15 miles west of Ushant, for I intended giving that noted sea-mark a wide berth. Our next port of call was Las Palmas in the Canaries. Except for the purpose of checking our untried navigation the sighting of any land on the way would have been unnecessary. It is 1,500-odd miles to Las Palmas, which we reckoned upon reaching inside three weeks.

With four of us available for watch-keeping—the cook very properly being exempt—we had an easy time. The day from 8 a.m. to 8 p.m. was divided into four watches of three hours each. Thus, without recourse to dog watches, one's watch changed automatically, and on every fourth day a man had practically the whole day off or the whole night in. In order to make life still easier, when sails had to be shifted we did it if possible at the change of watch. At nightfall we tried by shortening sail to ensure that the watch below was not disturbed. Naturally this did not always happen. A peaceful sky and a steady barometer might belie their promise, wind and weather might change without warning, so that that which might have been done in daylight and at leisure, had to be done in darkness, in a hurry, by men half asleep. More often a disturbed night was our own fault. Because of a natural dislike of slowing the ship when she was reeling off the miles it was too easy to leave our light sails up or the mainsail unreefed, to trust to careless hope and to use reason to thrust aside what we did not fancy.

According to the late Conor O'Brien, a complicated rig on an ocean-going yacht justifies itself in giving the crew something to do. Other than watch-keeping and sail-changing there is not much for the crew of a well-found ship on a long voyage under normal conditions to do, for the sail changing has neither the frequency nor the urgency that obtains in ocean racing. Naturally one tries to get the best one can out of the boat, but the comfort of the crew, the safety of the gear and the wear and tear upon it, are vastly more important than speed. The crew has to carry on for weeks or months and there is a limit to the amount of spare gear that can be carried or to the repairs that can be effected in mid-ocean.

Even so life was too hard for some of the crew, who during their trick at the helm needed cushions to support their body, an awning to cover their head, and a book to distract their mind. But at least one of us, John Van Tromp, had no sinecure. Those who invoke hunters, sharks, wolves, hyenas, or cormorants as examples of voracity have much to learn. Procter, and Michael Grove, too, when he had found his sea legs, could eat their way past any of these with hardly a pause for breath. And since neither Charles Marriott nor I would be described as delicate feeders the cook had his hands full in preparing meals and clearing up. In addition, by inclination and because he had more knowledge of it than the rest of us, John attended to the engine when needed and looked after the little charging engine. He also did any electrical repairs. They were often needed as the wiring throughout the ship was amateurish and the fittings not so waterproof as they should have been. He spent his spare time fishing and perhaps once in a thousand miles or so throughout the voyage his efforts were rewarded by a big fish. Those were red-letter days.

Procter was a good carpenter and handyman so that any such work fell on him, while I looked after the rigging. As I have said the amount of wear and tear that goes on at sea sailing night and day, particularly at night when sheets are eased or shortened and the necessary shifting of the anti-chafe material

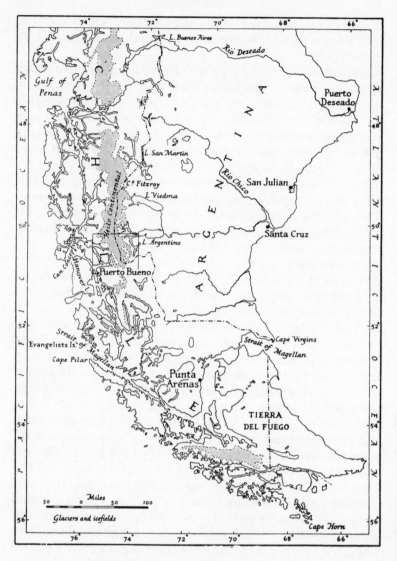

General map of Chile and Argentine Patagonia
(from *Mischief in Patagonia*, reproduced by permission of the Royal
Geographical Society)

("scotsmen") is overlooked, is a never-ending source of worry. There are few days when there is not any stitching of sails or splicing of rope and wire to be done. There can be no one who goes to sea for fun who takes no interest in the behaviour of the ship, the set of the sails, the ever changing pattern of sea and sky, sea birds which are seldom absent and the fish which, we found, were so seldom present. As long as the ship is moving, preferably in the right direction, one is seldom bored even in the most lifeless ocean and interest is quickly restored by the mere sight of another ship or another sign of life. Only in very light airs or flat calms, when there is no progress and there is nothing to be done or to be seen, is boredom felt, and the effect of such times upon the temper and morale of the crew is very obvious.

Our first night at sea passed peacefully for all except Mike Grove who mistook the rising moon for a sail approaching at speed, shone the torch on our sails, and was on the point of rousing me out. Next day when the wind had freshened from east-north-east we gybed over to the port tack and logged what proved to be our best run for many a long day, 140 miles. How thankful we were for a wind which gave us such a flying start and for a sea which as yet exacted no tribute. The subsequent shortening of sail by taking two rolls in the mainsail and handing the big Genoa served to mark our apprehensions rather than worsening weather; for in the early days we seldom failed to expect the worst, seeing menace in every cloud and a gale in every gust. But by the time we were well into the Bay of Biscay three of us who had not yet found our sea legs were in poor shape. The fair wind took us with a lessening speed right across the Bay and early on the fourth morning, with the wind falling light, we sighted land. During this run three of us had been busily taking sights, more by way of practice than in the expectation of getting trustworthy results. Before setting a course for the Canaries we had intended taking our departure from Cape Finisterre and to make sure of not missing it we had steered a little to the east. The land ahead was undoubtedly the north coast of Spain, somewhere, we thought, in the neighbourhood of Coruna. With the aid of binoculars, the hand-bearing compass, and the appropriate "Pilot", we speedily identified the Tower of Hercules, a square dark tower at the western entrance of Coruna bay. Procter, who two months before had been there in my old acquaintance *Iyruna* on her way home from Oporto, recognised it, and the adjacent features seemed to fit. After one wrong assumption it is remarkable how easily the neighbouring marks on a coast line can be made to conform and how long it is before discrepancies become so glaring that the original assumption has to be abandoned. Prominent buildings noted in the "Pilot" are cheerfully allowed to have been knocked down or put up since that invaluable guide was written; woods to have been planted or felled; and awkward hills which refuse to fit into the picture are either ignored or assumed to have been swallowed by an earthquake. Until at last common sense prevails and one is obliged sadly to admit that nothing fits and that one is looking at an entirely different piece of coast. We were all adrift. We were off Cape Ortegal, and in the evening, after we had sailed in desultory fashion some 20 miles along the coast, the Tower of Hercules was unmistakably identified by its light.

That we were out in our reckoning and had made a bad landfall was attributed to our being set in by the tide. The navigator can always attribute his errors—unless, of course, they are fatal—to abnormal tidal sets or the perverse behaviour of currents, whereas the man who leads his party into the wrong valley or on to the wrong ridge has no such scapegoat and is written down an ass. We should have to do better after taking our departure for the Canaries, for it would not do to miss *them*. We had two sextants, both, judging by their venerable appearance, immediate successors of the astrolabe. Both had Vernier scales, which are less easy to read than micrometers, and unless one had a fearful squint Procter's sextant was very difficult to read. Moreover, it was useless for taking star sights unless one discarded the telescope. But for £5, which was all it cost, one can't expect refinements, and it gave reliable results.

For working sights Procter used the popular Air Navigation Tables. One objection to them is that for a long voyage a great many massive volumes must be carried; for instance, for a

voyage like that which Conor O'Brien made, twenty volumes
would be needed. The objection I had to them was that until
the answer had been plotted on the chart it did not mean
anything. Following the example of the "Master" I used the
tables published by the U.S. Hydrographic Office, H.O. 211,
a slim volume of 50 pages. With this and a Nautical Almanac
one could circumnavigate the globe. Using these, in less than
five minutes one knew without plotting the distance and
direction of the ship's line of position from the dead reckoning
position. Charles, who in pre-war days had studied celestial
navigation at what he called the Military College of Nonsense,
was our acknowledged expert, at any rate, in the theory of the
subject. But he had refused to move with the times. He
preferred time-honoured methods employing logarithms,
haversines, cosecants, and God knows what, and these seemed
not only to take longer than ours but gave more scope for
human fallibility. The scope, in fact, was so wide that an error
of a degree or so in working became known to us as a
"Charles". On the other hand a good intercept or, if we were
working several star sights, a small "cocked hat", was called a
"Henry" in honour of the great Navigator. Sometimes when
three or even four or five were taking sights it became a little
difficult to reconcile the results or even to pick one's way
through the spider's web which soon adorned the chart. But I
had the last word, and by a combination of the theory of
probabilities, a knowledge of the instruments used, and of
those who used them, I decided which to accept and which to
reject and plotted our position accordingly. It sounds haphazard. A court of inquiry, had we ever had to face one, might
have taxed us with awkward questions, but such problems
kept everyone's interest alive and before we were through we
were at least competent.

It is astonishing how quickly a southward bound yacht,
even though it is not a flyer, reaches the warmer weather for
which the crew long. Sweaters and shirts are shed, shorts and
bathing bags appear, and the sun-starved northerner's passion
for getting his body well tanned by the sun is given full rein.
But perfect comfort must not be expected by folks who go
a-pleasuring. After a few more degrees of southing the sun-

worshippers are wearing dark glasses, rigging awnings over the cockpit, and taking refuge in the shade of the cabin where they do nothing but complain of the heat.

When we had outrun the Portuguese trades a westerly wind carried us along until in about lat. 35° we were caught up in the strong embrace of the true north-east trades. With a wind which never fell below force 4 (about 16 knots) and more often reached force 5 or 6 sailing was exhilarating. We lowered the mainsail and stowed the boom, hoisted the twin staysails and let her go. The sky overhead with little fleecy clouds sailing across was a pale reflection of the sparkling blue sea flecked with foam and dancing spray. Rolling became continuous and sometimes heavy as the pursuing waves surged by, lifting the counter with a friendly shove forwards and slightly sideways, before hissing past the rail and depositing a dollop of water on deck by way of salute. Steering was easy, for there was no fear of a gybe. Sheets had scarcely to be touched, and perhaps best of all with this rig the gear subject to chafe was reduced to a minimum. *Mischief* seemed to enjoy sailing before a wind that blew true and steady as the wind of a bellows, as much as did her crew. She frequently showed her pleasure by some very lively rolling. This rhythmic rolling, inseparable from down-wind sailing, becomes a nuisance, particularly at meal times, when a man needs two pairs of hands, or when any work has to be done on deck. Every few minutes the ship would glide gently into what would become a crescendo of rolling, each successive roll becoming livelier and longer until the dislodging of the helmsman from his seat or a loud crash from the galley, announced that she had had her bit of fun. Then she would sail demurely along until tempted by the laughing waves to do it again. One could almost hear her humming to herself:

> Roll me over, in the clover,
> Roll me over, lay me down, and do it again.

With the coming of the trades we began to see flying fish in abundance and sometimes we got a few on board. For this effortless form of fishing neither patience nor implements are needed, only rough weather. After a night of heavy rolling a search of the scuppers and under the dinghy at times provided enough fish for breakfast. Another welcome visitor was a little brown and white striped pilot fish which perhaps mistook us for the shark he usually attends. He took station a foot or two ahead of *Mischief*'s rushing forefoot and swam there tirelessly for something like 300 miles. Perhaps fish sleep while swimming, as do horses when standing up, but this little chap seemed neither to sleep nor eat food. We watched him carefully, noting in the log at every change of watch whether Fidelio, as we called him, was present and correct. We missed him sorely when he left us, as he did the night before we sighted the Islands.

We are never satisfied with the present. Change is what we really like and if there is too much of that we begin to long for stability. Content though *Mischief*'s crew were with life at sea, we eagerly awaited the approach of land, although I for one knew that making port would inevitably give me work and worry. After only 16 days at sea we looked forward with mounting excitement to our first port of call. What sort of a landfall would we make? Or again, would there be any land to see? Grand Canary, on which is Las Palmas, lies between the islands of Tenerife and Fuertaventura and is separated from them by channels 30 and 45 miles wide respectively. By making a bad shot either way, and attended by the mischance of thick weather, the unskilled mariner could easily whistle through either channel in a matter of hours and not see land at all. In clear weather the veriest duffer should be able to make his landfall, since the Peak of Tenerife (12,140 ft.) can be seen from 70 miles and the other islands have their own mountains.

By the morning of 22 July we had run our distance and in spite of a smoky haze we fully expected to see the Peak towering above it. No such welcome sight appeared. Only the passing of three or four steamers showed we were on course and probably nearing a port. Visibility became worse. We were sailing fast in rough water and we had to decide whether to run off westwards where we thought Grand Canary should be or to carry on and hope to see land later when the sun burnt up the haze. In the skipper's opinion, though it would not have been helpful to express it:

> Beyond the clouds, beyond the waves, that roar,
> There may indeed, or may not be, a shore.

We raced on until about 10.30 a.m. The weather was as thick as ever and as the fear of having overshot our mark had become unbearable we handed the twins and hove to under reefed main and reefed staysail, for it was now blowing hard. Thus we lay until about noon when Charles, who is gifted with remarkably keen eyesight, cheered us with a cry of "Land". Sure enough to the north-west a blurred shape showed darkly through the haze. We let draw and sailed towards it when it presently resolved itself into Punta Gando, the easternmost point of Grand Canary some 10 miles south of Las Palmas.

Our landfall had been good enough. Had we but had faith in our reckoning and turned west at 8 a.m. we should have sighted the town. As we were now near the south end of the island I suggested sailing round and up the west coast in the lee of the land. This was vetoed on the grounds that we should have a hard job weathering the north end, so we put about and began the long beat back. Weary work it was. It took us the best part of twenty-four hours to make good the ground lost in two hours, but early on the afternoon of the 23rd we dropped anchor off the Las Palmas Yacht Club. Domingo, a man who speaks English and is well known to visiting yachts, came off. He startled me by insisting that if we thought of going ashore all together we must employ a watchman, otherwise water-thieves, bold as brass and cunning as monkeys, would strip the ship to the last nut and bolt. One yacht, we were told, had had her entire lead keel removed. Having thus prepared his listeners for bad tidings Domingo added that the watchman's fee would be 15s. a night. I agreed to this blackmail, if blackmail it was, rather than abide the consequences of refusal. So Johnnie the watchman was installed that night and proved a good investment. He rowed us back to the ship at all hours of the night as well as rendering us many other services. Domingo acted his self-assumed part of ship's agent well, saw that we were not cheated too much, and was very grateful for what we gave him.

THE LONG HAUL:
LAS PALMAS TO THE MAGELLAN STRAIT

LEAVING LAS PALMAS in a sailing ship bound south is as carefree as stepping on to a train. As soon as we were outside we hoisted the twins and metaphorically sat back. By 5 p.m. our old acquaintance Punta Gando was abeam. We streamed the log and managed to snarl it with the fishing line. It took us two hours to sort out the tangle. As fishermen we were always rich in hope if poor in possession. We usually had a line out, sometimes two, and if these were forgotten when going about or in moments of crisis, as they sometimes were, the consequent lash-up was deplorable.

Our next landfall, we hoped, would be St Vincent in the Cape Verde Islands some 900 miles to the south-west. Thence we would stand on to the southward without trying to make much westing, aiming at crossing the equator in about long. 29°W. This was the track used in other days by sailing ships bound round Cape Horn. Where possible we followed the track for sailing ships laid down on the *Ocean Pilot Charts* published by the U.S. Hydrographic Office. There is a chart for each ocean for each month of the year showing not only the recommended track for steam or sail, but also the prevalent winds and currents, the seasonal limits of the trades, percentages of gales and calms, sea temperatures, normal barometric pressures, and much else.

For the next seven days we ran in the full swing of the trades. These were days of glorious sailing. The sun blazed down till the pitch in the seams bubbled, the dazzling white twins swayed and curtsied until their booms kissed the water, while the ship rolled lazily along on her run of more than a hundred miles every day. All this happened with little or no exertion on our part. We even had flying fish for breakfast every morning with no exertion at all. But the Cape Verde Islands which were rapidly approaching seem to upset the steadiness of the trades. The wind became fitful and one wondered whether or not the wind would be truer away to the west of the islands. But the idea of taking such a course would be rejected when one remembered what a fillip the interest and morale of the crew receives from the sight of land. For me there is something about islands that rouses a more lively interest than a mere line of coast, an aura of romance such as is expressed in Flecker's

A ship, an isle, and a sickle moon.

To sight one, even the smallest barren ash-heap, excites curiosity—whether or not there be a landing place, water, or even any life at all; and to be on one is to enjoy the delights of the sea without the disgusts.

Most of the Cape Verde Islands are ash-heaps, ash-heaps which with their warm colouring appear to be still smouldering. Early on 6 August we sighed the bold headland of Lombo de Boi, Bull Point, at the north-east end of Santo Antao. With light airs we sailed and drifted through the channel between it and St Vincent to the east, past the main harbour Porto Grande, remarking as we passed, the barracks, the prison, the hospital, all the tokens, in short, of civilization. We crept past the signal station on Ilheu dos Passeros dutifully making our number (the signal flags MKCP) and as usual evoking no response; for a yacht's signal flags are too small to be read at any distance. It is doubtful whether a set of flags is worth carrying. It was very hot and we had barely steerage way; so we ignored the warning given in the *Pilot* that sharks frequent the bay, dived overboard and swam about the ship.

The sun sank and the ruddy glow of the barren hills changed to violet and then to deep purple as we drifted along the rocky coast towards Ponta Machado, the western extremity of the island. On this cape there is a lighthouse called Donna Amelia, a name which occasioned some chaff, mostly at Mike's expense, concerning the lighthouse keeper's daughter. About two in the morning I came on deck, perhaps by chance, perhaps because of that instinct which is supposed to rouse the sleeping mariner when his ship is in danger, but probably because Mike had called me to report the Amelia light abeam. Abeam with a vengeance. The thing was virtually above us. We were so close that I could have sworn I heard the light revolving and had the lighthouse keeper's daughter been on watch she could certainly have blown Mike kisses. Though the ship still had way she appeared to my shocked eyes to be getting sucked into a small bight beyond the headland where evidently—though the *Pilot* forbears to mention it—there lurked what that exemplary work sometimes refers to as a *bastardo*. With the help of the engine we won clear and I was thankful to see Amelia's baleful eye gradually recede and eventually disappear.

Having cleared the islands we had only one more good day of trade wind sailing before the wind failed, leaving us still two degrees north of its normal summer limit. The Doldrums, the belt of calms and rain squalls that lies between the north-east and south-east trade wind systems, is furthest north and at its widest in August when it covers about five degrees of latitude. These limits are, of course, only rough and may vary even from week to week. With luck a ship might be only three or four days in the Doldrums before picking up the trades on the other side, or she might remain more or less becalmed for a fortnight or more, fraying the tempers of her crew as well as the sheets, halyards, and sails. We had a weary time. Instead of handing the sails we left them up, the sheets hard in and the boom amidships, watching every catspaw that ruffled the oily sea in the hope that presently we might be able to let draw. On some days rain squalls burst frequently and with great violence, but if they brought any wind with them it might be from any direction. It was fun turning out naked in this heavy rain for a fresh water wash. We filled one of our 30-gal. tanks with great ease and had lots of water for washing clothes. On our shore-going clothes green mould sprouted freely. When it was not raining a clammy heat enveloped us. Buckets of sea water or a bathe overside brought some relief, but this resource was of little avail when the temperature of air and sea became the same, 80°F.

In the old days patience, a virtue very liable to be fatigued by exercise, was the only real remedy for this state of affairs. Other remedies were usually tried, such as whistling, throwing a pack of cards into the sea, or sticking a knife in the mast. But in order to be really effective the knife should be stuck in by a clergyman and seafaring clerics were not common. We ourselves were not free from these beliefs. When whistling failed we threw coins—Spanish pesetas of very nominal value—overboard on the quarter from which we wished the wind to come. But on the whole it is more effective to make use of an engine and petrol. By using these freely and by taking advantage of every puff of wind we worked our way steadily south, making good about 40 miles a day. The longest continuous running of the engine was nine hours, and how grateful we were when we could shut it off. How we reviled the noise and the fumes in the cabin, and how we rejoiced in the succeeding stillness, with the musical ripple of water along the sides and the slat of the sails as they began to fill. Even with the help of the engine we endured eight days of these trying conditions until our boredom ended suddenly with a day of heavy rain, high wind, and steep seas. This violent but welcome change cost us the light Genoa. We had left it up too long and the clew blew out. When the following day dawned bright and clear we thought we had at last escaped from the Doldrums but in fact four more days were to pass before we felt the first welcome breath of the south-east trades in about lat. 3°N.

But this baffling region is not without its interest. Marine life which hitherto had consisted mainly of flying fish and Portuguese men o'war (the nautilus with its delicate coloured sail which abound in tropical and sub-tropical waters) became more varied. We thought it was about time. Accounts of voyages, all no doubt written by honourable men, in which bonito, albicore, dorado, and barracouta are seen or even caught on every other page, where the grim triangular fins of sharks ceaselessly circle the ship, and where whales rub their barnacles off on her bottom, had whetted our appetites and roused expectation to a height that was never to be realised. But on a day of oily calm, after a vast school of porpoises had played round for hours and finally taken themselves off, the helmsman did at last raise the cry of "Shark". So indiscriminating were we then that any large, unpleasing looking fish was labelled shark, and this may well have been one, for there are many kinds. He never surfaced but remained a few feet below and never far from our stern, a vague, green, disquieting shape. Horace, as we called him, was interested in food but in a languid sort of way. He followed us with some persistence for several days. Bathing stopped immediately, although I entered him in the log as merely a giant South Atlantic sea frog. Then Procter, the mildest of men, went berserk and harpooned an inoffensive dolphin gambolling round the fore-foot. By the time we had it on board the harpoon was bent like a hoop. Some of us had an uneasy feeling that the consequences of such violence might rival those that befell the Ancient Mariner. Nevertheless, we ate him and for the first meal or two felt grateful. After that it palled, for the meat is like venison, dark and very rich. Soon after this we caught our first dorado (also called a dolphin). This was literally a very different kettle of fish, glorious to see and glorious to eat. He is anything up to 5 ft. long, with a long fin running down his back, a Roman nose, and brilliant greeny-gold metallic hues which in the dying fish undergo quick changes. It is a fine thing to see him leaping ferociously after smaller fish, finer to see him on deck, and finest of all to have him on one's plate.

Quite apart from this choice of dark or white meat we lived well at this time. As an experiment I had brought a quantity of dehydrated food from the Ministry of Agriculture Ex-perimental Factory, Aberdeen—minced beef, spinach, carrot, cabbage, and meat and vegetable blocks. All were so easily and quickly cooked and so excellent (the cabbage and carrot might have been straight from the garden) that I regretted having made the vulgar mistake of not taking enough. Even on hot mornings we fortified ourselves with porridge as belly-timber, and in the evening we turned hungrily upon large helpings of potatoes, rice or macaroni in various guises, followed often by steamed puddings with which John had a happy knack. A little too much carbohydrate, perhaps, espe-cially considering the heat, but we had no dietitian on board to point out that we were probably digging our graves with our teeth, and we thrived well enough. The puddings traced their origin back to an idle day off the Spanish coast when I made a cake. The recipe was no secret, so I handed it verbally to John who speedily discovered that "Skipper's Mixture", as it was called, was equally adapted to baked cakes or steamed pud-dings. On Saturday evenings we had a drink, for not one of us was a rigid abstainer. Sunday was curry night. We felt obliged to limit this to one night a week on account of Michael whose appetite for curry was a little immoderate.

For some time now we had enjoyed the full glory of the southern sky at night—the Cross with its two pointers, Canopus, Fomalhaut, Achernar, Antares, and the two Magellanic Clouds glowing faintly and mysteriously like straying portions of the Milky Way. (These cloud-like clusters, though named after him, were known before Magellan's time.) Charles, whom we knew as the "Astronomer Royal" and to whom we referred, as it were for heavenly guidance, pointed out these and many lesser stars with curious names like Nunki, Shaula, and Kaus Australis. For sights we used the major stars and planets and left that temptingly easy target the moon for better men; for the working of her sights, with the numerous necessary corrections and the consequent increased opportunities for errors, generally gave startling results. In low latitudes there were few early mornings or late evenings when three or four suitable stars or planets could not be seen, but in higher latitudes we rarely got good star sights. In the North Atlantic there was usually cloud, poor horizons, or rough weather. If one quarter of the sky was clear, the horizon under it would be hazy, or clouds permitted such a fleeting glimpse of a star that even with the approximately correct angle on the sextant beforehand it could not be picked up, much less brought down to the horizon. Considering which exasperating circumstances, the navigator would exclaim against the Creator's arrangements in somewhat the same style as that credited to Lord Jeffrey: "Damn the solar system. Bad light; planets too distant; pestered with comets; feeble contrivance; could make a better myself".

On 29 August we crossed the equator in long. 28°W. and celebrated the event with a plum pudding. On 2 September a noon sight showed us that we were on the same latitude as Fernando Noronha and still some 90 miles to the east of it. But as yet the south-east trades, which we had expected would blow bold and true like the north-east trades, were weak and variable. Still we were getting southwards all the time and were encouraged by the sight of a steamer, the first we had seen for three weeks. We were about 50 miles off the Brazilian coast and we aimed to keep off until the time came for us to close the land north of the River Plate. We were pretty confident the coast *was* there because when we were in the longitude of Recife we had seen in the sky the loom of the lights of a large city.

Off Cape Frio, when the weather became appropriately cool, we found that one of our two big paraffin containers had leaked, so that we had only one gallon left to last us to Montevideo, still a fortnight away. We had therefore to reduce our hot meals to one a day and to forgo steamed puddings. Perhaps it was the denial of these sustaining rib-stickers that made us complain of the increasing cold. If we were feeling cold off the Brazilian coast, what would we feel like twenty degrees further south? The sea temperature had already fallen to 70°F.—no water for weaklings—and only the hardiest of the crew could any longer face the daily rite of three buckets over their heads before breakfast, hail, rain, or shine. Between John and me there lay an unspoken challenge as to which of us would bathe farthest south, and already each was watching the other hopefully for signs of weakening. We began to see more ships. A tanker, the *Ancap Tercero*, passed close and gave us three blasts on her horn. Not to be outdone in civility we replied with three on our hand fog-horn, hiccuping, as it were, in response to a thunder-clap.

On the morning of 28 September, after a fine run of 130 miles before a biting north-east wind, the wind fell light when we were some 50 miles off Cabo Polonio, where we expected to make our landfall. That we were not far from land was evident from the presence of seals. Having sighted what we thought was some wreckage or floating branches and altered course to avoid them, we found a party of seals asleep on their backs with their flippers in the air. Presently we were becalmed, handed the sails, and amused ourselves by watching the antics of a seal and two big gulls. While they sat side by side patiently expectant of scraps from the galley, the seal would suddenly shoot up between them. Squawking indignantly they would flutter off and settle down anew, whereupon the seal would play the same trick. So calm and so inviting was the sea that I rashly dived in before taking its temperature. This proved to be only 56°F.

Meantime the glass had been falling steadily and by morning we were bowling along in thickening weather with a strong south-east wind. Rice pudding for breakfast seemed to me an indication of worse to come. At 11 a.m. we sighted land and a little later identified a lighthouse as that on Cabo Polonio. The thrill and satisfaction of making our appointed landfall, of sighting a new continent after two months at sea, now gave way to concern that we might hit it. With the wind and rain both increasing, we spent a most anxious afternoon sailing fast along a lee shore, glimpsing it just often enough to raise doubts as to whether or not we were being set towards it. In the evening a brief clearing showed Cabo Santa Maria abeam, and that we were now well inside the estuary was evident from the nasty, yellow appearance of the water.

The River Plate estuary is 138 miles wide at its mouth, narrowing to 57 miles at Montevideo which is 60 miles from the sea. At its head the estuary is 25 miles wide. It receives the waters of six rivers, thus comprising the second largest system in the world. The discolouration caused by the silt can be seen 70 or 80 miles out to sea, while this mingling of tropical river water and the colder water from the southern ocean is marked by the presence of large numbers of petrels, albatrosses, seals, and sometimes penguins. The estuary is noted for its sudden and violent weather changes, for its thunderstorms and dust storms, for *sudestadas*, *zondias*, and *pamperos*, each of which has its own particular unpleasantness. The *pampero* is often preceded by the phenomenon known as *Baba del Diablo*, or Devil's Dribble, which fills the air with the gossamer webs of the aeronaut spider. The *zonda* is a norther; the *pampero*, as its name implies, arises over the pampas and is a line squall which strikes with suddenness and ferocity. The *sudestada*, coming off the sea, brings with it rain and thick weather. Since the estuary is shallow these storms quickly raise a short and nasty sea.

We were about to experience a *sudestada*. Early in the morning after a quiet night the wind rose steadily and heavy rain began driving over the livid water. For us the wind was fair—a wind the sailor is advised not to waste—so we shortened sail as far as we could and taking care to allow two points for leeway we laid a course for the light vessel marking the northern end of the English Bank. This great sandbank lies plumb in the middle of the estuary and in time past has taken its toll of many a ship. This liberal allowance for leeway could be regarded as a sort of insurance policy, for if the allowance proved to be too much and so caused us to miss the lightship we might perhaps sight instead a buoy lying some 8 miles to the south. But since the *sudestada* is accompanied by heavy rain and bad visibility the chances of our sighting a small object like a buoy, which in a rough sea is for half the time obscured, were not good.

In the early afternoon when we had run our distance and had sighted nothing, a change of course became imperative if we were to clear the bank. I had just decided to carry on for another five minutes when to our joy lynx-eyed Charles sighted the buoy about half a mile away on our port bow. With renewed confidence we altered course for the lightship, and at the same time the wind began to moderate and the rain squalls to become less frequent. For the very good reason that it was not there the lightship was never found, for as we learnt later it had been taken off station for repair. However, we soon made out the Isla de Flores some ten miles to the north, and as we passed the island a great box-like thing appeared above the distant horizon. At first we took it for a large ship distorted by mirage—mirage effects are common in the estuary—but when other rectangular shapes began to show on either side of it we realised that we were looking at the skyline of Montevideo still some 12 miles away.

As wind and sea subsided we shook out our reefs. Night fell and we enjoyed a lovely moonlight sail with the lights of the coast road and the eastern suburbs twinkling close on our starboard hand. At length we cut into the dredged and buoyed channel where we began to experience one of the problems of entering a strange harbour at night, the picking out of the aids to navigation from among the even brighter aids to dissipation, the neon signs and coloured lights of bars, night clubs, and such like. After an exchange of marine pleasantries with a steamer and its attendant tug in the harbour entrance, we motored in and dropped anchor at 1 a.m. on 1 October, sixty-four days out from Las Palmas and all well. Rum and cocoa were served in the cabin.

After a good deal of work in Montevideo and the temporary replacement of Charles Marriott by a young German because of a shoulder injury, Mischief sailed southward towards the Straits of Magellan. On 5th November they picked up the light on Cape Virgins that marks the westerly entrance to the famous Strait.

Off the entrance to the Straits the tidal streams are strong and confusing; for the flood stream makes north up the coast from round the Horn and also sets east through the Straits, and in the same way the ebb running south divides, part of it setting west through the Straits. So when the wind fell light we started the engine, fully determined that no false pride should stop us entering the Straits and attaching ourselves firmly to the bottom to save our being blown out or set out by the tide. Bernicot, who in 1936 in the cutter *Anahita* had repeated Slocum's single-handed circumnavigation by way of the Magellan Straits, had had a rough handling just inside the entrance and was twice swept out to sea in spite of all that sail and engine could do. Slocum, too, had no sooner rounded Cape Virgins than a south-westerly gale struck him and for thirty hours his sloop *Spray* managed to hold her ground with no more than a three-reefed mainsail and forestaysail. *She* had no engine and she was *not* driven out to sea; but then *Spray* was *Spray* and there have been few seamen like Slocum.

Inside the Straits the tidal streams are stronger and reach their maximum strength in the First and Second Narrows. In the First Narrows spring tides run at from five to eight knots and are not much less in the Second Narrows. Between the eastern entrance and Punta Arenas a sailing vessel or a low-powered steamer must therefore work the tides, anchoring when the stream is against her. By 10 o'clock that night, when the Dungeness light bore north, we knew we were fairly inside the Straits, and with a nice breeze coming in from north-west and with the flood under us we sailed happily westwards gaining assurance with every mile made good. Early in the morning, when the ebb began to run, we dropped anchor at the tail of the Orange Bank.

Coming on deck that morning with the vague, mysterious coast of Tierra del Fuego on one side and the bold headland of Cape Possession on the other, we felt our adventure had really begun. Until the tide turned we fished unsuccessfully and watched with interest some Commerson's dolphins. These were the first we had seen; they are smaller than most dolphins with black and white colouring sharply delimited, the white part including the flippers and the lower half of the head. When the flood began to make we weighed and stood towards Punta Delgada at the entrance to the First Narrows. As we neared it the wind dropped and we started the engine and with the tide running full bore we swept through the Narrows with a speed of something like 8 knots over the ground. The channel has a least width of 2 miles, the fairway is deep, and the shores steep-to but not high. An hour later we shot out of the western end and at the same time the engine failed. There was no wind but the tide still ran strongly enough to carry us to a safe anchorage in Santiago bay.

Instead of pressing on that night with the next tide we took a long night in. At noon next day we weighed again hoping to pass the Second Narrows while it was still light, for at this time of year it is light until after 10 o'clock. No sooner had we started, however, than the wind came in so strongly from dead ahead that we had to push the engine hard to get as far as Gregory bay, the next anchorage some 10 miles to the west. In Gregory bay there is a *frigorifico*, a mere collection of buildings with a tall, iron chimney and a wood jetty from which the frozen mutton is shipped. We anchored close off the end of the jetty where only a few children gathered to look at the strange ship, for at this time of year the place was not being used. As if a *frigorifico* was not a strong enough hint that times had changed we could see, as we looked across the Straits that night, the great flames of natural gas from the oil wells on Tierra del Fuego. Thus the voyager in these historic waters, aglow with such romantic names as Famine Reach, Royal Road, Pelican Passage, or Elizabeth Island (so named by Drake), whose imagination has been stirred and who yet cherishes the hopeful illusion that the low coast on either hand is still wild and strange, must here abandon such imaginings, now utterly extinguished by the horrid reality of a *frigorifico* on the one hand and of oil derricks on the other.

Expecting to reach Punta Arenas that day we got under way soon after midnight. Since the Second Narrows are much wider than the First the stream is weaker. In our eagerness to be off we rounded Gregory Point and were at the entrance of the channel before the east-going stream had stopped running. Until the tide turned progress was slow, but by five in the morning, when it was full day, we had cleared the western end. As we altered course for Punta Arenas, for the Straits here bend sharply southwards, we met a rare sailing breeze from the north-west. The day was wonderfully clear. To starboard lay Drake's well-wooded Elizabeth Island, with Queen Channel to the east of it and Royal Road and Pelican Passage to the west. Ahead Broad Reach opened out, its light blue waters ruffled by the freshening wind. Beyond it to the south lay high ground, the slopes green with forest and crowned with patches of winter snow. Far away in the distance, from west round to south, rose a jagged skyline of high mountains, the highest of them glistening with the convincing whiteness of perpetual ice and snow. So unexpected a vision was heartening. There at any rate was country still wild and strange.

As the wind gradually freshened and Broad Reach became covered with white-capped waves, *Mischief* sped along with a bone in her teeth as if eager to finish in style what had been a rather slow passage. The brown huddle at the foot of a bleak, reddish coloured hillside which we had long decided was Punta Arenas began to take shape. In the roads a big four-masted hulk lay forlorn and uncared for, and soon we could make out the jetty and we had to decide where to go. We were still sailing fast, a little too fast for accurate navigation, and presently a jar and a shudder warned us that *Mischief* had indeed reached Patagonia. But in a matter of minutes she had bumped over the shoal and we lost no time in handing the sail and dropping anchor a cable's length from the jetty. A pilot launch was soon alongside and towed us to the jetty where we tied up. We had at any rate astonished the natives. The slight contretemps had gone unnoticed by the ancient mariners and longshoremen who had gathered to see us come in, and who, as we heard later, had much admired our dashing approach, swift rounding-to and stowing of sails. To have made such an impression was gratifying, for it is not every day that an English yacht, or indeed any yacht, comes to Punta Arenas. It was perhaps a pity that our departure was destined to be the reverse of dashing.

In Punta Arenas Tilman waited with some impatience for the return of Charles Marriott, put up with the constant howling winds, and frequented "a saloon of severe aspect named the Bar Antartica". He also recruited a climber.

A young Chilean climber, Jorge Quinteros, recommended by the "Federation Andinismo de Chile", offered to come. He had climbed in the Central Andes and was a student of ballet and a bee-keeper. He spoke little or no English. He was prepared to fly to Punta Arenas for an interview without any commitment on my part, but I felt that if he came as far as that I could hardly send him back. So I decided to take him. After all a ballet dancer should have impeccable balance and Everest had been climbed by a bee-keeper*. But in asking him I made it clear that there would be a great deal more load carrying than climbing and that he would be away at least three months. When Jorge arrived on the 24th he did not seem much disconcerted by the rum-looking characters with whom he had thrown in his lot, by what to his eyes must have been the inadequate size of *Mischief*, or by the rather cramped bunk in which he was invited to spread himself and his gear. I think that thus to commit himself inescapably for a period of three months in the company of strangers and foreigners, in the totally unfamiliar circumstances of a small yacht bound on a voyage of some hazard, required more than common spirit. I am glad to say this gamble came off. I don't think Jorge ever regretted having joined us and our only regret was when he left. On the ship, of course, he was able to converse with

*Sir Edmund Hillary

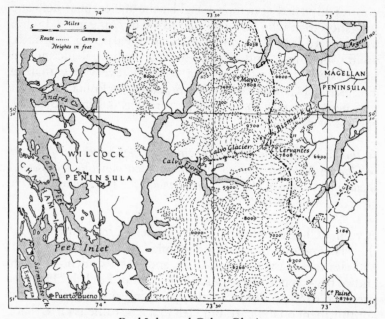

Peel Inlet and Calvo Glacier
(from *Mischief in Patagonia*, reproduced by permission of the Royal
Geographical Society)

Procter who put him in the way of things and told him what
had to be done. On the ice-cap journey talking was not so easy,
but there are occasions when it is an advantage not to be able to
exchange ideas—"the camel driver has his thoughts, and the
camel he has his."

On the morning of the 26th the S.S. *Arica* came alongside the
jetty bringing with her our missing tourist. Sailing time was
fixed for 2 o'clock. At 2.30 p.m. the crew began to assemble
and by 3 p.m. we were complete, a search party having
retrieved John from the Hotel de France where he was playing
the piano. By then a large crowd of friends, admirers, and no
doubt some critics, had assembled to see us start. After some
hasty last-minute photography we hoisted the jib so that her
head would sheer away from the jetty, and cast off the
remaining warps. For some as yet unexplained reason the jib
promptly fell into the sea and the next minute saw us stuck

hard and fast by the stern less than a ship's length from the waving crowd. The wise man sits on the hole in his carpet, but there was no covering our shame; the critics would need neither telescopes nor binoculars to discern our embarrassment. Having recovered the jib and unavailingly tried the engine which we had hitherto been too proud to use, we sent a warp ashore to the accompaniment of much friendly advice from the experts with the idea of pulling her off the mud. *Mischief*, who had so eagerly taken the ground on her arrival, seemed to have a liking for the place and would not budge. In the roads two Chilean cruisers lay at anchor and at this moment of crisis one of their picket boats was approaching the jetty at the good round pace common to picket boats, a sailor with a boathook standing rigidly to attention in the bow. Either by seamanlike intuition or at the instance of the loud instructions from the crowd, her helmsman grasped the idea that we wanted pulling off. Perhaps he thought we wanted shoving off, for putting his helm hard over, with little diminution of speed, he rammed us fair and square, projecting the still rigid, well-disciplined bowman half-way up our shrouds. It was a Saturday afternoon and one could almost hear the happy sigh of the crowd as they realised how wise they had been to spend it on the jetty. However, the aquatic sports were nearly over. With admirable fortitude *Mischief* uncomplainingly sustained this assault and rather surprisingly remained unmoved. But by now we had a line to the still quivering picket boat which, forging ahead, plucked us quickly into deeper water. With all speed we hoisted sail. Rounding the jetty and dipping our ensign to the cruisers, we headed south.

TO THE ICE-CAP

This streight is extreme cold; the trees seeme to stoope with the burden of the weather and yet are greene continually. Towards the South sea monstrous high hills and craggy rocks do exalt themselves, whose tops be all hoary with snow.

—*Hakluyt's "Voyages"*

STILL SOUTHWARDS! We had yet 50 miles to go before we
could round Cape Froward, the southernmost point of the
American continent in lat. 53° 56'S. We were sailing down
Broad Reach which continues south of Punta Arenas and is
some 20 miles wide. Gradually it narrows and leads into
Famine Reach where the Straits are only 5 miles wide. As if to
atone for the shambles of her departure *Mischief*, with two rolls
in the mainsail, went down Broad Reach at a great clip. The
flat, barren coasts of the eastern end gave way to bold, densely
wooded shores, while to the south rose the wild, snow-
covered peaks of Dawson Island. In the evening, as the wind
had freshened to force 7, we took another roll in the mainsail,
reefed the staysail, and set the storm jib. It was a short-lived
flurry; by midnight we were drifting past the Santa Ana
lighthouse with barely steerage way.

In the morning, there being no wind, we started motoring
in order to round Cape Froward. The glass was falling, the
western sky looked dirty, and we had no wish to be caught in a
gale from ahead off this notoriously stormy cape. We had with
us no Belloc whose love for the sea and sail was equalled only
by his hatred of machinery. "I would rather die of thirst", he
writes, "ten miles off the headland in a brazen calm, than have
on board what is monstrously called an auxiliary. . . For it is
with headlands as with harbours, if you have machinery
aboard your craft is gone." Whether it is done under sail or
power, the rounding of a great cape, more especially a cape
that divides two oceans, has about it something both solemn
and elating. Although it is a normal and long foreseen step, the
moment the cape looms in sight the pent-up hopes and fears of
a long voyage focus themselves upon its successful rounding.

Cape Froward is not like Cape Horn. The rounding of it,
unlike that of its more famous and tempestuous neighbour,
confers none of the traditional privileges such as spitting to
windward or drinking the loyal toast with one foot on the
table. Nevertheless, it is a noble and impressive headland, in
shape and size not unlike the Horn.

Having got fairly up to this defiant looking headland we
stopped the engine and sailed slowly past with a light north-
westerly breeze, passing near enough to see clearly the big

white cross on the summit. The wind then freshening from dead ahead we sought shelter in the attractively named Snug bay, about 5 miles north-west of the cape. The bay belied its name, for it is wide open to the west and it was to that quarter that the wind was backing. While lunching below we paid frequent visits on deck to see if the anchor was dragging. It is the kind of place of which the *Pilot* elsewhere advises the mariner that "anchoring in this bight must be prompted by necessity and not by any hope of tranquillity".

So far from tranquil were we that at 2 o'clock, in a rising wind and sea, we got up our anchor and sailed out. As Froward Reach is amply wide enough for manoeuvre we began to beat against wind, sea, and driving rain, for using the engine in such conditions was merely a waste of petrol. We sailed in this way all through the night, for although the reach is unlit there are no dangers and the iron-bound shores are steep-to. By daybreak we were off Pond Sound on the southern side and more than ready to seek shelter after such a wet, cold and anxious night. The necessity of putting the ship about at irregular and frequent intervals had meant that two of us had continually to be on deck, one steering and the other standing by. It was becoming clear that if the conditions met with on this first day and night west of Cape Froward were usual (as they were) a tough time lay ahead of us. The entrance to Pond Sound looked intricate and as we had not yet accustomed our weak nerves to threading tortuous passages beset with rocks, mostly within the proverbial biscuit's toss, we plumped for Port Gallant. This was reputedly one of the best anchorages in the Straits, spacious, sheltered, easy of access, and of moderate depth. Most often the depth is immoderate— a factor which rules out many otherwise safe and charming little holes where the mariner could hope to enjoy a care-free night. "No bottom at ten fathoms" was too frequently the leadsman's cry, and if one despaired of finding a better hole and went in close, by the time the anchor was dropped in 8 fathoms one found oneself within spitting distance of the shore, the ship having no room to swing.

Although it was late spring both the scene and the weather were wintry. The rain of the preceding night, falling as snow upon the grey hills around the bay, had clothed them with white to within five hundred feet of the sea; and as *Mischief* left the shelter of the bay to begin beating westward along English Reach she was assailed by furious squalls of rain, sleet, and snow. The squalls were prolonged, the intervals between them brief. But in these well-nigh land-locked channels there is never any sea to throw a boat about and *Mischief* was stiff and stout enough to sail happily in all but the strongest blasts under storm jib, reefed staysail, and reefed mainsail. In these waters this became our normal rig and we seldom had occasion to alter it. We had hoped to make Tilly bay, but after one of our hardest day's sailing, wind and tide defeated us. English Reach, the continuation of Froward Reach, is divided into two narrow channels by the Charles Islands which lie in mid-stream, so that the tides run strongly. Late in the afternoon, when the tide turned against us, we started the engine to help the sails. It was no good. Although at the start of a fresh tack we might be pointing at a mark on the far shore a good mile further west, inexorably the tide set us back. We barely held our ground, so after wasting much precious petrol on this treadmill we turned and ran back to Mussel bay where we anchored in 5 fathoms some 50 yards from the mouth of a small stream. We had made good only 10 miles. For a long day's beating against wind and rain, a discipline to which we had now become resigned, it was a small reward. Yet it was fascinating sailing; rounding miniature capes, peeping into hidden coves, tacking between rocky wooded shores backed by sombre fells of yellow heath and grey slabs, and over all the low, driving clouds. Desolate and forsaken as the scene was, it had the powerful appeal of an untrodden land and the bracing challenge of unsparing harshness.

Early next morning everyone went ashore to collect firewood, mussels and flowers. As it was our first landing on this wild coast we experienced a most satisfying thrill. As we ranged along the shore and a little way inland through bush and swamp, remarking the trees, the plants, the birds, a lake, and finally the mournful framework of a rude hut, we did indeed recapture something of "those first experiences, and felt as earlier men felt in a happier time". Firewood was needed for the cabin stove, now most necessary; the mussels of these coasts are famous for their size and succulence; while by collecting flowers I hoped to pay my modest tribute to science.

We sailed out as soon as the flood tide began to make. There was the usual head wind but the strong tide took us up to Crosstide Cape in three hours. Hereabouts three tidal streams meet—by English Reach from the Atlantic, by Crooked Reach from the Pacific, and by Canal Jerome from the miniature inland sea of Otway Water. Off the cape the wind died down and we had to start the engine to reach our chosen anchorage in Butler bay. According to the *Pilot* "for small vessels with local knowledge Butler bay affords anchorage on its western side over a bottom of rock more or less covered with mud". Even without local knowledge the information was enough. We were always amazed by the thoroughness of the sailing directions, for they were based largely on surveys by sailing vessels over a hundred years ago. The names of men like Fitzroy, Stokes, Lecky, Wharton, and their ships, *Beagle*, *Adventure*, *Sylvia*, *Nassau*, recur constantly on the charts. We were humbled by the thoughts of those men who had spent so many years in these tempestuous waters, hemmed in among islets and hidden rocks, riding out gales, drenched by constant rain, and who in open boats sought out and sounded all the various channels and anchorages.

In the evening after a day of rain and sleet, we dropped anchor in 4 fathoms only about 20 yards from shore.

"Mussels for supper and snow after" is the last enigmatic entry in my note of Butler bay. The following day, 1 December, we suffered a serious mishap. On a dry, dull morning we motored out and as there was no wind outside we kept the engine running. Two hours later a valve spring broke. The box of spare parts made up for us by the agents for our type of engine had no replacement. The engine could not be used except for short spells in moments of crisis or when making or leaving harbour. Peel Inlet looked an uncommonly long way off.

While the rain fell in great gouts we sat below in moderate comfort with a smart fire burning. As is a habit of cabin skylights ours leaked a little so that throughout our stay in the channels we had to keep the cover on. The canvas having been waterproofed with a preparation of my own making had a yellowish glaze, and the subdued light reminded us of sitting in an aquarium. It was not only the light that gave us this idea for most things about us were wet. The twilight of the cabin reflected our drooping spirits. We had expected bad weather but not quite so bad as that which we were now experiencing. Rain, bitter squalls of hail and snow, strong winds funnelling their way down the channels from dead ahead, were our daily and nightly portion. Perhaps we deserved it, for it resembled the Punishment of Gluttons in the *Inferno*:

> Ceaseless, accursed, heavy and cold, unchanged
> For ever both in kind and in degree:
> Large hail, discoloured water, sleety flaw
> Through the dim midnight air streamed down amain.

We had scarcely seen the sun since leaving Punta Arenas and the glass now stood at 28.75, well below the normal for that region. The breakdown of the engine also weighed heavily on us, and since it could not be repaired our 80 gal. of petrol on deck and the prospect of more at Puerto Bueno merely added to our exasperation. Equally worrying was the paraffin shortage. We had already begun to economise and those left on board at Peel Inlet would have to make do with wood. An almost painless method of economising had been devised by John in the form of what he called dual purpose pie. One must imagine a beef steak and kidney pudding (bully beef doing duty for both steak and kidney) crowned with a 6 in. thick roof of pastry. One ate half the roof with the meat and put the remainder aside to eat later with jam or treacle as the sweet. Since all ills are good when attended by food, we ate one that night.

Battling with engine problems and rain, Mischief *made it to Puerto Bueno, at the Pacific end of the Strait, and so up to Peel Inlet.*

Peel Inlet opens off Canal Sarmiento about eight miles north of Puerto Bueno round Cape Antonio. The northern side of the entrance is formed by the shore of Chatham Island and between cape and island, across the 6 mile wide entrance, are a few small islets. Off the shore of one of these a large object in the water arrested our attention, and when we realised it was not a boat but an ice floe we examined it with increased interest but with no great concern. A few miles up we passed the very narrow entrance to Pitt channel, a short cut leading to Canal San Andres and thence to the main channel. Several more floes, some of fantastic shape and delicate blue colouring, now drifted by close to the ship and were greeted with pleased cries, much as some ignorant clown might greet the first few ranging shots of a hostile battery. It is ridiculous to think that we went out of our way to photograph these feeble harbingers of the coming hordes.

When ahead of us a long line of what appeared to be white water was seen stretching almost from shore to shore, we at length awoke to the fact that trouble might be at hand. The mood of care-free happiness, encouraged by the near accomplishment of the long outward passage and the closeness of our objective, changed rapidly to one of extreme anxiety, and made me wonder where we could go should Peel Inlet be blocked. These weak fears, engendered possibly by a diet of mussels, proved groundless. That which from afar had looked like almost solid ice, dissolved on approach to a mass of small floes (technically known as "bergy bits") through which we had no difficulty in steering, though at a very slow pace. There were frequent leads of more open water and with a lookout posted in the bows to signal to the helmsman it was possible to avoid any serious collisions. If one appeared to be unavoidable a man with the boathook and another standing on the bobstay did what they could to deflect the floe. We were surprised, even alarmed, at the weight of impact of a floe no bigger than a small table. From the cross-trees it was possible to see well ahead and to plan one's course according to the shifting ice.

After some 6 miles of threading our way through patches of ice and occasional stretches of clear water we at last turned into a small bay to reconnoitre the approach to the next "sea-level" glacier. Waterfall bay, as we called it, was magnificent if nothing else. Quite near and high on our left a great white stream of ice swept round the foot of a black ridge to break into

myriads of cracks, seracs, and crevasses, many of them scintil-
lating with a vivid blue, as they plunged steeply to the
ice-strewn water. On one side was bare rock; on the other,
almost as steep, evergreen forest. On the other side of the bay,
the waterfall itself which in any other bay would have been
impressive, faded into insignificance before its stupendous,
frozen counterpart. Here we could approach near to the glacier
but we could see no likely landing place; and even suppose we
did land, an ascent of the ice-fall was obviously impractical,
while the rock on the left looked steep. The thought of having
to make our first carry on untried legs up such steep rock
daunted me. Perhaps it was that, as the time for abandoning
the snug shelter of the ship drew inevitably nearer, the more
ready I was to postpone it. Anyway it seemed wiser to enlarge
the circle of our acquaintance before we finally committed
ourselves, so without dropping anchor we left the bay.

Several miles further north the fjord opens out into a wide
reach, the eastern shore receding to form the entrance to what
is called on the map Calvo inlet. Inside the inlet we could see
three glaciers. There were several more in a very narrow
extension of Calvo which penetrated inland for several miles,
and yet another which terminated a mile from the sea on the
north side of the entrance. Here were infinite riches in a little
space. As the wide reach was free of ice we made sail and stood
over to an island in the middle of the entrance hoping to find an
anchorage. Here the water was deep, so we carried on and
closed the northern shore where there was ice. Soon we were
creeping through a narrow lead, with the shore close on our
port hand and thick ice on the other. We began sounding,
determined to anchor as soon as we found a reasonable depth,
for evening was drawing on. At last we got 11 fathoms and let
go the anchor; we were 50 yards from the shore and about a
mile from the nearest glacier. On the whole the day had been
fine with a few wintry gleams of sunshine. Thirty miles inland
from the main channel in the lee of the imposing range on
Wilcock peninsula, the absence of violent winds was most
noticeable. Indeed the comparatively fair weather we enjoyed
throughout our long stay in Calvo could only be attributed to
the shielding effect of this high land.

Our plan now was to take *Mischief* as near as possible to the glacier immediately ahead of us. After a peaceful night in the ice we motored very slowly for an hour and a half through thick floes before we anchored again close in to the bank in 6 fathoms. As our cable rattled out steamer ducks scuttled away, a penguin bobbed up, and from a nearby cave a sea lion roared in astonishment. After lunch the shore party went off in the dinghy to reconnoitre. The floes were too close together for rowing so we either paddled or hauled ourselves along with the help of an ice-axe with which the bowman reached out, striking the point into the floe ahead. Having passed close under the cave where the sea lion lived with his harem we found an easy landing place, but upon climbing a rock ridge we discovered that an arm of the fjord lay between us and our objective. At the head of this little arm was another branch of the same glacier, but the little arm was chock-a-block with ice and the way along the shore looked long and difficult. But on the other side, where the main glacier ended abruptly in a hundred foot high ice-wall, a little sandy beach beckoned us invitingly. The beach was within 50 yards of the left bank of the glacier, and dare we but force *Mischief* through the ice to anchor there, one problem at least—that of ferrying our stores ashore—would be solved. Whether a way up the glacier could be found was another thing. That part of it overlooking the sea was impassable, but we had already noticed what looked like a small moraine on the flank of the glacier nearest to the beach. It appeared that the beach with its sand and boulders was in fact the termination of the moraine.

Because of the tide and wind the ice conditions in the bay were seldom static. Our first sight of the cove off the sandy beach showed it to be free of ice and the water between reasonably open. After tea, when we began moving, more ice, including some very large floes, had drifted in. This was added to by the continual discharge of ice from the glacier snout, from which, with a thunderous roar, hundred of tons of ice crashed frequently into the water, setting up a young tidal wave. Hardening our hearts we drove the long-suffering *Mischief* slowly through a mile of thickly clustering floes, mindful only of her propeller. The shape of a floe above water

is no indication of what goes on below and there was always
the danger of a floe capsizing under our counter on to the
propeller as we brushed past. At last this frightening and
heartrending shunting of ice came to an end and by 8 o'clock
we had *Mischief* anchored in 7 fathoms only 50 yards from the
beach.

As anchorages go this one was more spectacular than safe.
Within a stone's throw of us there was on the one hand a
fantastically furrowed cliff of sapphire blue ice; on the other,
and equally close, a heavily forested cliff; while around us lay a
slowly circling mass of floes of alarming size, some of them as
big as a cottage with the garden thrown in. Although we had
reached the haven of our choice I was far from tranquil. It was
obvious that more reconnoitring must be done before the
shore party could disembark. It was more than possible that if
more ice drifted in the ship might not be able to leave or might
even be pushed on to the beach. Already the knocking about
sustained by poor *Mischief* and her tender was reacting upon
her owner as if he had suffered in person; indeed, what with
chilblains, back-ache, and a stiff knee his sufferings were at
that time not merely vicarious. Even Charles, as our short
excursion of the morning showed, was not as spry as he might
have been, for he moved with more dignity and deliberation
than the occasion demanded.

Next day, Friday 16 December, we went ashore to try our
luck on the moraine. Compared with Himalayan moraines it
was despicably small and failed miserably in offering the easy
going that they generally provide. (The absence of well developed moraines was a characteristic of all the glaciers we
saw.) About half a mile up from the shore, toiling mainly in
the trough between ice and moraine or moraine and jungle, we
met the first obstacle, a 20 ft. high wet slab up which obviously
the loads would have to be hauled. About a like distance
beyond this we met the type of obstacle we had half expected—a place where the ice so impinged against a rock wall
that it left us no way through, round or over. Thus we were
forced to seek a way on the glacier itself which at this point
proved more accommodating. We found it to be made up of a
series of transverse crevasses, the ridges between them being

sometimes very narrow and sometimes a yard or two wide. Where two crevasses merged together, as they often did, there was a void, and where two ridges met there was a pinnacle. On the whole it was a labyrinth which Charles tackled with more optimism than I felt justified, but after about an hour's hard work, finding a way mainly by trial and error, we emerged in mid-glacier on more or less unbroken ice. So far so good. Heading up the glacier in a crevasse-free trough we gained another 500 ft. of height before becoming entangled in a frightful jumble of seracs and yawning chasms. Above and beyond this devastated region we saw what appeared to be a flat shelf promising better going, but there was no reaching it that day.

The weather had been kind. True, it drizzled incessantly but it had been quite calm. When we got back to the shore at 6 o'clock we found that more ice had drifted in. Between ship and shore it lay so thickly that we had to haul ourselves back to the ship by means of a rope. We learnt that down here there had been a lot of wind which had brought into the cove some gigantic bergs. The ship's party had had an anxious time, watching helplessly as these monsters closed in scraping the ship's side and threatening to crush her, for the ice to seaward was by then too thick to permit escape. The pressure of the ice lifted the dinghy out of the water till it perched forlornly on a big floe. All they could do was to try to stop the bigger bergs from touching the rudder or fouling the bobstay, the bowsprit shrouds, or the bowsprit itself. As soon as the wind dropped, which it did as suddenly as it had begun, the ice began to drift out so that when we returned we saw only the aftermath of this heavy onslaught.

On the whole, despite the inconclusive nature of our recon-naissance, it seemed best for us to gamble on finding a route to the ice-cap by way of what we now called the Calvo glacier; for there are few ice-falls which time and perseverance will not overcome. The essential thing was to get the ship away as early as possible. The morning's inrush of ice had forced her perceptibly nearer the shore and the night's happenings emphasised strongly that this was no place to linger. About midnight an appalling crash close alongside brought us all on deck with a run. We were in time to see the water still boiling and surging and blocks of ice shooting up from below. One of our bigger neighbours had capsized and had broken up with all the turmoil and upheaval of water that would accompany the death throes of a stricken whale.

In the morning, except for two monsters which lay menacingly close, the cove was free of ice. Having made our decision we set about sorting stores and getting them ashore while the water remained open. In the cabin Chaos and old Night reigned. John and I checked food against food lists and filled paraffin containers, while the others weeded out their climbing kit from among sea clothes. Charles's impedimenta for journeying by land and sea for the first time lay remorselessly revealed. From time to time brief glimpses of his treasures had roused our curiosity and now Michael was able to complete the inventory he had thought it worth while surreptitiously making, either in furtherance of his sociological studies or with a view to equipping himself for some future journey on the lines of his illustrious model. A copy of this inventory which he kindly gave me, perhaps merits insertion here rather than in the obscurity of an appendix:

One tin of anchovies and two of sardines.
Palm and sail needle.
An old piece of canvas.
Yachting cap.
Tattered Balaclava helmet (looks like a crown of thorns)
Assorted empty tins of all shapes and sizes, mostly rusty.
Old pieces of string and cloth.
Assorted buttons.
Salt and pepper in empty first-aid tins.
A pair of pliers.
Rusty knife on an enormous khaki lanyard.

Dipping pen and ink bottle with huge cork in silver container.
Compass and binoculars.
Thick tailor's tape measure.
Assorted spices in small tins.
Dilapidated billy-can, half rusted through.
Old sweater and wind jacket, torn to shreds.
Patches with bits of trouser attached, once grey flannels.
A pack of cards, incomplete.
A sextant, too venerable to be cleaned.
Some maps and charts of S. America in general.

Selection of *Reader's Digest*.

A tin of pea-nuts.

Ancient camera, operated by guess work.

Bottle of quinine.

Home-made solid fuel burner with bits of "Meta".

A pair of mittens of very original design.

Badminton Library *Yachting*—very heavy.

Some whisky.

Hooded climbing jacket, home-made.

Although the glass was rising rain fell all day. We ferried the stores ashore, pitched the two tents, and left the stores inside. In the afternoon we made another reconnaissance but it did nothing towards clearing away our doubts. On the next day, with the willing help of the ship's party in carrying loads, we hoped we should be able to make a flying start.

So began the remarkable crossing of the ice-cap, the watershed between Pacific and Atlantic oceans; a six-week journey whose climax, for Tilman, was one of his "memorable bathes" in the icy waters of Lake Argentino on the far side. There were several narrow escapes before the moment when, from the beach in the Calvo fjord, her skipper again saw Mischief *"imperturbably solid and homelike even among such wild surroundings". She had been, in the interim, and under Procter's command, grounded and then trapped and battered by ice; the propeller was wrecked: so Tilman made for the open Pacific, and repairs at Valparaiso. The circumnavigation of South America was completed as* Mischief *passed through the Panama Canal; and after a call at Bermuda, romped home towards Lymington.*

By great circle course the distance from Bermuda to the Scillies is 3,353 miles. We did it in thirty-two days and for most of the way we had generous gales of wind and usually from a favourable direction. The passage was marked by a number of minor mishaps, attributable sometimes to our own folly or laziness and sometimes to the wearing out of the running rigging on the last few thousand miles of a twenty thousand mile voyage. The first, which might have been more serious, occurred a few days out early one morning in my watch. We had been running all night with whole mainsail and a twin boomed out. When I took over she was rolling and yawing wildly, but probably no more than she had been doing during the night. At length the gybe which I was beginning to fear happened. For a moment the wire boom guy held the boom high in the air; then it broke, and the boom crashed over wrapping the main sheet round the horse and breaking the back-stay tackle. The staysail was flat aback as well, so that when the crew tumbled up in response to my yell they were not a little startled by my new arrangements. With the main-sheet round the horse it was impossible for us to haul the boom inboard so that the sail could then be lowered. Taking a horribly rash decision I told them to stand by for another gybe. Back the boom came with a sickening crash, the main sheet unwound itself in a flash, and all was well. We then handed the mainsail, hoisted the twins, and felt much safer.

Towards the end of June there began a spell of dirty weather which was to last almost to the Scillies. Rain, high winds and rough seas combined to make life wet and wearing. The companion way was boarded up, the hatch cover closed, the skylight battened down—but nevertheless water managed to find its way below. Although the helmsman was partly pro-tected by the dodger rigged round the cockpit he still had the benefit of enough spray and solid water to keep him awake; and even the briefest of visits to the cockpit to survey the weather compelled one to be fully clothed. As one stood at the foot of the companion struggling into wet oilskins before going on watch, one would call hopefully to the helmsman for some words of comfort, for the least hint of a change for the better. But seldom were they forthcoming. Instead, more briefly and rudely worded, one heard:

> I tell you naught for your comfort,
> Yea, naught for your desire,
> Save that the sky grows darker yet
> And the seas rise higher.

The night of 29 June was particularly bad. The glass having fallen had apparently steadied. We had the trysail up and a twin boomed out. During the night the glass slumped to 29.2″ and at four in the morning, when we must have been doing 7 knots, we had to hand the sails and run under storm jib alone. When daylight broke on a grey wilderness of white-capped waves we successfully experimented with a couple of oil bags trailing from either quarter. We found that even the finest film of oil had a remarkably soothing effect when angry waves tried to break close to our counter. Towards the close of a dark and dismal day a German ship altered course to see how we were faring. She came very close to us but signalling was impossible as we were more often out of sight in the trough of a wave than in view.

Discomfort can more easily be borne when one is being driven homewards with such vigour. Every day we ran our hundred miles or more, whether under storm jib alone or with the trysail and a twin. Opportunities for taking sights had to be promptly seized. They were not common and on two consecutive days we could not take any at all. However, on 5 July, in improving weather, we found ourselves only 60 miles from the Bishop rock. That night we picked up the light and by breakfast time on a lovely summer morning we were off St Mary's. A year and a day after leaving we passed Falmouth, but by now we were enveloped in dense fog. For three days as we groped our way up Channel the fog persisted. Because of the tide we anchored in home waters for the first time in Swanage bay, but at last on 9 July we entered Lymington river and tied up at the yard where we had fitted out.

Next day the crew went their several ways and I was left once more to commune with *Mischief*. I will not pretend that at all times throughout this voyage we were a band of brothers. Patient Griselda herself and a company of angels would sometimes find their tempers strained to breaking point when cooped up in a small ship for months together. "Ships are all right—it's the men in them", was, I suspect, the thought of each one of us on many occasions; and I know for certain of a few occasions when the same idea was openly and more pointedly expressed. But we were old enough or sensible enough to bear and forbear, and to put the ship and the enterprise in hand before our own feelings. It was this loyalty to the ship, and not my management, that held the crew together and enabled us to bring a worth-while undertaking to a successful end.

It had been a voyage of 20,000 miles; and had proved the ship, the master, and the way of life that Tilman was to pursue for the next twenty years.

III

1959: Mischief Among the Penguins

Again Mischief *voyaged to the far South: the Crozet Isles in the Southern Ocean, mountainous, uninhabited, and unclimbed. After an unsuccessful attempt to reach them in 1957 (he settled for a circumnavigation of Africa, a 21,000-mile voyage) Tilman recruited a fresh crew in 1959. W. A. Procter came again; Roger Tufft; a Dutchman, Jan Garnier; Jim Osborne, a geologist; and John Lyons, who had crossed the Atlantic fifty-one times, playing the double-bass in the orchestra of the* Queen Mary. *First,* Mischief *herself required attention.*

FITTING-OUT

THE LONG-DRAWN-OUT preparations for a voyage have about them something unreal. Sailing day is distant and nebulous. The fear begins to creep in that one is preparing for an event that never will take place, and in face of the frustrations and disappointments that arise in finding a crew, this feeling of futility is almost justified. There were times when futility seemed the most welcome as well as the most likely upshot, when the idea of failing to start did not altogether displease. In fact, "Belial, clothed in Reason's garb, counselled ignoble ease." Is your journey really necessary? became the question. Why attempt to drag five other misguided men halfway across the world when it is obvious that most of our present-day troubles come from men not staying quietly in their room at home? But upon visiting *Mischief* to see how things are going, such weak thoughts are speedily banished. She and her kind were never built so that men should stay quietly at home. She breathes sturdy, eager confidence, a living embodiment of the truth that the sea is for sailing, that strenuousness is the immortal path and sloth the way of death.

After our return in July 1958 from the abortive attempt to reach the Crozet, *Mischief* spent the winter in her usual mud berth at Lymington. It was not until about November that I had gathered sufficient confidence to decide upon fitting-out for a second attempt, and as a preliminary had her hauled out for survey. Though the hull of an old boat like *Mischief* (built in 1906) may be generally sound, one needs to be always on watch for any slight symptoms of decay. Faults and weaknesses that might be safely overlooked for a season's sailing in home waters must be put right before undertaking a deep-sea voyage. A few days after she had been hauled out I heard the bad news that part of the hull had been damaged by teredo worm. I went at once to Lymington, where with Humphrey Barton, the surveyor, together with a shipwright armed with chisel and mallet, we spent a gloomy morning ascertaining the extent of the damage.

It was mostly confined to the planks forward of midships to about three feet below the water line. The planks had to be examined one by one for small holes no bigger than those made by a one-inch nail, the only visible signs of the worm's ravages. At all these suspicious holes a blow with the chisel would open up a small groove running along the plank, increasing gradually to the size of a man's finger. Each groove had to be followed up to the end until the full extent of the damage was exposed. Sometimes a whole plank had to be condemned, sometimes only part. Some planks were so riddled as to resemble a honeycomb, leaving a bare half-inch of sound wood in planks that were one and a half inches thick. Ignorance is bliss. Whether the attack had started back at Durban or at intermediate places such as Beira, the Comoro Islands, Aldabra or Aden, we must have sailed most of the way home in an unusually fragile hull.

In the days of wooden ships, the teredo worm was rightly dreaded as a deadly menace in tropical waters. No unprotected wood can resist it. In its home-made burrow it grows to a length of a foot, and some species are reputed to grow to six feet. No worms remained in any of the burrows we opened up, the only trace left being a coating of a hard, shelly substance. They rasp away the wood with minute teeth, visible only under a microscope, and the wood dust, after being acted upon by digestive ferments, is their food. As the hole of entry is so small it seems that the teredo gains its first footing when in the embryo stage, and consequently its existence and subsequent growth depend upon its finding a piece of wood as host. Why then are there such multitudes in being in the sea when suitable hosts are comparatively rare? I have had occasion to ponder over a similar question when being sucked dry by leeches in the Himalayan foothills. How do these revolting creatures survive when there are no men or animals to prey upon? For really bad leech-infested country is normally deserted for that reason, and no one travels through it if it can be avoided.

It was odd that we found no worms still in burrows, for no full-grown worm could get out through the tiny entry hole. They must have died on reaching colder waters and their bodies dissolved away. The only teredo worm I have seen was one solitary specimen which we found lodged in *Mischief*'s keel when I first took her over at Palma, Majorca. At that time her hull was coppered but we had to remove the copper in order to examine the hull, and it was so badly torn in the process as not to be worth putting back. This worm, five inches long and a half-inch thick, had got in where the copper had been torn by touching on a piece of coral rock. Copper sheathing is the complete answer to teredo worm danger so long as it remains in good condition. But it is not a thing you can fit and forget, for if there is a hole the teredo worm will find it.

Anti-fouling paint is an effective defensive measure if the paint is good of its kind and frequently renewed. But it is expensive, the best quality costing as much as £12 a gallon, while the amount needed to cover *Mischief*'s hull is nearly three gallons. When we had last painted the hull at Cape Town on the previous voyage in November 1957, I had on board a

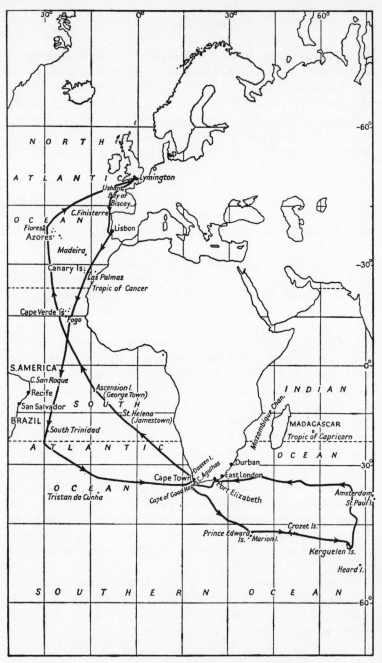

Lymington to the Kerguelen Islands and back
(from *Mischief Among the Penguins*)

5-gallon drum of anti-fouling paint of unknown origin which had been given me by a friendly shipowner a year earlier in Valparaiso. Naturally we made use of it and as things turned out we might as well have used face-powder. Two months later bare wood began to show along and just below the water-line. We ought to have done something about it but at none of the places we touched at on our way up the Indian Ocean to Aden were there any facilities for hauling out. So we pressed on regardless and ultimately had to pay for this penny-wise pound-foolish policy, and our subsequent neglect, to the tune of two hundred feet of new planking at a pound a foot.

This wormy digression, painful to write and painful to read, must be forgiven. Most people, especially the elderly, are too ready to discuss their ailments. I feel that *Mischief*, with the garrulity of age, would have much to say about her manifold complaints, the expensive operations she has undergone, the face-lifts and other attempts at rejuvenation. For it is with ships as with men:

> There is no fortress of man's flesh so made
> But subtle, treacherous Time comes creeping in.
> Oh, long before his last assaults begin
> The enemy's on; the stronghold is betrayed.

After taking advice I had already decided that *Mischief* should have a new deck fitted; and the cost of this so overshadowed everything else that the bill for teredo damage might be considered as merely "a trifling sum of misery new added to the foot of the account." But both Humphrey Barton and myself were fearful of what the removal of the old deck might reveal, of how extensive had been the ravages of time, rot and general decay in places that are normally hidden from view. They proved to be less than expected, but while the deck was off the opportunity to stiffen and strengthen the old boat was taken. Extra beams were put in; the half-beams in the way of the mast replaced by through beams; the half-beams each side of the cockpit were tied to the carlines with steel plates; and steel brackets were fitted to the ends of the main beams to tie them to the shelf. When suggesting these improvements

Barton wrote: "The general condition is better than I expected but there is not much holding the two sides of the boat together as the ends of the beams are in poor condition. The brackets should hold her together for many years to come." To which I could only say, "Amen, and so be it."

THE VOYAGE SOUTH

Once again Mischief *sailed down the Bay of Biscay, and to Las Palmas in the Canaries; leaving at last for Cape Town on 26 August.*

WE HAVE NEVER suffered from lack of wind in the vicinity of the Canaries. By breakfast we had reeled off ninety miles and in the three succeeding days we ran 360 miles. We had no complaints on that score but we had good reason to complain of the lack of life in the sea. In these waters we had been accustomed to catching an occasional fish, a dorado or a bonito, both delicious to eat. This time we caught none and were not destined to catch any, so that towards the end of the voyage we were too disgusted even to troll a line. Nor were the flying fish as numerous or accommodating as usually they are. It used to be an everyday occurrence, but now we rarely collected enough fish from the scuppers to give all hands a fish or two for breakfast. Dolphins, too, seemed less common than formerly. And the welcome break in the monotonous days of a long ocean passage which is made by a visit from a school of dolphin cannot come too often.

Those few species of fish which are neither frightened nor fierce are sad and solemn, whereas the dolphin, as befits its warm blood, seems to be always gay and frolicsome. It makes one laugh out loud to see them come scurrying after a ship they have just spotted, leaping into the air and turning somersaults as they come, as if overjoyed at the larks they're about to have. Scorning the dull wake, they make a bee-line for the stem, where a dozen of them begin to cross and re-cross in swift streaks of foam, missing by inches the plunging stem, the bobstay, and their jostling playmates. Everyone crowds in the bows, fascinated to watch these torpedo-like, olive-green

shapes with white bellies, the embodiment of lithe speed and
grace. Or to see another half-dozen, apparently waiting their
turn for a dance round the stem, take station just off the bows
in line abreast where together they rise, snort, and plunge
while maintaining their dressing like a file of soldiers. I should
like to see them having fun with a ship going at thirty knots.
Mischief provided poor sport for creatures that with a scarcely
perceptible flick of the tail shoot through the water like a
bullet. Soon they would disappear as suddenly as they had
come. Having had our amusement for the day, we would go
below and the helmsman back to the tiller:

> Though pleased to see the dolphins play,
> I mind my compass and my way.

We were in the full swing of the Trades, which could be
counted upon to carry us at least as far as the Cape Verde
Islands some 900 miles to the south. With the twin staysails set
we need hardly touch a rope and for the next ten days there
would be little to do but steer. In the big sailing ships there was
always plenty of work for crews that were proportionately
scanty. In fact one wonders how that maze of rigging, literally
miles of wire and rope, most of it out of sight from the deck,
ever got looked after. In our case there was nothing to be done
except the navigation and small repair jobs, both of which I
was glad to do for the sake of occupation and a liking for
"sailorising". Roger, too, soon picked up navigation and his
results were a useful check on mine. With five men available,
watch-keeping duties were extremely light, one spell of three
hours at the helm by day and two hours at night. There was an
ample collection of books on board—I will not call it a
library—from the *Odyssey* in the original Greek (Procter) to
geological tomes, Space Travel, Westerns, and the *Scragged in
her Silk Stockings* type. They catered for all tastes, and they
might have come off the sixpenny barrow.

Besides reading, most of the crew had an infinite capacity
for sleep which, in such circumstances, is of great value. Chess
was played too, and Jim was quite insatiable. Sometimes we
had to postpone changing sails until a game was finished, but
when he and Procter started playing chess on watch I had to

draw the line. Chess is usually a silent game but Procter maintained a running commentary for the benefit of his small public, who were anyway reading. It went like this:

"Let's see now. If I go there he'll take me with the bishop. No, that's not a good move. I'll just push this pawn up and wait for my plan to fructify. The situation seems not unpromising. . . . Hell! There goes my queen! I never saw that knight, Jim. Are you quite sure it was on the right square?"

Thus, day and night, with no help from us but a touch of the tiller, the ship rolled southwards, the long booms of the twins slowly describing wide arcs between sea and sky, the pursuing seas creaming along the hull and spurting through the scuppers at every roll. On the last day of August we had the Cape Verde Islands abeam sixty miles to the east and out of sight.

When we were twelve days out from Las Palmas, the Trades at last began to falter, twelve days of indolence and tranquil sundrenched hours until:

> Languor suffering on the rack of bliss
> Confess that man was never made for this.

As the wind veered and finally settled in south-west, while the sky clouded over and a steady drizzle began, we took in the twins and hoisted all plain sail. Between the North-east and South-east Trades are the doldrums, the two-hundred or three-hundred-mile-wide region where calms, light variable winds and rain squalls are to be expected. It shifts north or south according to the time of year and may be narrower or wider. On this occasion we were lucky, for we had fairly steady winds from south to south-west and by standing on the starboard tack we made good progress south or a little east of South. As the Equatorial current sets strongly towards Brazil, it is unwise to go on the other tack until one is sure of having picked up the S.E. Trades. On account of this current, southward-bound ships have sometimes been unable to weather Cape San Roque, in which case they have to make the circuit of the North Atlantic and try again. On the previous voyage we had stood on the port tack when we met these south-west winds and had fetched up between Cape San Roque and Recife. As we were bound for San Salvador, 300 miles to the south, we had to sail close-hauled or even tack in order to make it.

Thanks to some very heavy squalls of rain we were able to refill the forty-gallon deck-tank. The mainsail makes an excellent catchment area, and if it is reefed with one roll round the boom, the rain runs along the boom and trickles out by the mast. The man on water duty, usually stripped naked, slings saucepans on the boom and empties them into the tank. This is warm, wet fun, while at the same time we can wash clothes and have a freshwater bath. For Roger and me such baths were superfluous, for we made a solemn rite of pouring three buckets of sea-water over ourselves before breakfast, wet or fine. Having then combed our hair we sat down to breakfast with a warranted feeling of superiority over our frowsy companions, except for John, who had been called at 7 a.m., had probably already shaved, looked wide awake and was comparatively cheerful, sometimes too cheerful. When John banged a plate by way of a bell, Procter, like a lean, dishevelled fakir, would crawl sideways out of his blankets and slide into his seat, the blankets being left in *statu quo*, so that he could crawl back into them after breakfast. The only time, I think, he folded them was the day we got back to Lymington when he was about to leave the ship. We now had the table covered with some plastic material of a tasteful red, having advanced a long way since the days when we used newspapers. But this meant that there was nothing handy on the table for Procter to read, so he had to rummage among his blankets for his Greek Homer or, failing that, some Space Fiction.

Jim, whose bunk was above Procter's, and, therefore, rather close to the deckhead, had on this account very little freeboard for his face. Since there was no possibility of his first sitting up, he too rolled out sideways, but he did it circumspectly for fear of treading on Procter. By now he had a beard, and since his sparse hair hardly warranted combing, his appearance was less shocking. Jan, who never ate breakfast, put in a sort of token appearance, for it was a rule—enforced against some murmuring—that everyone should be up for breakfast whether or not he wanted any. Under the circumstances it was usually a sombre meal. There was no need to discourage hilarity, for it was never contemplated. Speech, if anyone was foolhardy enough to attempt it, usually concerned the prevailing weather or the ship's progress during the night. All this, of course, is standard practice at breakfast tables and there was no reason why we should depart from it even if we were on the high seas.

Since porridge uses a lot of water, on alternate days we had dried eggs. I confess that dried egg is best eaten in cakes, when one is not aware of it, but if well laced with pepper, or better still chillies, it can be eaten with modified ecstasy. I was shocked to find that Procter, who used to be omnivorous in the full sense of the word, could not face it. When both the bread and the "hard-bake" were finished we used Lifeboat biscuits for conveying the largest possible amount of butter and marmalade to the mouth. It was mainly out of consideration for these trimmings that we had to ration the biscuit.

For lunch we rang the changes on cheese, sardines, herrings, bully beef or Spam, with dates, Marmite or peanut butter as "afters". The cheeses were whole ten-pound Cheddars. Although packed in salt they did not keep well, becoming in time a little dry and more than a little strong. However, with a raw onion to qualify the tang they went down very well, at least John and I thought so. Onions always keep well and it is a time-honoured principle that one should never go to sea without one. Hard, white cabbages also keep, and for the first month or six weeks of a passage we used cabbage for salads. For tea we had biscuits and jam, sweet biscuits and occasionally cake, pancakes or soda bread, depending on the cook's benevolence towards us.

But the evening meal we regarded as our main hope and stay, like so many gross rustics "whose principal enjoyment is their dinner, and who see the sun rise with no other hope than that they shall fill their belly before it sets." It consisted of whatever dish the skill and ingenuity of the cook might concoct from ingredients limited to bully beef, sausages, Spam, rice, beans, lentils, peas, macaroni, spaghetti, potatoes and onions, helped out with dried vegetables and soups for flavouring. This would be followed by stewed prunes, raisins or apples, or a massive steamed pudding. The crew took it in turns to help the cook by drawing sea water, emptying the gash bucket and filling the stoves. He washed the pans too, while John did the plates and utensils. Sea water can be used for cooking potatoes, likewise for porridge and rice if sufficiently diluted, and all the washing-up is done with it. I had not been able to get any dehydrated meat such as we had on previous voyages. For cooking it is far better than bully beef, which is best eaten when cold.

The mainsail still had to come down frequently to have seams restitched. In the doldrums, when it was sodden with rain, this was no fun. Sewing wet flax canvas is a tedious job because the needle sticks and has to be dragged through with pliers, a method which sooner or later breaks the needle. Provided we could keep the sail full we had no trouble, but with a gaff mainsail a light wind is constantly spilled from the sail by the gaff swinging about. By means of a boom guy and a kicking strap the boom can be held steady but the gaff is impossible to control. The vang (pronounced "wang" by Thames bargemen), a rope leading down from the peak of the gaff, is useful when lowering the sail but it does not stop the gaff swinging. Thus while the boom remains steady the gaff swings and gives the loose canvas a flick like the crack of a whip which puts a fierce strain on the seams. If the wind dropped in the night, the helmsman had to make up his mind whether to call the sleeping crew to get the sail down or to whistle for a wind and wait hopefully. If he waited too long he might find, when he next flashed his torch over the sail, that several feet of seam had opened. In this respect a Bermuda sail is preferable as there is no gaff to torment the sail. On the other hand, the gaff rig is more efficient down-wind, the commonest point of sailing on an ocean voyage, and is much more pleasing to look at.

Owing to constant cloud and rain we got no noon sight for latitude until September 10, when we were four degrees north of the Equator. The weather continued uncertain and squally as we worked our way south, first on one tack then on the other, until on the 16th we crossed the line in Longitude 24 west. John celebrated the event with a particularly fine cake iced with Equatorial emblems. By crossing the Equator so far

east, we were well placed, being 500 miles to windward of
Cape San Roque, in spite of having been set thirty miles a day
westward by the Equatorial current. For a vessel bound south,
the South-east Trades are not very favourable until she is about
five degrees south of the Line, when they begin to draw more
to the east, thus allowing her to steer south without being
close-hauled all the time. When the wind freed us a little, we
set one of the twins in place of the working jib to give us more
speed. We got little benefit from it, for the same night, in a
squall, the clew split and the remnants we gathered in were not
worth putting together. Strong, squally weather with a rough
sea continued for several days and gave us a fine shove to the
south. Knocking off two degrees of latitude a day, by
September 27, when five weeks out, we had logged 3,000
miles and were half-way to the Cape.

After a stay at Cape Town for repairs, Mischief *sailed for the Crozet
in the Southern Ocean: Marion Island is 1,100 miles south-east by
east of Cape Town; once sighted, Tilman planned to run the last 600
miles east on the same latitude, to the Crozet Isles.*

We were about 500 miles on our way and had reached the edge
of the Forties. For two days running I had been worried by the
odd results our sights gave us—a degree or a degree and a half
of difference between the observed position and the position
we thought we were in by dead reckoning. Even though
Roger got much the same results I mistrusted them, for it
seemed more likely that we were making some stupid error
than that we could be a hundred miles wrong in our dead
reckoning. When it could no longer be denied that the sights
were correct and that, unless the solar system had gone
hay-wire, the dead reckoning must be wrong, I worked out a
sight with an assumed position a hundred miles from where
we thought we were, and the answer agreed within two or
three miles. Thus we had experienced a set of a hundred miles
to the north-west in three days.

Hitherto I had looked upon currents which set in unexpected directions, or currents which suddenly began flowing
where no current has yet been recorded, as the trump cards

which the prudent navigator keeps up his sleeve in case he makes an unsatisfactory landfall or if anything untoward happens to his ship. But whether such a card would be strong enough to play before a Court of Inquiry is more than doubtful. Nevertheless such unexpected sets do occur, as we had just seen, and when the compilers of the invaluable Admiralty *Pilots* state that a certain current always flows in a certain direction, they cover themselves by adding that sets in any other direction may also occur. The general circulation of water in the oceans, caused by the prevailing winds, the rotation of the earth and other factors, is well known. Thus in the Southern Ocean, where westerly winds prevail, the general drift sets east or slightly north of east. For example, a bottle thrown into the sea at Marion Island in 1958 was found on the coast of Victoria in 1960. But as well as this steady, unvarying drift, there are often day to day local variations—except in the case of fast-flowing ocean rivers such as the Gulf Stream or the Agulhas current. Thus in any region at any time currents setting in any direction may be experienced, caused probably by strong winds blowing for a short time from a direction different from that of the prevailing wind. These unpredictable variations are of more concern to the mariner than the general drift, and particularly to us in the Southern Ocean intent upon hitting off a small island. Even a castaway on a raft in the vicinity of Marion Island would be only faintly interested in the certain knowledge that in two years his raft might reach Australia.

Fortunately such strong local sets as we had experienced are not frequent. Navigation would be difficult indeed if every change of wind set in motion a fresh current, and I was already well aware of the difficulty there might be in finding the Crozet. Of all the unpleasant things that might happen to us in those lonely seas, this of missing the islands altogether, or, worse still, of hitting one in the dark, was what scared me most. They are small and scattered, their vicinity is sprinkled with sunken rocks, visibility is very often poor, so that, if owing to bad weather we got no sun sights, we might easily be blown to leeward of them before we knew where we were.

It is questionable whether the advice to ocean cruisers that they should frequently consider all the possible accidents that might happen to them or their boat and the appropriate action for dealing with any such accidents, is really the best. The time to consider them is before one starts so that all possible steps to prevent them happening can be taken. Subsequently an attitude of careless hope is, perhaps, permissible, for at least it allows the adventurer to sleep, eat, and enjoy the passing moment. Though, like most fears, it proved illusory, this fear of missing the islands was often present. Had I added to it the fear of losing mast or rudder, of developing a fatal leak, the fear that the next gale or the one after it would prove too much for old *Mischief*, or the fear that the bowl of my best pipe was about to crack—as it did—I had indeed supped full with horrors. And when a gale or trouble does start, though few of us are lofty-minded enough to do so, one might adopt the attitude of the skipper who, after giving the curt order "Call me when it moderates", used promptly to go below.

After an interlude of two passably fine days, the barometer fell again, cloud spread rapidly from the north-west, and rain set in. The mainsail was already reefed, so that we were able to collect water to replace that already used. There would be no lack of water at the islands, but it seemed a wise precaution in view of some of the possibilities mentioned above and the long time it might take a disabled boat to reach either Australia or some frequented part of the ocean. After its accustomed shift to south-west, the wind blew hard all night, during which we remained hove to in order to avoid losing ground to the north. An almost windless day followed this dirty night but by evening another depression was on the way. At three in the morning we had to gybe on to the starboard tack, the wind having gone south of west. An hour later, when I took over, the barometer had dropped to 29 inches; cold, rain, driving spume and a livid sky were the ugly ingredients of what I regarded as a hopeless dawn. We got no sights that day. As the glass rose, the wind backed in its usual way and again we hove to in order to avoid running away to the north-east before the sea.

But by nightfall we were lurching about with flapping sails, for when the guiding hand of the wind is lifted, the sea begins to run in all directions. What a place, we thought, either a gale of wind or none at all! The pattern of the weather is well shown by our runs for the last four days, which had been 113, 20, 105 and 14 miles. We were too small and too slow to take full advantage of the passing depressions; and since our course for Marion Island was more south than east we could not let her run as we might have done if bound eastwards. For the big clipper ships bound for Australia it mattered little whether the wind was north-west or south-west, and with speeds of twelve to fifteen knots they could probably keep pace with a depression and so carry a favourable gale most of the way.

The temperature remained at about 40° F., which, combined with the all-pervading dampness, we thought extremely cold. The sliding hatch remained closed, the weather-boards up in the companion-way, and all ventilators firmly plugged. Sparta, emphatically, began outside. Even if one merely wanted to poke one's head out to look at the weather, it was not wise to do so without wearing oilskins. Whenever it was calm, albatross used to gather on the sea around us, grounded, so to speak, by lack of wind. They can fly in light winds but in a gale they glide and soar with effortless perfection. In our small world Roger was the greatest living authority on the albatross. He was always being called upon to distinguish for us the Wandering Albatross, the Black-browed (so called apparently because its head is completely white), the Yellow-nosed, the Grey-headed, the Sooty Albatross and the Light-mantled Sooty. To the uninstructed, these are merely albatross which differ, as men do, in size or in the colour of their nose or hair. Just as some rock climbers like to make a small variation on an old route for the sake of giving it a new name, so ornithologists seem to have an itch to create new species or sub-species and to attach new labels. As well as the perplexity caused by minor differences and by the changes of plumage in immature and adult birds, the bird-watcher at sea is bothered by the fact that his quarry is nearly always in flight and that he himself is never stationary. To watch a fast-flying bird through a pair of field-glasses from a heaving deck is a hopeless task. I have been told that there is now a gadget, worked on some gyroscopic principle, that when attached to a sextant, camera, or field-

glasses, will hold them perfectly steady when the man handling the instrument is shaking with excitement or being
thrown about in a small boat. It sounds improbable but no
more improbable than those achievements of science before
which we bow low while hastily averting our thoughts from
their implications. But in the matter of the albatross family, I
think that the inexpert might follow the example of the
old-time sailor who reserved the name Albatross for the big
Wanderer and lumped the rest, together with Giant Petrels,
under the name Mollyhawk.

The calm lasted long enough for me to get an accurate noon
sight which put us in S. lat. 40° 24'. But by afternoon there was
plenty of wind for the albatross to take off and for *Mischief* to
be doing five knots well reefed down with a gale from
north-east. During the night it backed to north-west and blew
harder while the glass fell to 28.80 and by dawn we hove to. It
was a wild morning, the sea streaked with foam and the air full
of spray, but the sun rose in a clear sky. No weather seems
quite so bad when the sun is shining. We needed cheering too,
for we had not yet carried out the long deferred battening
down of the skylight cover; I had a plastic bivouac sheet rigged
over my bunk and in order to dodge the spurts from the
skylight those on my side of the table took their breakfast
standing up. On that bright but windy day, we might have
had a fine sail in a boat a little larger than *Mischief*, and with a
little more freeboard than our 2 ft. 6 ins. We did not venture to
let draw until afternoon, when the wind took off a little.
Owing to the amount of spray flying and the obscurity of the
horizon due to scud, I could make no use of the sun that
day.

On Sunday, December 20, in spite of an overcast sky, I got a
sight which put us thirty miles ahead of our dead reckoning
position, and at five that evening, fine on the bow, we sighted
an island. We were in some doubt whether it was Marion
Island, for which we were aiming, or Prince Edward Island
twelve miles to the north-east. Long and anxiously we peered
at it until at last we could make out Boot rock, a detached rock
200 feet high shaped like a jackboot which lies off the north
coast of Marion, and soon all doubts were set at rest when out

of the cloud wrack to the north the hard outline of the other island took shape. When sailing down there in a waste of water which encircles the globe, any land seems unnatural. When it does appear it has an unreal quality, even though one has gazed at it daily on the chart. It has an air of defying the sea, as if it knew that in that vast ocean land had no place.

I don't know what we expected to see, but from the disparaging remarks that passed I gathered that the crew were not pleased with the view of our first sub-antarctic island. Certainly Marion looked grim and sombre enough in the fading light, its 4,200-foot-high summit shrouded in cloud, the bleak lower slopes sprinkled with fresh snow sweeping down to the rock-bound shore. By dark we could see some lights in the huts of the weather station at the north-east end of the island, then about three miles on the beam. Having been unable to find at Cape Town a bulb for our Aldis signal lamp we were reduced to some ineffective flashing with a hand torch. It was no night for anyone to be sitting outside gazing seawards and I'm sure we were not seen. We hove to with the intention of closing the land at daylight to make our number.

But by morning we had drifted farther away, the wind was right off the land, and by the time the engine had been coaxed into starting (there was water in the cylinder), I thought we might as well push on.

On Christmas Eve the weather still looked settled. In those regions, however, changes are sudden, and I begin to despair of drawing any useful conclusions from the appearance of the sky. One sees the most lurid sunsets and predicts, quite wrongly, the direst consequences, and contrarily, after a lovely quiet evening sky, the dawn ushers in wind and rain. So it was now. By morning the wind had freshened, the sky become overcast and the barometer was slowly falling. In the course of the day the wind swung to south-east and the barometer dived to 28.7, the lowest we had yet recorded. Not only could we not lay the course but the behaviour of the barometer indicated that all kinds of devilment were in store. We hove to and nothing much happened. During the night the wind was recorded as Force 6 gusting to Force 7, but it might equally have been of hurricane force, for we had had a lot of mulled wine with our Christmas dinner and were not in an over-serious mood.

Next day I reckoned we were within fifty miles of the Ile aux Cochons, the westernmost island of the Crozet. It was rough and windy, but the glass was rising after its ominous fall of the previous day. On approaching the islands from the west, one needs to have either good visibility or to know within a mile or two the ship's position. Ten miles north-east of Hog Island are Iles des Apôtres, the group of pinnacled rocky islets where the *Strathmore* came to grief; to the south-east, six and ten miles respectively, are two groups of sunken rocks where the sea always breaks, known collectively by the French as "Brisants de l'Héroïne" or Heroine Breakers; and seventeen miles to the south is Penguin Island, a small barren rock 500 feet high no bigger than an overgrown fortress. And having got all hot and bothered about avoiding these dangers one learns that the charted position of Heroine Breakers and Penguin Island cannot be relied upon, for they are "believed" to lie about five miles farther to the south. Sixty miles to the east of this outer fringe, which to my heated imagination began to look like a *chevaux de frise* of rocks, lies Possession Island. My plan was to sight either Hog Island or Penguin so that we could verify our position and lay a course clear of all dangers, in particular the Heroine Breakers.

As we had been sailing briskly all afternoon, I hoped that before nightfall we might raise one or other of those islands. Hog Island is supposed to be about 2,000 feet high and on a clear day would be visible from a long way off. After supper, having seen nothing, I got a star sight for latitude which put us nine miles south of our dead reckoning. Through the delay at Cape Town and through taking longer to get here than we expected, we had overrun the full moon period. The night was moderately clear but, in view of the uncertainties regarding our own position and the position of the Heroine Breakers and Penguin Island, prudence required that we should heave to. At first light it happened to be clear, so I took star sights and went below to work them out. A few minutes later Jan, who was at the helm, gave a hail. Never was it more welcome. He had sighted Penguin Island about four miles to the south. So our luck was in. Whatever the weather might do now, we knew where we were and had a good chance of reaching Possession Island before nightfall. The weather seemed to have decided to take a hand. The glass began to fall and, as the day advanced, the wind rose and a succession of heavy rain squalls began driving across from the north-west.

At eleven o'clock I took over the tiller and remained there for the rest of the day. We were sailing fast under trysail and stays'l before a big quartering sea, and I was bent on having my fill of pleasure in sailing *Mischief* round an island that for the last two years had seldom been far from my thoughts. Ahead of us in the distance a great black squall seemed to squat as if intent on hiding something, and on this I fixed my gaze. The squall seemed to move very slowly. For some time I thought I could see something more solid than cloud and by noon I was sure of it. Perhaps the earlier sighting of Penguin Island had taken a little of the edge off this landfall, but not much. For here was the long-looked-for prize at the end of a 10,000 mile voyage, a prize with a true romantic flavour—a lonely island set in a stormy sea, and *Mischief* borne towards it on the crests of great following seas, with albatross wheeling in her wake.

It was mostly covered with cloud, but between squalls, when the sun touched it, we thought the island slightly less forbidding in appearance than Marion. We closed the land near Pointe des Moines at the north-west corner and then ran down the coast to round the southernmost point. Pointe des Moines takes its name from a detached rock resembling a monk's cowl which lies off it through which the sea has carved out a large hole. It was exciting sailing along this wild coast, with one eye on the seas chasing us and one on the look-out for breakers ahead. We were far too close, for once when I glanced astern I could see over the port quarter white water surging over a sunk rock which we had passed without noticing. Upon rounding the south corner of the island, we smoothed our water, for we now had land to windward. The wind, however, seemed to gather fresh fury from this obstruction and swept over the low cliffs to scoop water from the surface like the willy-waws of the Patagonia channels. A waterfall dropping over the cliffs hurled water in every direction except downwards.

There are two possible anchorages at Possession Island. Baie du Navire, known to the sealers as Ship Cove, lies on the east coast about two miles round the corner we had just passed. It is sheltered from all winds except easterly. Baie Américaine, the other anchorage, is on the north-east side of the island about seven miles' sailing from Baie du Navire. We intended anchoring in the last-named and when we first saw it about five o'clock that evening we had some doubt about it being the place, or how it came by the name of bay. The English word "cove" gives a much truer picture. On the chart it looks quite a snug hole, from the sea it looks anything but snug. We regarded with misgiving that slight indentation on an ironbound coast which seemed to offer so little hope of tranquillity.

There was nothing else in view, the other anchorage might be worse, so we decided to try it. The wind was blowing straight out of the cove and seemed to gain force by being funnelled down the valley which stretches inland. There was no question of beating in, we must either heave to until the wind moderated or motor in. The temptation to have done was so great that we dowsed the staysail and turned on the heat. The engine had to be kept going all out to make headway against the wind. If her head got blown off, as it did twice, I had to let her fall off and go right round to gather speed before she would head into it again.

We first let go in eight fathoms of water, only to find when we had veered enough cable that our stern was far too close to a ledge of kelp-covered rock. From shore to shore this U-shaped inlet is about 300 yards wide and indents the land for about the same distance. It looked a lot less in both directions and for practical purposes it was a lot less as it shallows fairly quickly and we needed room to swing. With the wind ahead and the rock ledge close under our stern, getting the anchor was a tricky business. In fact it was touch and go and we only cleared the ledge by going hard astern. Our next attempt was more successful and by about six o'clock we were anchored a hundred yards from a beach of black sand, white with penguins.

POSSESSION ISLAND

MISCHIEF BEING NOW firmly attached to the bottom, and there being no signs of dragging, we had a moment to look at our surroundings. *Mischief* has been in some rum places but never in any place like this. We seemed to be in a sort of zoo. King penguins not only covered the beach but extended up the valley behind in serried ranks; here and there among them lay huge slug-like creatures which we recognised as sea-elephants; and small colonies of gentoo penguins occupied the rock ledges, where a few fur-seals also lurked. The sand beach covered with the clamorous multitude of penguins extended only along the bottom of the "U". Seaward from there on either side the shores of the cove were formed by a rock shelf backed by low cliffs, and above the cliffs were slopes of what looked like lush grass. Numerous white dots sprinkled over the slopes were, as Roger assured us, nesting albatross. Behind the beach a valley with a stream running down led gently upwards and inland till it disappeared in the cloud. Out to sea, about ten miles away, lay East Island, which was likewise cloud-covered. To land on the beach looked deceptively easy. As we found later, it was most often a troublesome business and landing on a rock ledge proved the easiest.

The holding ground seemed to be good. We had down our "Fisherman" anchor of about 120 lbs. backed by ⅝-inch cable; and to make sure we laid out the sixty-pound "CQR" anchor on a stout warp as a kedge. Just as Procter got back with the dinghy from laying out the kedge, several long black fins, sticking three feet or more from the water, were seen approaching the ship in menacing fashion. They were killer whales, and anyone who has read Bowers' account of how these fierce creatures tried to get at his sledge ponies adrift on an ice-floe would not choose to be out in a dinghy in their company. They may be up to twenty feet long, hunt in packs from three to thirty in number, and are extremely voracious, preying upon penguins, seals, porpoises, the smaller dolphins and even whales. In the Antarctic they have been observed making combined efforts to break the ice or upset floes in order to get at seals. The pack of some half-dozen which we saw, having first circled the ship, went close inshore in quite shallow water, no doubt hoping to snap up a penguin or two.

"Sleep after toil, Port after stormy seas, . . . does greatly please." To be safely at anchor with the pleasant prospect before us of all night in was a great joy. As the wind had dropped we set no anchor watch, relying upon the grumbling of the chain and the noise the wind would make to wake us if it came on to blow. Only a gale from south-east or east would oblige us to clear out and gales from those quarters are rare. In fact we lay here undisturbed throughout our stay.

After a peaceful night and a leisurely breakfast, Roger and I had to be put ashore to make a reconnaissance. As was most often the case, cloud covered everything down to 2,000 feet, but we could find out what the going would be like and we had to choose a base from which to start. The waves breaking idly on the beach were so small that we landed without difficulty. But launching off the dinghy and pushing her clear of the breaking waves proved a wet job for us who had only knee-high gumboots. Later we gave it up and used a convenient rock ledge. Naturally Roger and I had to stop some time on the beach to inspect the zoo, hobnobbing with the penguins, sheathbills, skua gulls and sea-elephants, all of which, except the last, were just as eager to inspect us—the penguins out of curiosity and the skua gulls out of greed. A sea-elephant must have a limited range of emotions and curiosity is not one of them. If he has any others he is seldom awake long enough to exercise them.

Living on one's fat seems to be the chief requisite for life on a sub-antarctic island. Day and night, day in day out, the penguins did nothing but squawk at each other and nurse their eggs. Sometimes small parties might be seen emerging from the sea as though they had been fishing, but they were a tiny minority, probably only the lunatic fringe. The sea-elephants we never saw enter or leave the water except for a few who played about in the mouth of the freshwater stream. Young and old lay supine in luxurious attitudes of repose, dead to the world apparently, for days, weeks, or possibly months at a time. They were not thick on the ground but they were to be found everywhere, dozing away on this beach and many others, in mud wallows, or in the grass a mile or more from the sea, old bulls up to twenty feet long weighing a couple of tons, and sleek youngsters the size of prize sows. Perhaps those near the beach launched themselves off surreptitiously at night to pick up a few snacks, but those who lay inland, like cows in meadows, had, so to speak, swallowed the anchor, seemingly unwilling to be reminded of the sea and fish. Indeed, to shuffle inland for a mile or so, more or less on one's belly, and carrying two tons of blubber, is not an expedition to be undertaken lightly or frequently. The pups, born probably in September, had all been weaned, yet sleep seemed to be all the food they needed as it was of their parents. Both young and old go to sea in the southern winter in June or July and feed steadily and strenuously before returning to the beaches in the spring for the breeding season and the long fast which follows.

There is no fur on elephant-seals or sea-elephants, as they are equally well called. They were hunted and nearly exterminated solely for the oil their blubber yields. The long snout or short trunk which accounts for their name is only prominent in the old bulls. When angry or excited they inflate it. They have to be angry or excited before they make a good subject for photography and one has to approach very close indeed to rouse them. Then they rear up on their fore-flippers, opening their mouths very wide, and snarl ferociously while they shuffle away backwards. Should an aggressive old fellow decide to shuffle forwards one has to step back pretty smartly. The youngsters have better manners. They just lie with one eye open and the other half shut as one approaches, and if one begins stroking them they shut both and go to sleep again.

As is well known, penguins are sociable birds. The more they are together, and the closer the better, seems to be their guiding principle. Consequently we found it harder to make our way inland from the beach than to land on it. The sandy beach near the water was used mainly by the idlers as a sort of promenade where they assembled in small huddles to gossip, show off and generally keep an eye on things. But as soon as we left the sand and stepped on to the muddy gravel by the banks of the stream, we had to barge a way through several thousand close-packed penguins, their serried ranks covering perhaps two acres of ground and extending inland for a couple of hundred yards on both sides of the stream. Except that the stupid people who got in the way were little more than knee-high, it was like the rush-hour in a Tube station. Some birds were so astonished to see a man towering over them that they fell over backwards knocking down several others like ninepins; and if any tried to get out of one's way, they inevitably set in motion a wave which travelled to the outskirts of the rookery accompanied by a crescendo of clamour. But most of them stood firm and showed their dislike of being shoved by reaching up with their long, slender beaks to jab ineffectively at one's trousers. The smell and the state of the wet, muddy ground were both disgusting, but the birds themselves were clean, sleek, handsome. The king penguin is only a little smaller than the emperor, standing nearly three feet high. He has beautiful orange patches on the side of the head, extending down the neck and across the throat, where the orange shades off into the snow-white breast. Like the emperor, he has a dignified carriage and walks upright.

The majority of these birds were incubating eggs, the parents taking the duty in turns. The egg rests on the inturned feet and is covered by a broad transverse fold of skin. They manage it cleverly and can shuffle about, stumble, or even be knocked over without dropping the egg. Like the emperors, they lay only one egg, the incubation period being seven weeks. We saw no chicks and only one young one still in the down stage, who had probably been born the previous year and was evidently a backward child. Poor little Benjamin, as I called him, in his russet coat, who had no playfellows of his own age and who, I felt, had been orphaned soon after birth. Easily distinguishable by his small stature and comic coat, he was usually to be seen hanging round the idlers on the beach, among them but not of them. Later when I returned from the mountains, I looked in vain for little Benjamin. Alas! he had been knocked on the head, and perhaps it was better so. The sealers had a good name for these youngsters, calling them "oakum boys", as the colour of their coats is not unlike that of oakum.

After cleaving our way through the thickest of the rookery

we reached the outskirts, where there were merely a few hundred of the unemployed, the birds with no parental duties. At first we stuck to the valley following a track made by sea-elephants, skirting round many of their sleeping forms and the deep, treacherous mud-holes where they had wallowed. As the going in the valley was bad, the ground soft and wet, and thickly covered with a plant called "acaena" which grows a foot high, we left it to strike up to the ridge 500 feet above. Even at that low height all vegetation ceased and we found comparatively pleasant and easy walking over reddish lava and stones. Inland this broad ridge merged into another which was evidently the backbone of the island. On it were some high features where a few patches of old snow lay, but these were dismissed out of hand as being nowhere near 5,000 feet high. Farther north where a bank of cloud hung persistently over the ridge it looked more promising. We thought that under that cloud lurked the snow-covered peak we had come so far to climb.

It was a strange, bleak landscape of smooth, easy contours, its uniform drabness relieved only by the fresh green of the valley bottoms and in places by whole hillsides of a warm red colour. From the ridge we had a good view of the coast to the north-east and a bay, obviously American Bay, to which we decided to walk. It was about four miles away but there were four intervening ridges and their valleys to be crossed. At the mouth of each valley were small penguin rookeries and we passed numbers of nesting albatross and giant petrels.

Ridges or slopes from which the bird can easily take flight are preferred to the valleys, and the nests are substantial affairs of earth, moss and grasses raised well above the ground and about two feet across. Most of the birds were sitting on the single egg they lay and they remained undisturbed but watchful at our approach. I wish we had devoted more time on our walks to standing and staring. Had we hung about we might have enjoyed the sight of an albatross making its landing. When they alight on water they look comical enough with their huge webbed feet splayed out and the heels dug in to check their speed, like a man glissading down a snow slope. As one observer writes: "They appear to dread the act of alight-ing, flying round and round their nests close to the ground before they make up their minds, and when they finally do, often toppling forward on their beaks. At least half of them make a faulty landing, striking the ground violently with their breasts and turning turtle . . ."

American Bay looked wider than our bay and the protection it afforded no better. The beach of the same black volcanic sand is longer and is bounded at both ends by bold cliffs several hundred feet high, that at the southern end, the Red Craig, being strikingly red in colour. There was a large penguin rookery and great numbers of elephant-seal near the beach and far inland, for the valley which drains into the bay is wide and perfectly flat. The sealers, I should think, frequented it more than Baie du Navire. We found the remains of huts—two floors and a few upright posts—and a couple of big iron try-pots. A little way off was a post which may well have been a cross marking a grave.

For want of a better plan, Roger and I decided to make our first camp at American Bay. Bounding the next valley to the north we could see a long, high ridge leading up into the cloud which lay as if permanently moored over our suspected mountain. In the course of the day the cloud had lifted slightly, perhaps to the 2,000-foot level. Clearly something lay hidden there, yet from the general appearance of things we found it increasingly hard to believe in the presence of a 5,000-foot snow-covered mountain. Still it would be fun to camp on this beach in the company of elephant-seals and penguins, with a fire from the wood of the old sealers' huts, the Southern Ocean lapping at our feet.

Even without a load I found it hard work recrossing the ridges on the way back to the ship. For men straight off the sea it had been a long enough walk. We might have saved ourselves some walking and load-carrying by sailing *Mischief* round to American Bay, but I decided against that, reflecting that Jim would no doubt carry an immense load for us and that he would be able to make a second carry while Roger and I extended our reconnaissance. As we sat on the beach waiting for the dinghy we were, as usual, objects of interest to the penguins and the cheeky little sheathbills, the latter pecking at

Mischief at anchor (without topmast) in
Wodehouse Bay, Canal Sarmiento

Left: Bar Antartica, Punta Arenas "A saloon of severe aspect"

Below: Mischief anchored off Calvo Glacier

Above: Two pages from Tilman's notebook showing his provisions for Patagonian voyage: "No larger than the back of an envelope"

Left: Tilman on the Patagonian ice-cap

Roger Tufft, tickling an elephant seal

Baie du Navire, Possession Island: "A kind of zoo"

Mealtime aboard *Mischief*

Tilman in his bunk

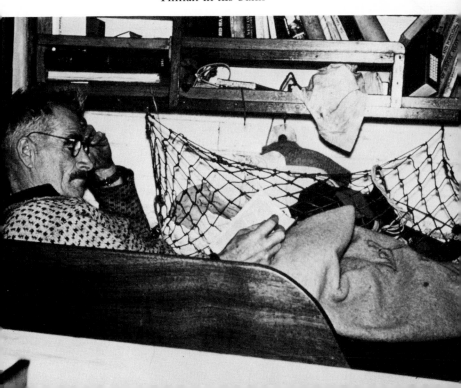

Taking a sun sight: when ice blurs the sea surface
a tin of oil provides an artificial horizon

Sailing between Greenland bergs

Greenland bergs

Oldest inhabitant of Igdlorssuit, with envied
sealskin trousers

our boots and thoroughly investigating our discarded ruck-sacks.

During the night the glass fell to 29 inches. We woke to find it raining and a south-east wind blowing straight into the anchorage. With the wind in that quarter we must stay on board in case it piped up, and I myself was heartily in favour of taking the day off. For breakfast we tried the penguin eggs collected the previous day. Provided one can stomach their resemblance to jellyfish, the fried eggs are not bad eating—certainly an improvement on dried eggs, though that is not extravagant praise. On the whole I concluded that the eggs of the jackass penguin, which in Cape Town are regarded as a delicacy, must be something different. Of the two I much preferred albatross eggs.

On behalf of a Californian Wild Life Society, Roger had undertaken to ring birds. The south-east wind did not blow hard, so in the evening he went ashore and began by ringing fifteen albatross. He was expert enough to do it single-handed, simply picking the great bird off its nest and holding it with its head and neck under his arm behind him. They squawked a bit but made no resistance. In the evening we had a second and more comfortable Christmas dinner of curry and Christmas pudding, this incongruous and possibly explosive mixture being mollified, assuaged and quenched by a bottle of Van der Hum. Our oil stove, which could not be used at sea, was now brought into action and made the cabin moderately snug. As there were no trees and no driftwood to be found we had done well to discard the three-foot-high iron stove we had used in the Patagonian fjords, where wood was plentiful. But one missed the fine fug its smoke and heat produced, just as one misses a coal fire when reduced to the miserable make-believe of an electric stove.

On the morning of December 30, a day of low cloud and drizzle, we assembled our loads and took them ashore by backing the dinghy close to a rock ledge. With a slight swell running one had to watch for the right moment and move smartly. The small colony of gentoo penguins which made these rock ledges their home kept strictly aloof from their larger neighbours. Generally known as Johnnies, they are distinguishable by a white band on top of the head. Formerly they seem to have been as numerous as the king penguins on these islands.

Because, I suppose, the island is so small that we should never be more than a day's walk away from the ship, the adventure of leaving her seemed nothing like so exciting as when we had left for the crossing of the Patagonia ice-cap, when we had cut ourselves off completely on the far side of a 7,000-foot-high glaciated range of mountains. Nor, fortunately, had we anything like so much to carry. All told we had about 150 pounds of gear including tent, stove, paraffin, personal kit, rope, and fourteen days' food, but we left thirty pounds of this for Jim to make a second carry the next day. Roger and Jim shouldered the main burden, matters being arranged by me so that the weight was in inverse proportion to age. We had now a better knowledge of the route, so that by 1 p.m. we had reached American Bay, where we pitched our tent on the sand under a low cliff. In spite of the wind, and the sand, which soon covered our belongings, it was a pleasant spot. A family of sea-elephants were our closest neighbours— good neighbours, too, for they never intruded—while penguins from the rookery were constant and welcome visitors.

PORT AUX FRANÇAIS, KERGUELEN

The shore party climbed the mountains of Possession Island (the French later named "Mont du Mischief" officially after her visit), and sailed on for Kerguelen, 700 miles east; explored the intricate channels and climbed a 3,300-ft ice-cap. With only two gallons of petrol left in reserve, they made for the French Antarctic base at the other end of the island.

OUR DESTINATION NOW was Baie du Morbihan, about seven miles away, which we expected to reach in a day and a night. We could stock up with water at the French base but I thought we might as well take some fresh food. I particularly wanted to try cormorant, which the *Antarctic Pilot* describes as being "rich in fat and meat and good eating." The opinion of my other authority, Chapman, is cooler: "I was once served with boiled cormorants," he writes, "but the dish left me with no taste for more." Boiling, of course, is no way to treat game birds, so Jim was sent ashore to murder a cormorant and returned in due course with two penguins. Waiving the small matter of a mistake in species, a mistake excusable in a geologist, we asked him, "Why two?" "Well, you see," said Jim apologetically, "one got in the way."

Baie du Morbihan is a magnificent sheet of water which with its numerous arms and inlets covers an area of nearly 200 square miles. From entrance to head the distance is twenty miles. The southern and western sides are fringed with many islands and the long fjords, which extend inland, provide many excellent harbours. Two expeditions for observing the Transit of Venus made their headquarters in the bay, and from 1909 to 1929 a French-Norwegian whaling company maintained a settlement at Port Jeanne d'Arc on the western side, where they built houses, workshops, tanks, stores, a factory and 200-foot wood jetty. All has long been abandoned and is now in ruins. The French base is on the north side of the bay and is wide open to winds from the west. It was probably chosen with an eye to the future in a place where there is enough reasonably flat land to build an airfield.

The small concrete wharf was thronged with men and as our anchor went down a boat put off. In it was M. Heurgon (Chef de l'Etablissement) whom I had last met in his Paris office in 1957; he speaks English, as he had served as a Flying Officer with the Free French air force during the war. After helping us to moor securely to a large buoy, his Breton boatman ferried us ashore. Our arrival could not have been better timed. It was a Sunday and happily the lunch hour. The large crowd on the wharf raised a cheer as we climbed up the ladder. Cameras clicked and ciné-cameras whirred, their principal targets being Jan crowned with a yachting-cap with a white cover and wearing a Newgate fringe, and Roger with his luxurious dark brown mane. With so much hand-shaking to do it was unfortunately impossible for us to return the fire, for our hosts were the more picturesque, with beards of all sizes and shapes and faces of all colours; for many of the staff, such as mechanics, gardeners and kitchen-hands, are recruited in Madagascar. One of the scientists, a short, stout man, had a real hard-weather, dreadnought beard, his face being completely concealed under a thick carpet or rug of hair surmounted by a pair of spectacles.

Dazed and feeling a little sheepish with the warmth of our welcome, we were bundled into a jeep and carried half a mile to the mess where M. Heurgon, his chief assistants, and the fifteen scientists lived; a big, light room, with double glass windows, central heating, settees and armchairs, and a large brick fireplace above which was a mural painting of Mount Ross. Fortified by brandy and soda, we then walked round to the main messhall, where on Sundays all sixty-seven souls assembled for their *déjeuner*, sitting at one long table and a cross table for the seniors and guests. There, amidst a prodigious convivial clatter, we embarked upon a meal such as only Frenchmen could conjure up on a desolate land.

Judge of our astonishment upon seeing scattered up and down the table whole bowls of tomatoes, lettuce and radishes, and to be assured that they were grown on the island. The long, crusty loaves of French bread were to be expected and were delicious, but the butter that we slapped on pretty freely was fresh, and that also, we were told, was made at the base. Likewise the potatoes, the mutton, the pork and the *pâté de la maison*, which we scooped out by the spoonful, were all home products. To men accustomed to thinking mainly in terms of rabbits and cormorants all these good things were as delightful as they were surprising. Wine, of course, circulated freely, and we concluded this memorable meal with a masterpiece of a cake, a variety of cheeses, coffee and brandy. Speeches were made, John had to be restrained from singing, and Jan, whose fluent French had made him popular, had to be carried out and put to bed.

Presiding over this magnificent affair and supervising everything was the chef in white apron and professional cap, dignified but vivacious, who sat just below the salt, where he kept a watchful eye on the dishing-up and the wants of the guests. He seemed to relish the responsibility of feeding this enormous family of hungry men and evidently enjoyed the life, for he had returned to the island four times. With his love of banter and quick jests I pictured him as a sort of modern Alexis Soyer, born to grapple with gastronomic problems from braising boars' heads to spitting larks or boiling tripe, equally at home cooking for an army in the Crimea or for the crowned heads of Europe.

Sternly overcoming the desire for sleep, those of us who were still on our feet took a walk round the establishment with M. Heurgon to see how all this fresh food was produced; for we were told that tinned and preserved foods played very little part in the diet. We went first to the garden, where a skilful and enthusiastic Malagasy showed us how he grows either in the open, in cold frames, or in a greenhouse, and for most of the year round, radishes, chervil, dandelions, parsley, cabbages, spinach, cress, potatoes and tomatoes. Additional soil has been put down, and manure from the cowsheds and piggery, as well as blood and offal, are liberally applied. Besides the milking cows and the piggery, there is a large poultry yard—wired overhead to protect it from skua gulls—and flocks of geese and ducks roam at large. For fodder they make hay and silage from the acaena grass which grows so abundantly, and they also feed to the livestock an oily meal, a waste product of the sea-elephant factory which we later visited. M. Heurgon, who is a fisherman, showed us a trout hatchery he has started with a view to stocking the streams, and an attempt to breed reindeer is also on foot.

The sheep are run on one of the many islands in the bay. We regretted having no time to visit them, for I felt that homage was due to the providers of the most succulent mutton I have ever tasted, mutton which combined the sweetness of the mountain, the fat of the valley and the tang of the saltings. Rabbits have long been a curse on Kerguelen as they have been elsewhere, and an attempt to kill them off by introducing myxomatosis failed owing to the absence of fleas to spread the disease. Partly owing to the rabbits there is not enough herbage on the main island—at any rate near Port aux Français—to support even sheep. The flock now numbers several hundred, of which more than a hundred are exported annually as surplus. When one island is eaten out the sheep are moved to another, a system of rotation of islands, so to speak, instead of a rotation of crops. We saw no sheepdogs about and I imagine the job of getting a few hundred sheep on board a tank-landing craft is no mean one, calling for unlimited patience and cunning. We noticed two of these craft at the base, their main use being that of ferrying stores ashore from the relief ship.

Apparently these sheep have begun to thrive only comparatively recently and against all expectation. Xavier Reppe, a journalist, has written in *Aurore sur l'Antarctique* a popular description of all the lands comprised under the name "Terres Australes et Antarctiques Françaises," including St Paul and New Amsterdam, Adélie Land, Kerguelen and the Crozet. In it he has some amusing stories about the livestock of Kerguelen which I hope are true. He is a man who, like myself, is not displeased to see the scientists and savants confounded by the unlearned, as very rarely they are. Up till 1955 experience, tradition, biologists, botanists and oecologists all agreed and decreed that sheep would not do on Kerguelen. The woe-begone, emaciated appearance of three experimental sheep sent out and borne on the establishment at Port aux Français seemed to endorse this conclusively. A visiting expert who examined them declared that their teeth had rotted away and that owing to the lack of calcium in the soil this was inevitably to be expected. One of the menials, however, a man who knew something about sheep as he had been a shepherd in the Pyrenees, declared that the only trouble with the sheep was their extreme old age. And enquiries showed this to be the case, for the bureaucrat who had the task of balancing the island's stringent budget had ordered the sheep to be bought in the cheapest market. The same ex-shepherd then visited an islet where in 1952 four other sheep had been dumped and written off. When with difficulty they had been rounded up, for they were completely wild, they were found to have multiplied themselves three times and the largest weighed 200 pounds.

Another problem which baffled the combined brains of the savants at the time of our journalist's visit to Kerguelen in 1955 was the infertility of the duck eggs. The birds themselves did well enough but they obstinately refused to breed. Lack of minerals in the soil, lack of vitamins, insufficient sun, insufficient moon and all kinds of obscure biological anomalies were canvassed and analysed as possible explanations. The true explanation was imparted discreetly to M. Reppe by a humble labourer who told him in confidence that *"les imbéciles"*, as he called them, had not perceived that they had eaten all the drakes, for from the very first these had been sent to the table as the finest birds. Nevertheless, even in those days some of these sub-antarctic farmers knew their business, and M. Reppe seems to have appreciated their efforts as much as we did. At their Christmas dinner in 1955 they ate a pig weighing nearly half a ton. Or to put it less grossly and more gracefully, as he does: *"Nous avons sacrifié un sujet qui pesait 320 kgs. Mais la specialité la plus prisée des gourmets est le cochon de lait farci, que le chef Perrimond réussit à merveille."*

M. Heurgon insisted on our taking all our meals with him, so next morning we went ashore for breakfast. Before leaving the boat we bent another chain on the mooring buoy, for it was blowing very hard from the south-west.

The yolk of my breakfast egg was of such a violent red colour that I suspected my sight had been affected by the lunch of the previous day; but M. Heurgon explained that the colour was due to feeding the hens on sea-elephant's liver, and suggested that we should visit the factory where the carcases are processed. A small private company is licensed to kill up to 2,000 seals a year, but the number actually killed is generally less than a thousand. They are shot on beaches several miles away from the factory, the carcases being hauled overland by Weasels. After the inside has been removed the remainder is chopped up by hand and fed into a hopper, whence it passes into large cylinders like pressure cookers. At the end of the process all that remains of a sea-elephant is oil and a brown mealy substance. This meal, rich in oil, makes a valuable feeding stuff for the livestock.

By afternoon the wind had increased so much that when I tried to row off alone to do some small job on board I had to give up the attempt, and finally regained the shore several hundred yards to leeward of the jetty. At night the wind had abated sufficiently for three of us to get back on board. There had been a cinema show after supper, so it was late when M. Heurgon drove us down to the wharf in the jeep. Jeeps, like yacht-dinghies and maids-of-all-work generally, are apt to suffer from neglect. This one had no lights, so our friend the Breton boatman sat on the forward end of the bonnet to act as navigator and look-out. Our driver seemed to place implicit confidence in the penetrating powers of a seaman's eyes as we shot off with true French *élan* in pitch blackness down the road, or where the road was thought to be. Navigating at that speed, the look-out in the bows never had a chance. As we hit the reef—a dump of empty oil drums—he was projected violently from the bonnet to the top of an oil drum without time to utter a Breton oath, let alone a warning. The jeep, of course, sustained no damage that mattered, but the boatman sprained his wrist.

I had appointed next day, February 2, as sailing day. Besides feeling that we were imposing too much on French hospitality we wanted to get home in good time. Roger, insatiable in the pursuit of hard experience, had plans for joining a friend in Spitzbergen for the latter half of the summer; and Procter, besides having his bees constantly on his mind, wanted to be home in time for his children's holidays. In the morning our friendly Breton, in spite of his damaged wrist, made several trips in his boat ferrying off water to fill our tanks. As a Breton, and therefore a seaman, he took great interest in *Mischief*. His motor launch gave him plenty to do. Besides making trips to various islands, particularly the island where the sheep lived, she was employed in fishing—another way in which M. Heurgon fully exploited the local resources.

At our farewell lunch we were again impressed with how well and sensibly these Frenchmen lived. But then no men with a M. Perrimond to cater for their bodily needs and to educate their palates would be in danger of becoming what a gifted gastronome has described as "Gobble-and-gulp-people, who in their melancholy ignorance swallow a *Potage à la Comte de Paris*, or a *Risolette à la Pompadour*, with the same frightful nonchalance as a sailor will devour his pea-soup, or a rustic bolt his bacon." For *hors d'oeuvres* we had salami and *pâté à la maison*, both home-produced. Our hosts (God forgive them) then offered us snails; but some superb mutton chops with fried potatoes and salad made full amends for this lapse. With the cheese we were persuaded to try honey—pure, unadulterated honey—and needed no second persuasion. We should have preferred to linger over the coffee and brandy but we had to get not only ourselves on board but a whole cargo of good things given us by M. Heurgon, the chef, the doctor, the priest and many other well-wishers. These comprised eggs, fresh butter, bread, potatoes, radishes, lettuce, tomatoes; enough chocolate to last each of us all the way home, and for Jan a like amount of cigarettes; jars of the famous *pâté* and tins of sauerkraut and fruit. Besides that we took on board all the petrol and paraffin we needed, a six-gallon carboy of red wine and a one-gallon jar of Martinique rum. All we could do in return was to take all the letters they could write in two days to Cape Town for posting. The whole party were due for relief in November; but meantime communication with their families was confined to a telegram of so many words which each man was allowed to send fortnightly.

With a hearty cheer from the crowd the last boatload of men and stores at last left the quay. With a fair wind we hoisted sail, let go our moorings and sailed out, accompanied for a time by M. Heurgon in the launch. It had been a most enjoyable and impressive interlude. We left full of admiration for M. Heurgon and his men, the efficient way in which this far-flung French outpost was run, and the keenness and high morale of its occupants.

I must say this state of things, the friendly, cheerful atmosphere, came as a surprise. On landing at Port aux Français I had half expected to find *cafard* oozing out of the windows of the men's huts, for among a party of nearly seventy men of varying rank—officials, scientists, tradesmen, labourers—confined for twelve months on a barren island and living at fairly close quarters, there is bound to be friction. Especially in the case of Frenchmen, who are perhaps more effervescent and therefore likely to go flat more quickly than are Englishmen.

The life is monotonous, the climate harsh, the scenery severe, and it is the job of the base leader and his assistants to see that morale remains unaffected by these conditions. Of

M. Heurgon's assistants in this difficult task I should give a high place to M. le Chef. On an expedition, where there is generally a sense of struggle and achievement, men will accept a scanty and monotonous diet. A man working at the base on Kerguelen has no such sense to sustain him. When a man is tired of food—not to mention brandy and baccy—he is tired of life, but no one, not even a Frenchman, could tire of the fare provided by a man of Perrimond's genius.

After sailing back to Cape Town, Mischief turned homeward again; a voyage not without incident. . .

Once more I experienced the relief and joy of being at sea again, free from the fetters of the land, with nothing ahead but an almost endless vista of carefree days, no bills to pay, no engagements to keep, no newspapers or telephones; the ship, a snug, secure little world, day by day bravely pushing her way over the trackless ocean. Sitting at the tiller while we headed out past the breakwater, enjoying these trite but pleasing reflections, I suddenly saw flames issuing from the fore-hatch of our snug, secure little world. Jan, I thought, must be making tea. On reaching the galley I found the double-burner Primus the centre of a small inferno and flames were licking up the wood-work surrounding it. Jan brought the galley fire extinguisher into action while I threw a blanket over the stove for good measure. The effect was slight. A fleeting and horrifying vision of yet another return to Cape Town crossed my mind, or even of *Mischief* abandoned, on fire off the breakwater. But our second fire extinguisher hastily brought into play did the trick. Beyond the melting of the lead sheet on which the stove stood, some burnt paint and my severe fright, no harm was done.

Off Robben Island we streamed the log, by midnight we had Dassen Island abeam, the loom of Cape Town faded, and by next day it was a hundred miles away. From this flying start we never looked back and in the first week we logged nearly a thousand miles. But we had one black day, Sunday April 10, which I entered in the log as Black Sunday. We were on the fringe of the South-east Trades, which prevail farther south on the African side of the South Atlantic than they do on the other side. The wind backed slowly during the night from south-west, through south, to east of south, which brought it right aft; so that an hour before breakfast, when it was getting light, the helmsman gybed her. The boom guy prevented the boom crashing over and we escaped without damage. Worse, much worse, soon followed. I was at the tiller after breakfast when suddenly an overpowering but delightful aroma of rum billowed up the companion-way. Our precious rum jar, still nearly three-quarters full, had broken adrift and smashed. The smell of rum that pervaded the ship for the rest of the day was a constant turning of the knife in the wound. Smells, I think, recall past scenes more surely than sights or sounds. The smell of certain kinds of petrol fumes, for instance, always bring to my mind the Western Desert. Now, throughout the day, we were reminded of the sundown hour, the glasses, the lemons, the sugar bowl and the rum jar (still nearly three-quarters full)—until at sundown came the moment of truth. But even now our cup of sorrow was not full. With the wind aft, we changed the rig, and while hoisting the old twin, some bungling resulted in it giving one mighty flog and splitting from head to foot. It looked beyond repair but later we buckled to and sewed a foot-wide strip of old cloth the whole length of the sail.

After a call at St Helena (where no doubt the rum was replaced) and a curious incident when the bilge water began to pump out bright green, due to marker dye in an inflatable dinghy pack, Tilman was back in home waters: "the last thousand miles seemed a mere flea-bite".

It took us five days to work our way up from Ushant, taking sights on the rare occasions when the sun appeared, for we had not yet seen any land. At last on the night of June 28 we picked up the loom of Portland light and on the following night we sighted the Needles light some thirteen miles away. We missed the tide that night, but next day, with the flood under us and the lightest of westerly breezes behind, we sailed up Lymington river, sixty-five days out from St Helena.

When *Mischief* had been stripped of her sails, stores and gear, the crew were free to go their several ways, no doubt glad to have seen the last of each other. Eleven months is a long time for six men to be cooped up in a small cabin with frequent, unavoidable spells of leisure and boredom to be endured. As well as being thankful, I am always amazed that *Mischief*'s several crews, picked up at random, strangers to me and to each other, thrown abruptly together with an invitation to like it or lump it, yet contrive to live and work together on tolerably good terms. One firm bond is no doubt the sea and ships, and especially the ship in which they serve. As Conrad says: "The ship we serve is the moral symbol of our life," and there could be no better symbol of service than old *Mischief*; symbol of work faithfully performed, first as a working boat, then as a pleasure yacht, and finally, in a very minor way, as an expedition ship.

Only once has one of the crew left me on the outward passage, before completing what he had undertaken to do. Anyone, with or without a sense of loyalty and responsibility, will see an ocean passage through to the end, even if only for the reason that there is no getting off. But to make a series of long ocean passages, such as *Mischief*'s recent voyages have entailed, some other bond is needed to hold men together. Such a bond may be found in the goal the party has in mind, and I like to think that the more distant and seemingly unattainable the goal, the stronger is the bond.

IV

The Far North

───────────

After the two great southern voyages, it occurred to Tilman that—to paraphrase Prince Hal—"they provided an intolerable deal of sea to one half-pennyworth of mountain, while Greenland, excessively mountainous, is only a month's sail away". The Greenland voyages would be shorter, and cheaper; the crews easier to find. With Charles Marriott (who this time volunteered to cook), David Hodge, Terence Ward, Michael Taylor-Jones and John Wayman, he set out for Godthaab and the West Greenland coast, hoping to reach Disko Island, in Lat. 70° N. The days of Trade Wind sailing and flying fish on deck were, for the moment, over. They made their way up the Irish Sea to Belfast, and on 25th May 1961, caught the north-going tide for the first voyage to Greenland.

1961: FIRST GREENLAND VOYAGE

THE NORTHERLY WINDS that might have sent us far on our way had we passed south of Ireland still persisted. But at sea as on land, the truth of the Spanish proverb, that whichever way you go there is a league of bad road, is generally borne out. At sea one must accept whatever winds blow, for it is not often possible to cheat the wind like a "vile politician seeking to circumvent God". Readers of *Typhoon* may recollect that a similar view was held by that sturdy seaman Captain Mac-Whirr, a man who "as if unable to grasp what is due to the difference of latitudes, always wore, at home or in the Tropics, a brown bowler hat and black boots". He had a contempt even for the laws of storms and thus expressed it to his mate at a moment when his ship was about to be all but overwhelmed by a typhoon: "All these rules for dodging breezes and circumventing the winds of heaven, Mr Jukes, seem to me the maddest thing."

When the tide turned against us as well as the wind we could make no progress so we ran into Red Bay where we anchored. There is little shelter from northerly winds in this deserted bay but at any rate we were out of the tide. In the evening the wind veered so that we could steer north and with the tide now under us we went like a scalded cat. The tides in the North Channel run at three knots. At midnight, north-west of Rathlin Island, I came on deck to find her moving backwards, the sails all aback and the tiller lifeless, the sea around seething as if about to boil. We were in the tail of a race, probably in the vicinity of Shamrock Pinnacle. In order to get steerage way we had to start the engine.

Having at last rounded the corner of Ireland we had the wind free and could steer west. By eight o'clock next morning, a big sea then running, we had Inishtrahull Island abeam three miles away. We did not lose sight of the Irish mountains for another two days, but we were now in the open ocean with nothing between us and America two thousand miles away. When presently the wind again headed us we had trouble persuading *Mischief* to go about, the sea being so rough. At the second attempt we got her round but not before the flogging jib had shaken one of the sheet blocks out of its strop. When the wind dropped at midnight we rolled about with the boom slamming wildly. In such circumstances the question is whether to call all hands to get the sails off or to leave things as they are in the hope that the wind will soon come again. Experience teaches that leaving the sails up seldom pays but hope generally triumphs over experience, as Dr Johnson remarked of a man marrying for the second time. Although we steadied the boom to some extent by bowsing it down with the handy-billy, by 2 a.m. a large rent had appeared in the sail so down it had to come. I had hoped that this sail, the weaker of the two we carried, would have taken us across. It had already given so much trouble that we decided to change it, a decision easier to make than to carry out on the deck of a small boat in a rough sea with no sail to steady her. Having first prised the second sail out of its bin in the galley we pushed it by main force into the cabin and on to the deck through the skylight. There are about 700 square feet of canvas in the sail, a lot of canvas to unroll while trying to sort out the head and the foot, the tack and the clew. Having bent it on and hoisted, we bundled up the old sail as best we could and stuffed it below, wet as it was.

On May 30th we had our first good day's run when we logged 120 miles, and on the following day we did 94 miles. We felt we were getting somewhere, for Cape Farewell, the southern tip of Greenland, was less than 1,500 miles away. We began making absurd calculations, little thinking that another thirty days would elapse before we rounded that noted cape. Cape Farewell is 59° 46' north and 43° 53' west, but the mariner is advised not to go north of 58° 30' when passing it on account of the ice which accumulates off the cape. This meant for us roughly a course of west-north-west, a course that we could seldom lay, the wind blowing most often from somewhere between north-west and south-west. We sailed on the tack that allowed us to point nearest to west-north-west and changed to the other tack when that looked the more profitable. If both tacks were equally bad we chose the port tack whereby we got farther north where degrees of longitude measure fewer miles. In the Northern Hemisphere the Great Circle course, which is the shortest possible, lies to the north of the rhumb line course—the course that looks the shortest on a Mercator chart but in fact is not. Sailing thus, generally well off our course, we might log a hundred miles and yet make good less than half that in the direction of Cape Farewell, or even nothing at all.

Meantime the jib halyard continued to be troublesome. The sea being reasonably smooth, I went aloft and changed the block. Later we reverted to using the sheaves on the mast, and finally to the block again. It was unsatisfactory but by using the winch on the mast we could set the halyard up taut, twists and all. I must have been feeling energetic because after that I showed Charles how to make a cake, a task well within the capacity of a man who had spent two years at the Military

College of Science. In fact he was already doing well and even beginning to reach out for the higher branches of his present profession. He is blessed with a cast-iron stomach. If the boat is knocking about a lot, as it was the next day, one does not expect anything but the simplest fare for supper. Defying the weather, Charles produced a rich stew with dumplings the size of cricket balls floating in it. I was about to add "like half-tide rocks", a phrase that might have cast doubts on the wholesomeness of Charles's dumplings. We still had some fresh bread left. Ordinary bread keeps for about ten days at sea before sprouting a green mould. I suppose sliced bread wrapped in cellophane might keep longer but such bread, even without a green mould, is hardly worth eating. Having finished the fresh bread we go on to what I call "twice-baked", thick slices of bread or rolls that have been in the oven a second time. This seems to keep indefinitely, only its bulk prevents one from carrying enough for the whole voyage. Baking bread at sea for a crew of six on paraffin stoves is not feasible on account of the time, labour, and paraffin oil needed.

Nothing could be more different from Trade Wind sailing than sailing in the Atlantic in the latitudes of the fifties. No two days are alike, and for that matter the night that follows the day will generally see a change of some sort in the weather. However peaceful the sky may appear as the sun sets, it is a rash gamble to leave the Genoa up if one wants to pass an undisturbed night. Sunshine and rain, winds and calms, reefing and unreefing, followed each other incessantly and at brief intervals. Happily in summer the worst conditions seldom last long. What moderate gales we had were generally over in twenty-four hours, and it was rare for a calm to last more than a few hours.

Sailing to windward in a rough sea is generally wasted effort. For two days we steered NW by N. making little or no westing, so we hove-to and had a quiet night. When we let draw we tried her on the starboard tack and in the course of another two days lost about forty miles to the east. I found this discouraging. Besides the lack of progress I was worried by the wear and tear caused by prolonged beating in rough weather. On previous voyages we had generally managed to make ground in the required direction however hard the wind blew. The crew did not seem to mind. Having had no experience of long spells of down-wind sailing they took our slow, arduous progress as a matter of course. But they felt cold, cold accentuated by the general wetness, for there was usually spray flying or rain falling, or both. For the two-hour spell at the helm they adopted the unseamanlike practice of wearing gloves. Woollen gloves were so soon saturated that they devised ingenious waterproof mits from plastic bags or pieces of canvas. Under these conditions none of us looked forward to a spell in the cockpit holding the brass tiller or the equally cold, wet tiller line. How fast the time passes on watch depends much on how the boat is sailing. When close-hauled in a lumpy sea—which means in effect that she is going up and down in the same hole—the hours seem interminable, whereas if she is going fast in the right direction with the log spinning merrily they pass like a flash. Perhaps the watch passes most quickly when one has to really concentrate on steering her, when running with the wind dead aft and the imminent threat of a Chinese gybe hanging over one.

On this passage we seldom had any inducement to sit about on deck and in the North Atlantic there is seldom much to see except a waste of grey water devoid of life or ships. We were now north of the northernmost steamer track used by ships bound for Scandinavian ports round the north of Scotland. The last ship sighted, an ore carrier called the *Afghanistan*, had altered course to have a look at us and gave us three friendly blasts on her siren by way of encouragement. We returned the compliment with three dismal squeals from our hand fog-horn. The few birds seen, we wrote off as gulls, for we knew no better and had on board no keen bird-watchers such as we had on the later voyage. Most of the way across Terry Ward trolled a line—not, perhaps, such a hopeless gesture as it may sound, for on the way home, in fine, warm weather, I saw some tunny leaping. When there was no work on deck most of the time had to be spent below, usually flat on one's back reading or sleeping. I am told that in a steamer, where there are rivets in the deckhead, an alternative occupation is to count them.

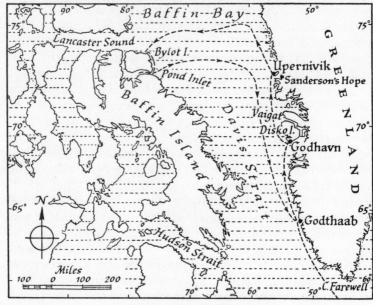

Bylot Island, Baffin Bay, 1963
(from *Mischief in Greenland*)

The fight that we had to get westwards and to round Cape Farewell can best be understood from the brief entries I made in a diary for the latter half of the passage. All bearings, by the way, are true. My hopes and fears are not set down, for I have generally found that in the event these are made to look damn silly.

Tuesday, June 13th. Steering north yesterday till wind backed in the evening. Early this morning wind backed farther to south-west and glass fell to 28.9. Reefed before breakfast when we were doing 6½ knots. A sight at 9 a.m. put us in Long. 33° 14′ west. A new canvas bucket washed overboard. Glass down to 28.7 and a flat calm since 5 p.m. Handed sails and hoisted again at 8 p.m. when wind came in hard from north. Reefed. Had to run off to south-west owing to wind. Reefed again and handed jib. Blew hard all night.

June 14th. Sea rough and fresh head wind. Steering south-west. Gybed later and steered north.

June 15th. Wind fell light in night. Lowered main for repair at 4 a.m. and at 6 a.m. hoisted with all reefs out. Wind south, steering west-north-west, steady rain and glass down to 28.7. No sun, no sights for last twenty-four hours. Very cold on watch. My feet always cold. 4 p.m. glass down to 28.4. Wind backed to south-east, rain stopped, and sun came out. Wind fell light, violent rolling, handed sails. Hoisted in the night with wind from west. Barometer flattened out.

June 16th. Very fresh wind. Took reef out of main but soon had to reef again. Strong wind all afternoon and evening with barometer rising. Overcast. Steering north.

June 17th. Same dull windy weather. Went about in the evening and then about again to steer north-west. 10 p.m. wind freshening, reefed. Midnight reefed again and hove-to.

June 18th. Sunny morning but wind about Force 8. Weather sheet of backed fores'l parted. Got sail down with difficulty and hoisted storm jib in lieu. Nut came off starboard shroud shackle bolt. Now about N. lat. 58°.

June 19th. Blew hard all day but some sun. Wind moderated by evening when barometer rose and rain set in.

June 20th. Reached N. lat. 59° 05'. Went about in the after-noon but by night on port tack again steering north-west. Wind from west-south-west has hardly varied a point since Saturday. Now about 150 miles west of Farewell. All complain of cold.

June 21st. Still beating against WSW wind. Sunny until afternoon when some fog came up with a harder wind. Mains'l down for stitching. Went about steering south. Small Danish ship *Nancie S.* bound east stopped while we hove-to to speak them. Asked them to report us but don't think they heard as we had no megaphone. The wind has been at WSW for five days. We sail north-west up to Lat. 59° and then go about again. No sign of any ice but still 100 miles west of cape.

June 22nd. Still beating but did better steering west by north until heavy rain started and wind headed us. Now about 70 miles south-east of Cape. Glass falling at night so reefed and dropped jib to slow down. We may be farther north than we think.

June 23rd. All plain sail steering north-west. Noon sight disappointing, not so near cape as we thought. Lat. 58° 58′ Long. 42° 10′. Went about steering south-west. Strong wind and rough sea, twice failed to stay and had to gybe her round. Strop of jib halyard block on mast parted. Too rough to do anything so now are without jib. 6 p.m. sighted first iceberg ½ mile on port bow. About 30 ft high. My seaboots filled with water when getting jib in.

June 24th. Wind freshened yesterday evening. Reefed. About 11 p.m. a tear in leach of mainsail opened so had to get sail down. Quite a job. Under stays'l only, so can only steer south. Same hard, cold wind all day. Mains'l sodden but repaired with herring-bone stitching a long rub caused by the topping lift. Tear in leach still to do. Had trysail up and steered south-west, but a snap sight this evening showed we had lost 13 miles to east. Poor outlook.

June 25th. Same wind all night. Very cold on watch. Some sun today. Got sail patched and hoisted by midday. Renewed stays'l hanks which were all worn through. Now down to Lat. 57° again and evening sight put us 43° 10′ west. Wear and tear continues. Jib outhaul stranded, ditto halyard, also stays'l sheet and wire of port topping lift. Not happy about the mainsail.

This was about the nadir of our fortunes. From a position not far from Cape Farewell, in three days we had been blown a hundred miles or so to the south. Whatever the crew may have thought about it, certainly at this time the breeze of anxiety began to ruffle my brow. We had about three weeks' water left, and Godthaab, the port for which we were aiming, was still nearly 500 miles away. At this comparatively early season the more southern ports of Greenland are difficult to approach on account of ice—the ice that is drifted round Cape Farewell and up the west coast by the Greenland current. We might surely expect more favourable weather in Davis Strait but we were not there yet; in my gloomier moments I even saw us having to run for Iceland to refresh—almost as far away as Ireland. I was worried by the wear and tear occasioned by constant beating and the wet conditions. Wet, sodden rope, with never a chance to dry, seems to fray much more readily, and wet, sodden canvas is hell to repair. The last job on the mainsail had cost David and me several hours' work. Such troubles were not serious except that cumulatively they tended to slow us down still more. Happily the crew remained unperturbed, though I warned them that with only three weeks' water left there was a limit to the time we could spend beating about off Cape Farewell. But better things were now in store for us. Cape Farewell had exacted its tribute. We had paid our footing.

They rounded Cape Farewell at last, and after a few days' stay in Godthaab, sailed north again through the Davis Strait.

The next time we closed the land we found ourselves at the mouth of Disko Bay. Disko is a large island separated from the mainland by a strait called the Vaigat which extends about sixty miles north-westwards and has a least width of six miles. To go north by way of the Vaigat was longer than by the open sea but we preferred the longer way on account of the scenery, both sides of the strait being mountainous. Moreover Disko Bay and the strait are famous for huge icebergs, some of them up to 300 feet high, carved from the great glaciers of Christianshaab, Jakobshaven, and Ritenbank. These glaciers descend from the ice-cap itself which from here northwards reaches right down to the coast. All along the coast south of Disko there is a strip of ice-free country varying in width from one mile to one hundred miles. The widest part lies inland from Holsteinborg and is of some value as a breeding ground for reindeer.

The mouth of Disko Bay was as far as we got on our passage to the Vaigat. For the best part of a fine, sunny morning we beat up and down across the wide mouth without making any progress. The blue, iceberg-strewn waters of the bay were flecked with white horses by a fierce wind whistling out of the

Vaigat. Bowing to superior force we eased the sheets, pointed her head north-west, and went out to sea like a train. The more northing we made the better the weather became. Clammy fog and cold rain were forgotten as one clear, sparkling day followed another, the sun shining perpetually from a cloudless sky. At this time of year, north of Lat. 69°, the sun never set. After sinking towards the west, he hesitated as if in thought, before beginning once more to climb—very strangely to our unaccustomed eyes. We found this phenomenon extremely agreeable. It made the night watches as pleasant as those by day, caused no alteration in our daily life, and abated not a jot our ability to sleep. The brilliant weather we now enjoyed, and continued to enjoy more or less unbroken throughout our stay in these northern parts, seemed to have set in when the sun first remained above the horizon all night, as if before his unceasing vigil the malign spirits of fog and rain dare not show themselves.

The one drawback to these halcyon days was the absence of wind. That north-easterly blow in Disko Bay was the last we were to have. For the rest of the way to Igdlorssuit, a small Eskimo settlement sixty miles north of Disko, we drifted and motored. In these circumstances we had no qualms about using the engine for hours at a time. On deck its subdued rumble can easily be tolerated, but in the cabin the noise is barely endurable for the space of a meal. So we often stopped it at meal-times and never dreamt of running it at night, or what our clocks told us was night. Off Hare Island, near the northern entrance of the Vaigat, we began really to see icebergs, spewed out by the tide from this narrow strait in their hundreds to begin their slow journey northwards across the head of Baffin Bay until halted by the winter's sea-ice. Icebergs of all shapes and sizes, some like fortresses with sheer sides, others with pinnacled towers like glistening cathedrals, all floating serenely on the stillest of blue seas.

Now that we were approaching our journey's end, where Charles and I would have to gird up our loins for action, instead of being filled with joyful anticipation, flexing our muscles, doing a little quiet limbering-up on deck, both of us went about our work like a couple of cripples. I had a gathering on one hand and could still feel my rib when breathing—an unavoidable act at most times and more than ever necessary when climbing. Charles disclosed for my inspection a toe which looked as if it had been frost-bitten and required immediate amputation. Naturally he took a more serious view of this than I did and wanted me to make for Umanak, a small town where, according to the Sailing Directions, there was a hospital. I demurred strongly to this. As the Arabs say, the camel-driver has his thoughts and the camel he has his. We were already later than we should have been, and by the time we had been to Umanak (sixty miles away) and back, and Charles had had his foot looked at and probably been told not to put it to the ground for a month, we should have wasted a good many days.

So to Charles's chagrin and with some slight misgiving on my part we held our course for Ubekjendt Island and the settlement of Igdlorssuit in Lat. 71° 30′. Ubekjendt is a name given by the Dutch whalers and means "unknown"; Igdlorssuit is Eskimo and for that language is a comparatively short name. A brief glance at the map of these parts had served to disgust me with Eskimo names. Their length and their doubled consonants combine to make up words that no ordinary man's tongue is able to pronounce. For their repellent appearance we must, I suppose, thank Hans Egede who coined the orthography for his translation of the Bible into Eskimo. Igdlorssuit lies on the east side of Ubekjendt Island, an island that rises to over 2,000 feet. In my eyes it looked rounded, featureless, dull; but Rockwell Kent, an artist and a writer, who in 1933 built a house at Igdlorssuit and lived there for a year, had viewed it with far different eyes, the eyes of an artist, a man with a soul, as opposed to a man personifying, as a French writer has put it, "*le mépris de vulgarisation, du clubalpinisme et des yahous.*" He, Rockwell Kent, thus describes Ubekjendt:

Both by the suggestion of its name and by its position and character—its seagirt isolation, the simple grandeur of its stark snow-covered table-land and higher peaks, the dark cliff barrier that forms its eastern shore—there is the glamour of imponderable mystery about the island which dignifies it even at the gateway of a region of stupendous grandeur. Its cliffs, proclaiming inaccessibility, preclude the thought of human settlements. When, therefore, on approaching its more mountainous north-eastern end, where, just ahead, steep mountain walls rise sheer from the water's edge, the barrier ends, the shore sweeps inward in a mile-wide crescent of smooth strand and, cupped by mountains, there appears a low and gently sloping verdant foreland, jewelled with painted buildings, one's spirit, in sudden awakening to a need, exults in grateful consciousness of its fulfilment.

When we rounded the northern end of the island and started down its east coast in search of the settlement, we wondered much as to what we should see. At the time I had not read Rockwell Kent's book and, as I have said, the island appeared to me an uncommonly dull and barren lump. But it was in the nature of the settlement we were mainly interested, not the island. Obviously we could not hope for igloos, for there was no snow below the 2,000-foot level. Perhaps we expected to see semi-troglodyte dwellings of stones and earth, their blear-eyed and smoke-grimed inhabitants, clad in furs and reeking of blubber, crawling out to greet us with cries of "Pilletay, Pilletay" ("Give, give"), as we read of their doing in accounts by McClintock and other early explorers in search of the North-west Passage. It was therefore with mixed feelings that we finally brought in view a row of some twenty gaily-painted wooden houses (Rockwell's "jewels") straggling along the beach and in the background what was obviously a church. However, we were cheered when with the aid of binoculars we made out numbers of husky dogs, kayaks, sledges, and racks of drying shark-meat. We felt that the last item should have been blubber, but shark-meat it proved to be.

To show what we could do we caught some fish for breakfast before we turned in that night. They were what are called fjord cod, smaller and less firm-fleshed than their fellows of the open sea, despised by the natives but welcome to us. Although we expected to be here several days, and

although one could see from the boat pretty well all that
Igdlorssuit had to offer in the way of sight-seeing, we lost no
time in going ashore fully armed with cameras. In fact we
spent five days here, mainly on account of Charles who was
now lying up nursing his foot, still convinced that only a visit
to Umanak would save it. Like the rest of the Greenlanders the
people of Igdlorssuit are far from being pure Eskimos, yet they
and their way of life appeared to us more like the real thing.
The huskies, of which each family had some twenty, the
sledges lying about, the kayaks carefully stored high up out of
the dogs' reach, the racks of shark-meat drying in the sun, the
women sewing skins on a new-built kayak, all these led us to
believe we were seeing life in the Arctic, even while we
trudged along the sandy beach sweating in the sun and cursing
the heat and the mosquitoes. A walk of about half a mile, the
sea on one hand and on the other a gravel fan sparsely covered
with grass and a few flowers (Rockwell's "verdant foreland"),
brought us to the heart of Igdlorssuit life—the store and the
post-office, and the shed where barrels of sharks' liver were
stored. At least the revolting stuff we watched being weighed
was, I am told, shark liver, and several times up the fjord we
saw the fins of these creatures sticking out of the water. The
store, owned by the Greenland Trading Company, buys all
the sealskins and shark liver brought in and sells all that the
community needs in the way of food, clothing, household
goods, beer, tobacco, tools, implements, fishing gear, rifles,
shotguns, ammunition, and fuel for their motor boats. Thus
although their occupations have not changed and they still
live, though indirectly, by their skill in sealing and fishing, yet
their way of life has greatly changed from the self-sufficiency
of the old days when the seal provided their clothing, boots,
tents and boats, food for men and dogs, fuel for cooking and
heating, and oil for lighting.

The three or four motor boats anchored off the settlement
were used for going to various islands where at this time of
year seals might be found. Generally a kayak was carried on
board for use in the final stages of the hunt. Hunting so wary a
creature as the seal calls for no little skill and patience even with
modern firearms. The only evidence of seals we saw were

mere fleeting glimpses of a head poked above water and immediately submerged. The best chance of a shot is when they are hauled out on a berg or floe, or ashore on an islet. They must be shot through the head or they will roll into the water and sink or escape. In winter they are netted or harpooned at breathing holes, or stalked on the ice, the hunter behaving as much like a seal as he can and taking hours over the stalk. A few seals were still being got in July when we were there. I remember seeing a dory with two seals tied behind being towed along by a team of huskies. The beach is steep-to and the water so calm that there was no difficulty in keeping the dory afloat while the dogs walked along the beach. The seals are not the fur-seal, but the skins of these ringed and hooded seals are valuable to the fur trade. As privileged visitors and prospective buyers we penetrated to the back premises of the store where the skins were kept. We were not allowed to buy the quality skins—lovely, silvery fawn skins in prime condition which were reserved for export to Denmark—but we all invested in a few of the lower quality at prices in the region of £1, depending upon the condition. From his purchase Terry Ward knocked up a useful pair of bedroom-slippers. My thoughts were running on sealskin trousers and the figure I should cut in them at home. This novel idea never came to fruition though it seemed to me to be a more proper use for sealskins than the elegant coat for my sister that, as I should have anticipated, they eventually made.

Husky dogs and children, alike, swarmed in Igdlorssuit. Both seemed to be well cared for, the dogs being fed daily on shark meat. In late winter, when the fjord is finally frozen over, when hunting parties go out and when visits are paid to neighbouring settlements, the dogs earn their summer keep by pulling sledges. For the children our visit was a godsend. They played on and around *Mischief*, showed off for our benefit in a kayak, and followed us diligently on our walks. Apparently the sensible arrangement prevailed of closing the school entirely for the summer months. The children were well clad in European clothes—brightly-coloured anoraks were a favourite—as were their elders, apart from one or two old-timers and the young he-men who affected sealskin trousers.

Nearly everyone wore sealskin boots. One woman on seeing me approach with a camera darted into her house and re-appeared in full-dress costume, with beaded vest and beauti-fully embroidered white sealskin boots reaching well up the thigh. This dress, we were told, was worn on Sundays for church, but in summer, by a less sensible arrangement, the church, too, seemed to be closed. Both in manner and appear-ance the people struck me as being very like Sherpas, the same short, sturdy figures and Mongolian features, their brown cheeks suffused with red; cheerful, happy-go-lucky, and al-ways ready to laugh either at us or themselves. The oldest inhabitant was a delightful character; a man like a barrel, as broad as he was long, who walked about (sealskin trousers, of course) aided by a stick, a benign smile on his leathery, wrinkled face and a short cutty pipe stuck firmly in his toothless mouth. They shopped freely at the store buying sugar, flour, jam, sweets, tinned meats and fruits, so that their normal diet seemed to be as humdrum as our own. It must be a sad change from their former régime of blubber, seal meat, and sea birds. In time one can get used to anything and no doubt they still eat enough of these natural, wholesome foods to prevent them from getting scurvy. They certainly looked healthy enough and in little need of the services of a sort of district nurse who visited them about once a fortnight in a small motor vessel from Umanak which brought also mail, stores, and passengers.

Having undertaken to collect plants for the Natural History Museum I spent most of my time botanizing around the settlement where flowers might be found growing up to the 500-foot level. I now had lumbago—"a trifling sum of misery new added to the foot of my account"—so that I had to be careful when bending to dig out a plant for fear of not being able to straighten up. Really, I thought, I should be far better employed exploring the Brighton front or Cheltenham from a bath-chair rather than Greenland; to be joined there no doubt, in the very near future, by Charles, provided that vehicles of that kind were procurable on easy terms. But Charles was now on the mend. Our second-hand accounts of life's busy scene in Igdlorssuit would no longer serve. He must see for himself. So rising from his bed of pain he announced his intention of going ashore, and in order to save him a long walk we rowed the dinghy to a landing place just below the store. The populace, scenting something unusual afoot, had gathered in strength and they were well rewarded for their pains. In yachting cap and gumboots, his beard a sable silver, monocle in eye and supported by an ice-axe, Charles stepped ashore like a slimmer edition of King Edward VII landing at Cowes from the Royal Yacht. The crowd were speechless with delight. At last, they thought, the captain of *Mischief* had condescended to visit them.

On the same afternoon, having extracted Charles from the thick of an admiring crowd, we got our anchor and sailed out. The wind soon died. After drifting on to a large iceberg and fending off with the boat-hook we started the engine. We had about forty miles to go to the anchorage I had in mind, a bay at the root of the Qioqe peninsula with the remarkable name of Kangerdlugssuakavaak. "Kangerd" means fjord—the fjords between which our peninsula lay were called Kangerdlugs-suaq and Kangerdluarssuk. Since most of the forty miles would have to be done under the engine we anchored for the night on the south side of Upernivik Island off the snout of a dying glacier. In the fjords it is difficult to find water shallow enough to anchor in without being perilously near the rocky shore. Usually the most likely place is off a glacier, or a stream that emerges from a glacier, where silt and débris have accumulated.

Early next morning a small floe got under our bowsprit and we had to move to another anchorage. I spent an hour ashore looking for plants. In West Greenland there are several hundred species of flowering plants, grasses, and ferns. In our short visit we collected only some sixty species but many of the flowers were no doubt over by the time we arrived. There are many familiar forms such as buttercups, dandelions, saxifrage, campions, poppies, harebells, willow herb; and of the larger kinds, creeping willow, dwarf birch, crowberry, and bilberry. As we motored up Kangerdluarssuk, with the Qioqe peninsula on our port hand, we met with a bitter wind

blowing straight from the ice-cap. The day was unusually
cloudy with cloud down to about 500 feet so that we saw
nothing of the mountains but their lower cliffs, broken occasionally by steep and narrow valleys filled with ice. At its
upper end the fjord widens. In the middle lies the small island
of Qeqertak; in the south-east corner a massive glacier de-
scends from the inland ice, filling that part of the fjord with big
icebergs; and in the north-east corner was the bay with the
long, unpronounceable name where we proposed to stay, a
bay well protected from drifting ice. We dropped anchor in
seven fathoms off a wide gravel fan left by a retreating glacier.
Even so we found the stern touched the bottom about twenty
yards from the shore. We had to lay out a kedge anchor astern
to keep her lying parallel to the beach.

David was eager to set foot on a glacier, so next day he and I
took a walk up the valley which runs right across the root of
the peninsula to Kangerdlugssuaq fjord on the north side. In
winter this valley is used as a sledge route. Rockwell Kent
describes a journey made in January from Igdlorssuit to
Umanak when, owing to open water, they could not sledge
direct to Umanak and had to sledge up the northern fjord, haul
the sledge over the peninsula by this valley, and continue
down the southern fjord and along the coast to Umanak. A
short walk up the gravel fan brought us on to the glacier itself
which, fortunately for David, for he had on only shoes, was
smooth, unbroken ice covered with gravel and flat stones.
After about three miles of easy going, passing on our left the
mouth of the valley whence the glacier descended, we reached
the moraine on the far side of the glacier and were soon on the
low divide looking down to the northern fjord. Thick mist
covered the fjord while we basked in sunshine. On the evidence alone of this short excursion I began to fear that we had
come to the wrong place for a climbing centre. Certainly the
glacier led into the heart of the peninsula in the direction of the
bigger peaks, including Punta Italia, but its ice-fall, filling the
valley that we had passed, seemed to me an effective barrier.
The peaks were too far to be climbed from the boat so that we
should have to carry loads up the ice-fall, and besides that they
looked inaccessible from the glacier head. I did, however,

notice a peak of about 6,500 feet which was within reach and which could be got at by way of a steep but ice-free valley less than a mile from the anchorage.

Charles, too, had been out for the day exercising his foot. When we compared notes I gathered that in his view this ice-fall was a minor obstacle. In the course of many years of climbing, mostly in the Himalaya, the times I have failed to come to grips with some peak on which I had set my heart, having been balked and forced to retreat by some ice-fall, are sad memories. Most ice-falls, I admit, can be overcome with time, patience, or possibly ladders, as, for example, the ice-fall leading to the West Cwm on the south side of Everest. But unless the goal beyond is all-important they are best left alone by small parties like ours, especially if loads have to be carried up them. Charles, as I have said, did not agree. He judged this ice-fall to be, so to speak, a piece of cake, and persuaded me to try it in spite of my conviction that we were wasting our time. He concluded by saying there was nothing he liked better than worrying his way through an intricate ice-fall. My reply, couched in phrases that might have shocked anyone but Charles, was that I thoroughly disliked messing about in them. However, since I had had my way over the little matter of not going to Umanak I thought that this harmless whim of his should be humoured.

Accordingly next day we started up the ice-fall. I must say Charles did his best while I studiously refrained from any discouraging remarks and even tried to show the enthusiasm I did not feel. As we got higher even a one-eyed man might have seen that there was no likelihood of finding a route up any of the big peaks beyond had we surmounted the difficulties of the ice-fall, but Charles was so engrossed in mastering it and showing that it could be mastered, that the uselessness of doing so hardly occurred to him. Nothing daunted, Charles pressed on, only a little astonished to find that after one terrace had been laboriously gained there was always another above. We lunched precariously, surrounded by crevasses and seracs in hideous confusion. Shortly afterwards, when we were still some 200 feet below what really was the top we were stopped by a series of gaping crevasses, around, through, or over which, Charles had to admit there was no way. He had had his fun, so on the way back to the boat I pointed out the 6,500-foot peak I proposed we should tackle next day. The steep valley leading to it narrowed higher up to a gully packed with snow. By way of the gully we could reach a high snow shoulder and possibly the rock peak beyond. We could not see what lay between shoulder and summit but the mountain was well worth trying. In spite of the encouraging example of a so much older man, I had some misgivings about my own ability to emulate Piero Ghiglioni's feats. I asked Charles how he felt about climbing 6,500 feet in the day. Many years ago, at a much higher altitude, I had climbed 6,000 feet and back in a day; and Charles, searching his memory, thought he had done as much before and could no doubt do it again.

The condemned men ate a hearty breakfast—cod steaks, if I remember right—and at 8.30 we had ourselves rowed ashore. Not the least blessing of climbing in Greenland is that one can start at a reasonable hour; no turning out in the small hours, as one must in the Alps, to cook and swallow some food, that were it food for the gods would be revolting at such a time, and then to stumble out into the cold darkness guided by the feeble light of a candle lantern. All this to avoid being benighted, of which in Greenland there is happily no fear. Some loose scree in the valley took a little of the shine out of us but when we reached the gully we found almost continuous beds of hard snow up which we could kick our way. We lunched just below the shoulder, having climbed about 3,000 feet. We continued kicking steps until when about 500 feet below a flat snow ridge at the foot of the final rock peak we were obliged to cut steps. Charles, who was in front at the time, thought we might avoid this by making use of some old avalanche snow off to our right. When this proved delusive we came back and I took over the step-cutting, for Charles, even at this early stage, was beginning to suffer from mountaineer's foot—the inability to put one in front of the other.

At four o'clock we came out on the level ridge whence we looked straight down to the waters of the fjord and across it to the great glacier rolling down from the inland ice. A mountain prospect from a high place is enthralling but to look out over sea and mountains is, I think, even more moving—to feel at once the immensity of the one and the steadfast, unchanging nature of the other, both indifferent to man's presence and yet to many men an inspiration and a solace. However that may be, that which concerned us more than the majestic view was the formidable aspect of the rock and ice ridge which sprang upwards towards the summit almost from where we stood. There were nearly a thousand feet of it. It might improve on acquaintance, but to two tired men it looked sufficiently daunting. Charles now admitted that he had shot his bolt and while I might have gone farther I did not feel capable of looking after him as well as myself on what would evidently be the hardest part of the climb. Reluctantly, and keenly disappointed, we accepted defeat. For all that it had been a day of rare enjoyment, of strenuous endeavour in glorious surroundings and in flawless weather with only our own feebleness to blame for our failure. At 8.30 that evening, dejected and humbled, we rowed back to the boat.

While Charles and I had been amusing ourselves on the mountains the crew had set about giving *Mischief* a new look. At Godthaab we had not been able to find any cream-coloured paint like that on her topsides. At David's suggestion we bought instead some bright yellow paint; he thought that with black bulwarks and yellow topsides she would look pretty rakish so this new colour scheme was now adopted. All Danish ships plying to Greenland, and all the local fishing boats, are painted a standard red-lead colour, presumably to make them conspicuous when among ice. Personally I liked the new colour scheme, but when we returned to Lymington, where yachts are either glossy white or nothing, I failed to detect any gasps of admiration from frequenters of the Yard.

After more climbing, and another visit to Godthaab, Tilman sailed home to Lymington, confirmed in his taste for Greenland waters. The following year, he mounted another expedition, this time to the Arctic coast of eastern Canada. In his reading, he found a historical precedent for his travels in the far north: the Elizabethan seaman John Davis, who sailed in 1585 to Exeter Sound on Baffin Island, and named a mountain rising from the Sound Mount Raleigh. Tilman's plan was to climb it.

1962: IN THE FOOTSTEPS OF JOHN DAVIS

NOWADAYS WHEN PRETTY well every nook and corner of the earth has been explored, only large-scale Antarctic expeditions, helped by aircraft and Snowcats, and hindered, perhaps, by the pressing needs of science, may still hope to make fresh discoveries. The individual with a taste for discovery has for the most part to content himself with following the tracks of early explorers, obtaining a vicarious thrill from making the landfalls they had made. On our last voyage we had by chance made the same landfall at Cape Desolation as Davis had when he rediscovered Greenland. This Elizabethan seaman and explorer therefore roused my interest.

Davis's search for the North-west Passage was no doubt instigated by Sir Humphrey Gilbert's famous *Discourse* published in 1576. The loss of the little *Squirrel* in 1583 with Sir Humphrey and his companions must also have made a deep impression, coming so soon after he had penned the famous words with which his *Discourse* closed, words which in those brave days rang like a trumpet call: "That he is not worthy to live at all, that for fear or danger of death, shunneth his country's service or his own honour; seeing death is inevitable and the fame of virtue immortal." On his first voyage Davis, as we have seen, after making his landfall at Cape Desolation anchored in what he called Gilbert Sound, the present Godthaab, where he had friendly intercourse with the Eskimos. Crossing the Strait he discovered and named Capes Dyer and Walsingham, and anchored in Exeter Sound; and finally explored Cumberland Sound in the belief that it was a strait and possibly the desired passage.

In 1586 with the same ships *Sunneshine* and *Mooneshine*, and *Mermaid*, a larger vessel of 120 tons, he landed first at what is now called Old Sukkertoppen. Having again entered Cumberland Sound he sailed down the coast, explored the Labrador coast, and returned home bringing with him some salt cod and 500 sealskins. For his third and last northern voyage in 1587 he had the old *Sunneshine*, another vessel *Elizabeth*, and the clinker-built pinnace *Ellen* of twenty tons. In Gilbert Sound he made a heroic decision. To satisfy his backers by making the voyage pay, he dispatched the two bigger ships to the Labrador coast to fish while he continued his exploration in the barely seaworthy *Ellen*. He went north as far as the great cliff now called Sanderson's Hope in Lat. 72° 12′, or as he wrote, "Sanderson his hope of a North-west Passage, no ice towards the north, but a great sea, free, large, very salt and blue, and of an unsearchable depth." A northerly wind drove them westwards where they encountered the "middle pack" and were forced once more into Cumberland Sound. Sailing south down the coast off Hudson Strait they met with "a mighty race, where an island of ice was carried by the force of the current as fast as our bark could sail". On these three voyages Davis charted long stretches of coast on both sides of the Strait and much of the Labrador coast and took regular observations for the variation of the compass. As Clements Markham wrote: "Davis converted the Arctic regions from a confused myth into a defined area. He not only described and mapped the extensive tract explored by himself, but he clearly pointed out the way for his successors. He lighted Hudson into his strait. He lighted Baffin into his Bay. He lighted Hans Egede to the scene of his Greenland labours. His true-hearted devotion to the cause of Arctic discovery, his patient scientific research, his loyalty to his employers, his dauntless gallantry and enthusiasm, form an example which will be a beacon-light to maritime explorers for all time to come."

Of many remarks made by Chinese sages of the past one of the less pithy (but one that I like) is that of Chang Cha'o: "If there are no famous hills then nothing need be said, but since there are they must be visited." Mt Raleigh by its association with John Davis merits fame and as an objective it had for me other desirable features. True it was not very lofty, but lofty enough for a man of whom it might be said that years have tamed his mountain passion without clouding his reason. Besides its romantic name and romantic association it was a

nountain lying upon a wild and desolate coast, a coast that
vould be hard to reach. Indeed when I had read all that I could
bout the ice conditions in summer on that coast I did not rate
ur chance of success highly and was prepared to be dis-
ppointed. *Mischief*'s hull has not been strengthened in any
vay to make her fit to shunt ice, as she would have to do if we
ried to force a way through loose pack-ice. We should
ierefore have to wait until the ice had cleared away from the
oast, and much depended upon our experiencing a favourable
eason.

*he crew were Hans Hoff, Michael Rhodes, Roger Tufft, Roger
Brown, and cook Shaun White. It was on this voyage of 1962 that
Mischief and Tilman had their first encounter with the pack-ice that
vas to become so familiar. Exeter Sound on Baffin Island was
npossible to enter at the first attempt; so Tilman sailed southwards,
nd turned west again for Holsteinborg on the Greenland coast.
Tilman, in any case, had broken his false teeth and sought repairs.*

bout two in the morning Roger Brown called me to say we
vere among floes. I went up and took the helm for we were
ailing fast in smooth water under all plain sail. That it was
oggy goes without saying. At first I thought these floes were
ierely a few stragglers and that we should soon be clear,
lough the smoothness of the sea might have warned me that
iere was pack-ice in the vicinity. In fact if the sea suddenly
ecomes smooth it is a pretty sure hint that there is pack-ice to
vindward. If loose floes are scattered over a wide area any
vind tends to regroup them and as the wind rises they collect
1 belts running in a direction at right angles to the wind. As
ve were sailing with the wind just forward of the beam we
vere likely to become more involved, as we very soon did.

At first it was fun dodging the floes but, sailing as fast as we
vere, this presently became too hazardous. All hands were
alled to get the mainsail off and we jogged along under stays'l
lone. We had erred in not turning back on first meeting ice,
or by now it was all round us and we were forced to follow the
iost open lead in whatever direction it might take us.
Although the sea was smooth a perceptible swell added to the

difficulty. At one moment we would appear to be followin
an open lead and suddenly floes would heave in sight on top o
the swell. After two hours of it we had got nowhere and wer
still unable to see in what direction to steer to find open water
Then the lead we were following narrowed and began to clos
ahead of us. We downed the stays'l to lessen the impendin
impact and at the same time noticed with alarm a big tabula
floe, much bigger than *Mischief*, making straight at us. It wa
undercut all along the water-line where even in that murk
light the ice shone balefully blue, and as it came towards us
travelling faster than we were, it brushed aside the smalle
floes in its path. This big, blue bastard, as we immediatel
christened it, seemed bent on our destruction. For one or tw
confused minutes we were hemmed in and to my heate
imagination seemed to be lifted up and riding on ice. Then
having started the engine, we began slowly making headway
The floes thinned, the sea became rough, and at last we were i
open water. Hard by lay a big iceberg, as white and fresh
looking as if it had just broken off a glacier. Under its lee w
hoisted sail and resumed our course. By the time we ha
brewed coffee and turned in, leaving the helmsman to carr
on, it was five o'clock. I suppose an experienced ice navigator
instead of taking fright at the approach of this threatenin
monster, would have moored his ship to it and allowed it t
clear a path for him through the raft of floes.

    This ice, we thought, must have been the tail-end of what i
known as the "middle-pack", the great tongue of loosel
packed ice that stretches down west of the centre axis of Davi
Strait from Baffin Bay to beyond Cape Dyer. We reckoned w
were about eighty miles from the Canadian coast when w
encountered it. The old whalers trying to reach the "nort
water" in June or early July often got into serious trouble i
this "middle-pack". In the year 1830, out of the fleet c
ninety-one British whalers, nineteen were lost and at one tim
there were 1,000 men on the ice, men whose ships had alread
been nipped and sunk or whose ships were beset. It wa
known in whaling history as "Baffin Fair". On such occa
sions, thanks to the presence of so many ships, few lives wer
lost, but some terrible scenes took place. Once a ship wa

ipped and making water fast so that she looked like sinking, he men would remove themselves and their gear to the ice, he rum casks were broached, and all discipline came to an end. And apparently it became a custom or tradition that a ship so ipped should be set on fire.

By the evening of August 5th, a lovely, calm evening, we vere once more off the Greenland coast about twenty miles north of Holsteinborg. Early next morning, keeping a wary eye on the diminutive Jacob's Skaer and other dangers, we lowned sail and motored through the harbour entrance. The main harbour looked so small and so full of shipping of various kinds that we went on to have a look at the inner harbour. This vas large enough and completely empty, for it is cut off from he town, so back we went to the busy main harbour. A friendly police boat (one of three similar boats that were newly arrived at Godthaab from Denmark when we were last there) varned us that in a vacant hole we were making for there urked a submerged rock. We had to go right in close to a floating jetty where the smaller fishing boats lay, where we dropped anchor and laid out a warp to the shore. We were barely clear of the fairway; I felt that sooner or later one of the many fishing boats which were constantly coming and going would fail to notice *Mischief*'s long bowsprit. Luckily it was a period of neap tides. Had it been springs we should have been on the bottom at low water.

There was no place here for the sea-weary mariner to go to wash the salt out of his mouth except a rather dreary coffee bar. Beer could be bought only over the counter at the general store and, as we soon learnt, could not be bought at all until a fresh consignment arrived. When in harbour we liked to have our evening meal ashore and Mick heard from a friendly Dane that we might be able to muscle in, as it were, at a hostel where some seventy Danish technicians and workmen had their meals. Just as at Godthaab a lot of constructional work was in hand, new houses being built, roads made, and drains laid. Accordingly, on our first evening we repaired to the hostel. As George Robey used to sing: "My word, it was fine; they were just going to dine; my reception gave me quite a shock." They were all so delighted to see us, or so we imagined as we slid

modestly into some vacant seats at the foot of a long table. A
very good meal we had, too, conversing brightly with our
neighbours, behaving with decorum, and finally paying our
bill. Next morning I went up to the hostel to warn them that
we should be dining with them again that evening. I was
confronted, however, by the manageress, a large, square
rigged Danish woman, strikingly masculine in face and figure
who at once gave me a curt "no" and with whom I felt no
inclination to argue.

Some further slight embarrassment awaited me later that
morning when I set out to find the dentist. At the quay a
drunken Greenlander attached himself to me and refused to be
shaken off. Every passer-by had to be stopped and told who
his distinguished friend was, and presently they were being
told, too, where I was bound for, the drunk having discovered
my destination when I asked a Dane where the dentist lived.
At the door of the dentist's waiting-room I tried to shut him
out but he followed me in and introduced me loudly to each
member of the small suffering assembly. The noise he made
brought the dentist herself into the room. Hastily explaining
the matter and thrusting my broken teeth into her hand I
withdrew before she had time to ask who my drunken com
panion was. But I had not yet done with him. I had to go to his
house where, in a neat room with a polished wood floor, he
made me sit while he cranked up an ancient gramophone and
turned his wireless on at full bore. This brought in his wife
who after viewing with distaste her polished floor, followed
him with a floor-cloth as he walked about wiping away marks
left by his muddy gumboots. Finally, seeing no end to it, she
made him sit down while she hauled his boots off and threw
them out. He had not brought me to his house purely out of
affection. Presently he went out of the room and returned with
his wife's regalia—high, embroidered boots, shirt, collar, the
lot—which he offered to me for £30. Upon my declining this
bargain he asked for a 2/- tip for having shown me the dentist's
house!

The drunk's house was perched perilously on a rock above
the road and the floating jetty, a wooden staircase giving access
to the road. It must have been one of the first houses built, for

now they extend inland as much as a mile from the harbour. The floating jetty always presented a busy scene, particularly if a boat came in with a load of whale meat or reindeer meat. This would be cut up into large hunks, weighed, and sold on the spot to a crowd of eager buyers. Behind Holsteinborg and its adjacent coast there is a stretch of broken, hilly country of nearly a hundred miles between the coast and the inland ice, a piece of country well stocked with reindeer. Hunting, we were told, is permitted for two months in the year, August and February. When we tired of watching the activity on the jetty we used to walk round to the other side of the harbour where cargo was landed from lighters and where the larger fishing boats landed their catch for the curing factory. The shore gang handling cargoes consisted of women. At the curing factory the cod were hauled up in baskets to be gutted by one gang of men and filleted at adjacent tables by another. Inside the factory were high stacks of alternate layers of salt and fish which in the curing process have to be moved and restacked with, I suppose, as much expert knowledge as would be required for curing tobacco or maturing Stilton cheese.

From there, Mischief returned to Holsteinborg, and crossed a second time to the Canadian Coast; Tilman did achieve his object of climbing Mount Raleigh, described by the Elizabethan seaman John Davis in 1585 as "a brave mount the cliffs whereof were orient as gold". Sailing homewards, Mischief's time was close to Davis's own.

It had taken us thirty-four days, only a day better than Davis's ships *Sunneshine* of fifty tons and *Mooneshine* of thirty-five tons, which returned to Dartmouth from Exeter Sound in thirty-five days. In his day almost every voyage undertaken had been a romantic adventure. As we read the accounts of them they did distil for us the essence of romance—the gay pursuit of a perilous quest. In more humdrum times, by following in the track of John Davis, we had sought and at times slightly savoured this elusive essence.

1963: BYLOT ISLAND CROSSING

"When you strike oil, stop boring," said Tilman; and having found such rich cruising and climbing ground in Greenland waters, he returned there in 1963. The plan was to cross the icebound Bylot Island, off the NE Coast of Baffin Island, in Lat. 73°N. His crew was strong: Ed Mikeska, a professional seaman, Mike Taylor, Bruce Reid, Stephen Pitt and Bob Sargent. After the passage north to Godthaab and up to Upernivik in the Arctic Circle, they set off to cross the Davis Strait to Bylot. Tilman fully expected to dodge through pack-ice—"a course that would make an eel dizzy"—but found problems, too, with the eccentric magnetism of the Arctic.

ON THE 18TH, when by dead reckoning we had reached Lat. 74° 40', we met with ice all along our port hand. For two hours we steered north along the edge until I grew impatient and decided to try conclusions with what after all might be merely a narrow line of floes—much to the dismay of Ed who had a wholesome respect for ice having spent some time bashing through it in an ice-breaker. Forewarned by recent experience I did not persevere too long. We turned north-east and soon reached open water again. On a day of little wind, the sea calm, in a region of no strong currents, there is no danger in poking about among loose floes always provided one has room to turn. *Mischief* unfortunately needs a lot of space in which to turn. But it would be unwise to persevere long amongst ice floes without being able to see open water ahead or at any rate quite certain it was there. On a day of wind, the sea rough, and the ice on the move, it would be courting disaster to be amongst it in a small, unprotected vessel. That day we saw a number of seals on the floes and I was glad they had the sense to dive into the water before we got close enough for a shot.

In the night we had some wind and made good eight miles to the west. All morning the light wind held, increasing to a fresh breeze by afternoon. The sun peering vaguely through the overcast enabled me to take a sight which put us in 75°N. 66°W., about half-way across Baffin Bay. Ice then appeared about a mile away on the port hand but so far our progress had been fairly painless. It looked now as if we had reached the North Water and that the ice showing up to the south must be the edge of the Middle Pack. When ice appeared dead ahead late in the evening our hope momentarily died but having come up with it we found it to be merely a long line of scattered floes projecting from the main body of the pack. Beyond lay more open water. In climbing it is notoriously a mistake to write off by mere inspection a seemingly impossible route. One must come to grips with it. In the same way ice floes that in fact are widely scattered, when seen from even half a mile away from the deck of a small boat—or even from the crosstrees—appear just as unbroken and impenetrable as heavily congested pack-ice. All next day in light winds and showers of sleet we sailed west over perfectly open water, only a strong ice-blink to the south denoting the whereabouts of the pack. The sun made a fitful appearance and our noon position I put at 74° 40′N. 66° 40′W. There happened that day to be a partial eclipse, so that we were delighted when the sky cleared to allow us to watch the progress of the shadow which began at 5 p.m. and lasted until 7 p.m. A huge iceberg afforded us another remarkable spectacle by heaving itself majestically out of the water as if about to capsize. At each ponderous roll one side lifted and the other sank by twenty to thirty feet. By estimating the number of cricket pitches that could be placed on it end to end some of us reckoned it about 300 feet long, others 500 feet. This led to arguments about its tonnage and estimates varied even more widely from a million tons to ten million. There is scope enough for error because the proportion of ice above water to that below varies greatly with the type of berg. A blocky, precipitous-sided berg has about five times more of its volume below water, than above, while a much pinnacled so-called "picturesque" berg, has only twice as much. As I write this, surrounded by slide rules and assisted by a young relative familiar with hypothetical logarithms and hyperbolic functions, I have worked the sum afresh and find that our rolling iceberg, give or take a few tons, weighed 450,000 tons.

In the evening ice-blink could be seen ahead as well as to the south. Ed swore there was ice to the north, too—ice all round, in fact. But he took the same lugubrious view of ice as he did of the weather. Having read more than once *Letters from High Latitudes* and being familiar with it, I was reminded of Wilson, Lord Dufferin's personal servant, who moved uneasily about the deck with the air of Cassandra at the conflagration of Troy. Cassandra Wilson used to wake his master something in this fashion:

> "Seven o'clock, my Lord."
> "Very well. How's the wind?"
> "Blowing a gale, my Lord—dead ahead."
> "How many points is she off her course?"
> "Four points, my Lord—full four points."
> "Is it pretty clear, Wilson?"
> "Can't see your hand, my Lord—can't see your hand."
> "Much ice in sight?"
> "Ice all round, my Lord—ice all round."

At midnight we came up with the ice that earlier had been betrayed to us by the "blink", a yellowish-white appearance of the sky produced by the reflection of pack-ice on the clouds. It proved to be another projecting cape which we presently rounded and resumed our westerly course. Throughout that next day we met scattered floes, so widely scattered that for the most part we could maintain our course. From sights I reckoned we had about 120 miles to go. Seals were fairly plentiful, sticking their heads out of the water or basking peacefully on the floes, and since we were under sail the latter took little notice of our passing. The crew seemed anxious to have one shot and equally in favour of casting me in the role of murderer. I must have been talking too much of my misspent youth in East Africa, of elephants and rhino, for they evidently took me for Buffalo Bill, or such a marksman as the famous elephant hunter Neumann who, because he invariably killed all his game with the one shot, earned from his Swahili followers the sobriquet *Risasi moja*—one cartridge.

When voyaging single-handed through the Patagonian channels Slocum felt that in the loneliness of those waters life of any kind should be held sacrosanct. I, too, felt reluctant to reduce the seal population by even one. But public opinion was too strong so, consoling myself with thoughts of fresh meat, I took Nissen's rifle, from which no shot had yet been fired, and lay down in the bows. It would not do to bungle it, the eyes of England, so to speak, were upon me. Waiting until the ship had glided quietly to within about a hundred yards of our unsuspecting victim, I fired. The seal hardly moved. It had either been killed outright or very hard hit, but I gave it one more round to make sure it did not slip away into the sea.

We hove to, launched the dinghy, and Bruce and Mike went off with rope and ice-axe to retrieve the body. The ice-axe was needed to cut a landing place on the floe. It proved to be a big harp seal. Stephen made a good job of skinning it and then put together a wooden frame where he stretched the skin to dry. The skinning is comparatively easy but cleaning a sealskin, removing all traces of blubber, is most laborious and trouble-some for the amateur. With various implements we whittled away day by day and still there were bits of blubber all over the skin. Finally it was left for the expert hands of an Eskimo at Pond Inlet who quickly made a proper job of it. We enjoyed the liver and we dutifully ate what little edible meat there was. To enjoy seal meat, perhaps one should be sitting in an igloo or smoke-blackened hut after a day's sledging, a blizzard raging outside, devouring it in one's fingers after slightly warming and smoking it over a blubber lamp.

On July 22nd we ran all day through patches of fog before a light wind. Both fog and wind increased at night (there was, of course, no darkness) till we were reaching at five knots with a spanking breeze at north. Seeing a few floes about we put an extra man on watch. At 1 a.m. the fog cleared and at 2 a.m. (ship's time) I took a meridian sight of the sun in the north. True, the sun was too low for a reliable sight but I liked the notion of taking a meridian sight in the middle of the night. On a fine, clear morning a bank of cloud away to the west hinted at the presence of land.

Before the weather closed down again, as it did before noon of the 23rd, I thought we had about forty miles to go to Cape Liverpool at the north-east corner of Bylot Island. At 4 p.m. I got a snap sight which was probably useless on account of the fog, but taking everything into account I reckoned we were only about twelve miles from the cape. Whereupon I altered course to WSW. hoping to fetch the land near Maud Bight which is twenty miles west of the cape and well inside Lancaster Sound. In view of the probability of ice in the sound, the reputed uselessness of the compass, and the paucity of reliable sights, this was a considerable act of faith. We were certainly near some part of the Canadian Arctic, we might even fetch the coast of Bylot Island. Beyond that it was anybody's guess.

> Beyond the clouds, beyond the waves that roar,
> There may indeed, or may not be, a shore.

About an hour later, the fog still thick and Ed on deck steering, the rest of us below were startled by an agonized yell, a yell like that from a covey of angry screech owls giving tongue together. Whether it heralded triumph or disaster I could not determine but knowing who had uttered it I surmised the latter. Tumbling up on deck we saw, a short 200 yards away, at about the limit of visibility, a low range of sandhills.

In Lecky's *Wrinkles*, of which I had a copy on board, there is a remark to the effect that "there is nothing so distressing as running on shore, unless there is also present some doubt as to which continent the shore belongs." We were not quite in that predicament. We were comfortably far from the beach—we had lost no time in anchoring—and in my opinion this was undoubtedly Bylot Island, though what part of it was, of course, a question.

Taking a map of the island I rowed the dinghy ashore. Not that I expected to meet any natives, hostile or friendly, of whom I might ask our whereabouts, or even any of the notices found nowadays on most beaches—"Deck Chairs 2d.", or "Bathing Prohibited". But on the map which, with regard to the coastline, is pretty detailed, there might be some identifiable features. Just west of Cape Liverpool, for instance, there was marked a lagoon where a river debouched. The cape itself is not significant enough, it is merely a bend in the coastline, a slight protuberance, as Dr Johnson might have called it. As far as could be seen in the fog the coast ran straight roughly from south-east to north-west, as the coast near Cape Liverpool does run. In a hurried walk along the beach in both directions I met several small streams and finally a backwater which a liberal-minded man might have called a lagoon. Back on board, with more confidence than I really felt, I assured the crew we were off Cape Liverpool. After supper some of us landed again for further exploration. The fog remained thick and apart from some old bear tracks we saw nothing else of interest. We set an anchor watch.

Though we could make Cape Liverpool our starting point for crossing the island, Bruce and I preferred if possible to start from Maud Bight, twenty miles further west, where a large glacier came right down to the coast, thus offering a broad highway to the interior. At this time of year at that low level the glacier, we thought, would almost certainly have a surface of dry ice, free from snow, on which we would be able to move at a good pace. At Cape Liverpool the nearest glacier was eight miles away from the beach.

Early on the 24th—the fog as thick as ever—we got our anchor and started sailing a little north of west with a good breeze at north. Very soon we began meeting icebergs and large flat floes, evidently at the entrance to Lancaster Sound. With one of these we had a terribly close shave. In the absence of any visible land it was difficult to tell whether we were being set up or down by any current. Stephen was at the helm pointing reasonably clear of a 100-foot-high ice monster with a ram like a battleship. Only when we drew near did I realize that we were being set down towards it very fast indeed. By then we were too close either to gybe or to go about. We could only hold on and pray that we were going fast enough to miss it. We shot by with about ten feet to spare. My knees still knock when I think of this near miss.

When the sun showed at 10 a.m., the horizon below it seemingly clear enough for a sight, I took one which showed that we were about ten miles east of our assumed position. My ideas about Cape Liverpool had to be revised. We must have been well to the south-east of it. The clearing, during which we had seen no land, lasted but a short time. Tacking towards the land we met more floes, stood out again, and continued tacking off and on until the wind died. Having started the engine we once more closed the land where we could make out fast ice (winter ice still fast to the shore) and beyond, very dimly, a low coastline. As we followed the edge of the fast ice westwards we were gradually forced away from the shore by its increasing width until finally the fast shore ice merged with heavy floes and blocked the sound. At 6 p.m. we had to abandon any hope of reaching Maud Bight or of penetrating any further west in Lancaster Sound.

Coasting back along the edge of the fast ice, keeping a sharp look-out for seals, polar bears, and somewhere to anchor, at last at 8.30 p.m. we found a little ice-free hole where a river debouched. We anchored there, only a few yards from the shore, with fast ice on either side of us. The strong current from the river which had kept the opening clear of ice also prevented us from swinging. We had barely done congratulating ourselves on finding this snug hole when the fog rolled away in dramatic fashion, revealing a wide stretch of brown tundra and beyond it a tangle of snow mountains brilliantly lit by the westering sun. A hasty inspection of our surroundings showed that the river formed an undoubted lagoon and that its course, parallel to the coast, agreed with that on the map near Cape Liverpool. This was decisive. We had already more luck than we deserved and I had no mind to push it any further by trying to force our way to Maud Bight. As Swift said: "There is no piece of knowledge in fewer hands than that of knowing when to have done." Bruce and I could very well start our journey from here and we had already marked down a glacier that would take us inland. Naturally the crew were all agog to set foot at once upon this barren and almost unknown shore. They proposed to walk after supper and for once I was quick enough to seize the advantage. Their energy could be harnessed. "When they bring you a heifer be ready with the rope", as Sancho Panza was fond of saying. Accordingly Bruce and I quickly made up some light loads which we carried inland for a mile and a half where we dumped them. On returning to the ship I took a sight, hoping to verify our position. Either I was too tired or there was too much refraction, for the working of it made no sense at all.

In contrast to the general run of the weather ever since Upernivik, and especially of the last few days, we enjoyed on July 25th and for several subsequent days bright, cloudless weather. There were no flowers and hardly any birds to rejoice and sing but even the bleak tundra assumed a more kindly aspect. But the thin ice that formed overnight round the ship reminded us of how far north we were and of the briefness of the arctic summer. I considered food for eighteen days a sufficiently liberal allowance for Bruce and I to take for the fifty-mile crossing. One had to assume that nothing untoward would befall either of us and that the boat would be there to pick us up. Food, together with our personal loads, tent, cooking gear, paraffin, and rope would, we reckoned, add up to about 160 lbs. The 15-lb tent was a big item and I had canvassed the idea of sleeping in snow-holes. But I like my comfort and in view of the sort of snow we were to encounter I am glad we did not try. Many years ago I may have been able to stagger *downhill* under an 80-lb load, and judging by what one reads in climbing journals this seems nowadays to be a standard load, especially among New Zealand climbers. One sometimes wonders whether the loads are weighed or whether they merely feel like 80 lbs—as indeed I could swear was the weight of any load that I now attempt to carry. However, on this journey I had no intention of competing in a weight-carrying contest. About 40 lb would be more than enough and the idea of adding to it by taking Peter Nissen's rifle never so much as crossed my mind. We hoped that for the first march, with the help of two volunteers, we could carry everything as far as the glacier. After that we should have to relay until we had consumed enough to be able to carry what was left in one lift.

Accordingly on the 25th Bruce and I, Stephen and Bob, set out for the foot of the glacier about eight miles away. Ed had the job of taking *Mischief* round to the settlement in Pond Inlet and I felt she could not be in safer or more capable hands. The settlement is on the south side or Baffin Island side of Pond Inlet, more or less opposite and separated by ten miles of water from the snout of the Sermilik glacier, the glacier by which Bruce and I hoped to descend to the south coast. The Sermilik is one of four glaciers on the south coast which have names. These and Mt Thule are about the only names on the map apart from the capes and bays of the coastline. I told Ed that we expected to reach the south coast about August 12th and that on either side of that date he was to look out for smoke signals at 8 a.m. and noon. If after the lapse of a week nothing had been seen he would have to sail over and look for us up the Sermilik. On shore we had noticed nothing much with which to make smoke. Perhaps on the south side there would be more vegetation, at the worst we could burn the tent.

The crossing of Bylot Island, through soft snow, took Tilman and Reid fifteen days. Mischief, *under Ed Mikeska's command, was to sail round to the Pond Inlet shore of the island and pick them up; but failed to appear.*

At its snout the Sermilik glacier is over a mile wide. Only the western corner of it is still washed by the sea, for it is receding and has been receding for a long time as the huge and very old moraine on the left bank showed. It took us a long time to climb this moraine and having reached the top we saw what in our snow-weary eyes looked like a lush meadow. What a contrast, too, was here from the bare, brown, stony waste that borders the north coast. Besides grass and a few flowers we noted with satisfaction an abundant growth of heath that promised to make for us a lot of smoke. Having carefully chosen a site, before erecting the tent we laid down a springy mattress of heath. We promised ourselves soft lying after what I think, taken all in all, had been the hardest fifty miles I had ever done, certainly the slowest. If we were not now in ecstasy it was at least comfort.

We had put the tent about 300 feet above the beach, fully high enough for a fire to be seen from sea level at ten miles' distance provided someone looked for it in the right direction at the right time. Tired limbs and a cold east wind kept us inside except for the time spent gathering a supply of heath for the fire. Although the next morning broke fine, a bank of fog still hid the opposite coast. When it cleared later we could make out even with unaided eyes the square outlines of buildings and a steamer at anchor. She was making a lot of smoke, evidently preparatory to sailing, for she presently moved off westwards towards Eclipse Sound. We guessed she must be the annual supply ship visiting the settlements at Pond Inlet, Arctic Bay in Admiralty Inlet, and Resolute on Cornwallis Island. We spent the morning building a big cairn on the beach and gathering driftwood to augment the fire. At noon the great moment had come. It was a substantial blaze comparable, we imagined, to the beacons signalling the arrival of the Armada and, we hoped, with an equally galvanizing effect. For what it was worth we also flashed a mirror and then settled back confidently to wait. An hour elapsed and nothing happened. Except for a few lonely icebergs the ten-mile stretch of water remained obstinately blank.

In the afternoon I took a walk uphill and then gained the beach below Castle Gables by way of a steep gully. As we had guessed from the air photographs this peak is merely a serrated ridge of rotten rock. Walking back by the beach I found evidence of old camp sites—a sheltering wall of stones, tins, bits of box-wood—relics perhaps of the American party of 1954. I collected more driftwood. At noon there had been a lot of wind blowing the smoke away horizontally, so that evening when the air was still we made more smoke.

On the next day we varied our tactics, lighting three fires in widely separated places instead of one big blaze. We had them going just in time, as a belt of fog crept slowly westwards along the Baffin Island coast. Albert Harbour, the best anchorage in Pond Inlet ten miles east of the settlement, had already been blotted out. We were already a little puzzled and as we gazed across the sunlit, smiling sea where nothing moved we debated the absence of response to our signals. If they had chosen to lie at Albert Harbour they would not have seen our smoke that day and might be too far off anyway. But it was unlikely that the crew would stop long at that empty harbour, however good the anchorage, with the hospitality of the settlement and fresh faces so close at hand. We found it hard, too, to believe that our smoke was not visible from the settlement or had not been noticed. Besides the crew who would be looking out, there would be numbers of keen-eyed Eskimos, quick to spot anything unusual, and probably with nothing better to do than ourselves but stare across the sea. There remained only the disturbing possibility that *Mischief* had not arrived, that she had been delayed for some reason, or even caught in the ice. There was no ice in sight now but a fortnight earlier conditions might have been as bad or worse than those we had encountered in Lancaster Sound.

As a result of these reflections we took stock of our food. The few luxuries we had started with—porridge, jam, butter, marmite, peanut butter, and chocolate—had been eaten long since, and on our arrival, thinking that we should be picked up in a day, we had made pretty free with what was left. We found we could now have ten biscuits each for that day and the next and that the pemmican, tea, sugar, and milk would last the same time. We had nothing else bar one slow-burning candle and so far as we knew the resources of the island were nil. And if *Mischief* had failed to arrive no one at the settlement would even know of our existence. Thus we faced the prospect of starving, with the added refinement of starving within sight of plenty. Obviously before that happened we should have to bestir ourselves. Bruce's air mattress was in good condition—a lash-up of that and driftwood might carry one of us safely across if the sea remained calm.

That night it blew hard from the east and continued blowing next morning. But the sun shone cheerfully as we surveyed the same prospect of wind-swept, sunlit, empty waters, and since cloud hung low over the Baffin Island side we need light no fires nor expect any rescue that day. We moved the tent to a more sheltered hollow and I went for a walk along the beach to the west under the front of the glacier. Bruce seemed sunk in lethargy or was perhaps reserving his strength for a voyage by raft. I can well understand the fascination of beachcombing, especially for a man on an island where the only evidence that there is life elsewhere on this planet is to be found on the beach. I found and discarded all kinds of worthless treasures—the runner of a sledge, a broken oar, whalebones, curious pebbles, the skeleton of a seal. The beach, too, was cluttered with bergy bits cast up by the gale. I took home some sea water which in the absence of salt we were using to flavour the pemmican, and that evening, in the last of our pemmican, we used too much.

Next morning, having made a smoke signal at 8 a.m., we retired to the tent for breakfast. As we were finishing this frugal meal, a mug of tea and three biscuits, thus leaving only seven in the larder, we heard the noise of an engine. In a flash I was outside the tent to see in the distance two small boats. We castaways had no need to wave shirts or light fires to attract their attention. They were obviously heading for our beach and presently two canoes, one large and one small, powered by Johnson outboard engines, landed and out stepped two Eskimos. The man, Kudloo by name, had a smattering of English. A party of Eskimos were apparently camped about five miles west of the Sermilik engaged in hunting seals or perhaps narwhal. They had seen our smoke and had had the sense or the curiosity to come and investigate. They must have been recently at the settlement because they knew of *Mischief* and they did not need to be told what we wanted.

In no time at all we had packed up, carried the loads to the beach, and dumped them in the big canoe, generously bestowing our remaining biscuits on Kudloo's companion, a young lad. In accord with my sense of fitness these chaps should have come in kayaks, though a kayak would not have helped us much. An umiak would have done—the large skin boat light enough to be carried, formerly used by Eskimos for ice-sea travel, propelled by rudely fashioned oars, while Kudloo and his companion should have been wearing sealskin anoraks and bearskin trousers, reeking emphatically of smoke and blubber. The only concessions Kudloo made towards my ideal were a pair of sealskin boots and a short cutty pipe which remained stuck in his mouth, the bowl close under his nose. The canoes were fine jobs of light plywood construction made in Canada, the big one capable of carrying several tons. The lad had to take the smaller canoe back to their camp. He had also to take with him, though Heaven knows why, some of the ice with which our beach was liberally strewn. I noticed he was choosy about what he took, discarding after a brief glance several pieces that to my inexpert eyes looked like perfectly good ice.

This done we all embarked and shot off at a good five knots
When about halfway over both wind and sea got up and
began to think Kudloo might be well advised to turn and run
for Bylot Island to await a better day. I pondered, too, how an
air mattress would have fared in these conditions. But Kudloo
drove on, pipe firmly clenched in his teeth, quite regardless of
the spray drenching both himself and his passengers. Soon we
sighted a mast and a familiar yellow hull and two hours after
leaving we were alongside. Having given Kudloo a well-
earned five dollars we climbed on board and surprised the
crew still at their breakfast. We thought they looked a bit
sheepish.

They had arrived about July 28th, the first ship of the
season, followed a week later by the supply ship Bruce and
had seen. During the last few days they had, of course, been
looking out for signals and apparently had looked in the right
place, but they had seen nothing. With no one now at our
camp site to make smoke the matter could not be tested, but
Bruce and I had to admit that against the dark background of
the moraine our smoke might have gone unnoticed. Nevertheless we remained secretly convinced that their combined
vision, even assisted by binoculars, must be singularly
myopic. At any rate all our anxiety had been needless, though
we were not to know it. In the course of the next week, seeing
no signals, they would have sailed over to look for us. But
whether before this happened, Bruce and I, with nothing to
eat, would have decided upon a raft, and which of us would
have embarked on this dicey voyage, are questions that I am
glad we did not have to answer.

1964: A LANDING ON SURTSEY

*After the notable crossing of Bylot Island, Tilman resolved on another
northern voyage.* Mischief, *however, was surveyed and declared
unfit for long voyages, and he sadly thought of parting with her
Finally he had her half rebuilt instead—all upper frames doubled—
and kept her. "This piece of folly having been committed, I began
thinking of committing another. . .". Instead of returning to the*

amiliar West coast of Greenland, he made his objective the more
langerously ice-strewn waters of the East coast, and aimed for the deep
Skjoldungen fjord (Lat. 63°). This objective failed, but the voyage
was full of incident. The crew of Mischief were to be the first British
visitors to the newborn volcanic island of Surtsey.

HAD IN mind a visit to the new volcanic island which had
appeared off the south-west coast of Iceland on November
4th, 1963. To say the island "appeared" is a mild description
of its tumultuous birth, a birth attended by violent explosions
which hurled clouds of smoke, steam, ash, and pumice
thousands of feet into the air. By the next day, when wind
blew away some of this cloud, it could be seen that an island
had emerged from the sea. *Notices to Mariners* of January 23rd,
1964, contained the following warning: "A submarine volcanic eruption has formed an island about half a mile in
diameter and 250 feet high, in position 63° 18′N. 20° 36′W.
Eruption is continuing and mariners are warned to keep clear
of the area." By April the island had grown to nearly a mile in
length and 500 feet in height. It had been given the name
Surtsey and the volcano itself was christened Surtur, after the
Fire Giant Surtur of Norse mythology, who comes from the
south when the world ends and burns up everything. In view
of the overcast skies, the rain, and the fog that are common in
those waters, I was not at all confident of being able to find this
exciting island, let alone make a landing.

By the 24th June we were some fifty miles east of the
Westman Islands or Vestmannaeyjar, Surtsey lying to the west
of them. Of this group of islands twenty miles off the south
coast of Iceland only Heimaey, the largest, is inhabited. The
islands are remarkable for the wealth of bird life on their
cliffs—puffins, fulmars, gannets—of which large numbers are
taken by the islanders for food. Much now depended upon the
weather. That afternoon we had a bit of a blow which soon
subsided and the sunset looked promising. In northern latitudes, however, when the sun sets towards midnight and
dawn follows soon after, a fine-weather sunset might equally
be interpreted as the "red sky in the morning when the sailor
takes warning". But June 25th proved to be our lucky day,

bright, calm, and clear. At 6 a.m. we sighted the stacks and skerries of the westernmost islands and hard by them a great plume of cloud drifting away from a hump-backed island, its easy contours contrasting strangely with its wall-sided neighbours.

We spent the whole morning coming up with it and a large part of the afternoon poking about along its eastern shore for somewhere to anchor. To our surprise the shore shelved so steeply that close to the beach we found 4 fathoms of water and when we let go the anchor it merely slid off or through the ash into deeper water. As holding ground it was no better than a heap of flour. Finally we gave up and were content to let her drift while we launched the dinghy for Roger and I to go ashore. A small surf breaking on the beach did not hinder our landing though it did give a little trouble when we came to launch off.

The beach, of reddish-black sand or fine pumice, offered firm walking and even at that early period it had acquired some litter in the way of tins, bottles, and bits of wood. Beyond the narrow beach the ground sloped upwards to the summit at an angle of about 30°. On this ash slope it was like climbing a sandhill, two steps up and one down. I classed the climb, in Baedeker's words, as "fatiguing and not rewarding", for the crater into which we finally peered belched merely smoke and fumes instead of the cauldron of molten, fiery lava that I had expected and hoped to see. There was a beacon on top, no doubt for survey purposes, so that evidently ours was not first ascent except, no doubt, the first ascent by a British party. The whole place smelt like a coke oven. One sensed, too, that the thing was alive and growing but I must say I was staggered to see later in *The Times* of October 9th a picture of Surtsey and to learn that it had by then grown to 800 feet high.

V

1966: Back to the South: The Unhappiest Voyage

After failing to reach Skjoldungen fjord in 1964, Tilman spent the autumn and spring skippering an expedition schooner, Panatela, *to Heard Island in the Southern Ocean. Flying home in the Spring of 1965, he assembled a crew and successfully sailed* Mischief *to the icebound coast of East Greenland, and anchored ten miles up Skjoldungen fjord.*

The following year, 1966, saw the start of a miserable voyage, back to southern waters. The preface to Mischief Goes South, *written between clenched teeth, makes clear the skipper's own feelings.*

Writing about the recent voyage was like turning a knife in the wound. I had to exercise iron control. Instead of cheerfulness continually breaking in, as it should, plaintiveness and spleen were uppermost in my mind. But the latter do not make for either edifying or interesting reading. I have therefore suppressed my feelings and hope that the tone on the whole is moderate and the language of strictest reserve.

An anecdote of Swinburne told by Hugh Kingsmill in his book *Invective and Abuse* is relevant. Swinburne, who thought he had been affronted by Emerson, had written him a letter. "I hope your language was quite moderate," says his close friend Gosse. "Perfectly moderate," replied Swinburne, "I merely told him, in language of the strictest reserve, that he was a hoary-headed and toothless baboon, who, first lifted into notice on the shoulders of Carlyle, now spits and splutters from a filthier platform of his own finding and fouling. That is all I've said."

PASSAGE TO MONTEVIDEO

The objective was Smith Island in the South Shetlands: a change of policy after the Greenland voyages.

WHAT ORNITHOLOGISTS, speaking *ex cathedra*, as it were, like to tell us about the habits of birds sometimes takes a lot of swallowing—an inelegant phrase, but apt enough in this context. For instance, one Forbush affirms in his whimsical way that the Arctic tern "nests as far north as the most northern Eskimo live, while in winter its tireless pinions beat along the distant shore of unexplored lands of the Antarctic continent." I am more willing to concede this because recently *Mischief*'s movements have been equally erratic, though less rapid, sailing off the east coast of Greenland in 1965, and in 1966 beating her tireless pinions far down in the Southern Ocean. With less compelling reasons than the Arctic tern has for its long journey, such behaviour may seem strange, especially after I had decided that from my point of view Greenland waters were the ideal cruising ground and that there was no need to look elsewhere.

A man must be allowed to change his mind. As Benedick remarked: "When I said I would die a bachelor, I did not think I should live till I were married." It is a mistake to get into a rut. Fired by the divine spark of discontent or out of cussedness, after five voyages to Greenland waters I felt in need of change. No doubt the most striking change would have been a cruise to the West Indies or the South Sea Islands, regarded as the Islands of the Blessed by most right-minded yachtsmen who, if they live in England, pine, not unreasonably, for sunshine, hula-hula girls, and bananas. Something could be said against such places but my main objection is that they have no mountains, or only mountains that are covered with a lush growth of tropical vegetation, suitable for bushwhackers but not for climbers. Instead my thoughts turned to the far South, to Antarctic islands; and since this would be a longer and more arduous undertaking than a Greenland voyage it was a case of now or never, before *Mischief* and her owner grew any older. Many would say, I suppose, that both should long since have been in a museum.

The South Shetlands were highly attractive—remote, inaccessible, mountainous. The fact that they were inhabited was a
slight drawback. At least on one of them, Deception Island,
there are British, Chilean, and Argentine bases. Smith Island
offered a supreme challenge to the sea-going mountaineer; a
party would be starting from scratch, without fore-
knowledge of a possible landing place—there might well not
be any—or of any route up the mountain. But apart from the
island and its problems, the voyage alone would be an ambitious undertaking for an old 30-ton cutter with a skipper
verging on the Psalmist's age limit. An old boat can, of course,
be strengthened. But the man whose strength is diminshed by
age can only strive to emulate Beowulf's well known exhorta-
tion:

> Harder should be the spirit, the heart all the bolder,
> Courage the greater, as the strength grows less.

To find crews for *Mischief*'s first three voyages, which were
all of twelve months' duration, had involved me in much
effort and trouble. On the whole the results had been highly
satisfactory so that none of this effort had been wasted. There
must be plenty of men of the right stamp who would come
forward if they knew what was afoot or if one could make
contact with them, but the publicity that could easily be had
and that would solve this problem is not all that welcome. One
would like to have the benefit without paying the degrading
price, like an American firm that proudly proclaims: "We
eschew publicity but we know how to use it." However,
despite this desire to let things speak for themselves, a policy
that in these strident days might also pass for reticence,
Mischief's voyages have become better known. For each succeeding voyage the need to shop around for crew or to
advertise, became less. To find crews for her most recent
voyages I had really exerted myself very little, merely lurking
in my fastness behind the Welsh hills, vetting the letters of
hopeful applicants, and sallying forth at intervals, like a spider
from his web, to inspect and secure another victim. One had to
take them on the principle of first come first served, for it was
not reasonable to defer a decision for long. This often had

unfortunate results. Sure enough, when the muster roll had been filled, a man with better claims and in every way preferable, had to be turned down.

In spite of this inevitably haphazard method of collecting a crew—for it could not be called picking one—on all the Greenland voyages we had been a reasonably happy ship. On a comparatively short voyage of four to five months it is easy enough to:

> Be to their faults a little blind
> And to their virtues ever kind.

And this cut both ways, the crew being prepared to tolerate anything I might do or say seeing that they had not to endure or suffer me for all that long. The crew's ability to get on with each other and to work together is more important than what seamanly qualities they may have.

My system, if system it could be called, had worked well enough so far. Even if it could be arranged, a short preliminary voyage to try out the crew would have little value. They would be on their best behaviour, zealous and willing to an embarrassing degree, and if one did take a dislike to one of them, a replacement would still have to be found at short notice. Always on past voyages the crews had soon shaped up to their jobs, took whatever was going in the way of food, and made themselves as pleasant as they knew how. I hope I did the same, though no man can be expected to make bright, chatty remarks for five months on end, much less for twelve. It is sometimes difficult to say "Good-morning" and quite impossible to continue the conversation beyond that. Doubts have been expressed as to whether the Christian virtue of good temper is binding on a man before breakfast. There is a story, quite apocryphal, of a pre-war voyage to India in a P & O liner with a Himalayan climbing party. On reaching the open sea from Tilbury the writer is reputed to have exclaimed, "H'm, the sea", and on nearing Bombay, after a silence of eighteen days, to have startled his expectant listeners with another profound remark, "H'm, the land". But no one goes to sea in a small boat in the hope of leading a social life.

Naturally the finding of a crew for a twelve months' voyage is harder than for one of only five months. Fewer men are able or willing to spare that amount of time. There are therefore fewer from whom to choose. Whether this means that the chances of picking a dud are greater or lesser I am not a mathematician enough to say, but the presence of any such will inevitably be that much more difficult to tolerate. For the sort of voyage now in prospect, where conditions would be tough, at times perhaps even daunting, the quality of the crew, their reliability, their devotion to the ship they served and their sense of obligation to finish what they had undertaken to do, became of prime importance. Again, unlike a Greenland voyage, there would be stops in strange, sunny, exciting lands where the temptation to swallow the anchor is strong. Places where:

> Slumber is more sweet than toil, the shore
> Than labour in the deep mid-ocean, wind, and wave,
>   and oar;
> Oh rest ye brother mariners, we will not wander
>   more.

Besides the attractions of the shore there may be other yachts which, at any rate in port, seem to offer more ease and comfort than hellship *Mischief*, and whose skippers appear to be less of a bastard.

Finally, the crew consisted of a student, Roger Robinson; John Ireland, a Liverpudlian; Tom O'Shaughnessy, an Irishman, who was to be cook; and a photographer called Mike Edwards. The most experienced seaman was the fifth crewman, David Shaw, a merchant marine master on leave. Tilman "took to him at once—red-haired, sturdy, quiet and self-reliant". Once again, Mischief sailed to the Canaries and turned westwards towards Montevideo. Then came tragedy.

The wind varied greatly in strength, one evening a flat calm and in the succeeding night enough wind to split the genoa. During the evening calm, the weather bright and sunny, we piped all hands to bathe and skylark. Skylarking was the word, ducking each other, diving from the rigging, belly flops and bottom flops. And for supper we had what we called a cheese flop followed by a jam sponge. Flop consisted of potatoes, cheese, and onions churned together and baked. At last on August 19th, in Lat. 8°N., we had the rain we expected and needed. With a roll in the mainsail water trickles off briskly to be collected into saucepans and buckets hitched at various points along the boom. Later we rigged the canvas skylight cover under the boom like a canvas bath. A watering party, stripped naked, stands by to empty the saucepans and buckets into the deck tank. The single roll that we had put in the mainsail for collecting water soon had to be increased on account of wind, the prelude to a black, wet, thoroughly unpleasant night. This bout of rain lasted for 24 hours.

The wind now settled down at south or a point or two either side of it, the very direction in which we hoped to steer. Whichever tack we sailed on, owing to leeway, we could make but little to the south, perhaps 10, or at the most 20 miles of southing as a result of 24 hours' sailing. Why worry, one might ask, South America lies to the west so why not steer west? The snag is that a ship which fails to cross the Equator far enough to the east is set to the west in the grip of the Equatorial current at the rate of 20 miles a day until it finds itself hard up against the coast of Brazil. In the days of sail a square-rigged ship that found itself unable to weather Cape San Roque at the north-east corner of South America might have to fetch a circuit of the North Atlantic in order to try again. One is well advised not to go on the port tack to start steering west until south of Lat. 4°N.

Notwithstanding, our reluctance to sail in the opposite direction to our destination overcame reason. For the next two or three days we steered stubbornly westwards on the port tack, always hoping that the southerly wind would free us by hauling more to the east. In fresh winds and a moderately rough sea we were going west at the rate of 80 miles a day and very little to the south; and it was in these unsatisfactory conditions that a most unexpected and inexplicable tragedy overtook us. Coming on deck at 07.40 on August 27th, I found the ship on course, the helm lashed, and no sign of the helmsman. It was hard to believe but it did not take long to satisfy myself that David, who had the watch from 06.00 to 08.00, was not on board. After a hasty look in the peak, the galley, and the cabin I gave the alarm, turned out all hands, and gave the order to gybe. In a few minutes we were sailing back ENE on a reciprocal course with all hands up the shrouds scanning. The sea flecked with white horses, dark cloud shadows moving slowly across it, the sea that for the last few weeks we had sailed over so care-free and unthinkingly, had suddenly assumed a pitiless aspect.

We soon noticed that the patent log had stopped rotating and on hauling in the line we found that this had broken about two-thirds of its length from the counter. It is by no means unusual to lose a rotator; on the present voyage we lost two. Either it is bitten off by a shark or a porpoise, or the line frays at the point where it is attached to the rotator. But the line is less likely to break or be bitten through at any other point, accordingly we assumed that it had broken when David grabbed at it, or even later on when his weight on it had combined with a sudden lift and snatch of the counter to put too much strain on the line. The entry in the logbook by the man whom David had relieved at 06.00 was 1,830 miles and the log had stopped recording at 1,831. In short, we concluded that if the line broke when David grabbed at it, as seemed most probable, this must have happened about 06.15, so that he had been overboard for an hour and three-quarters. My heart sank. In so far as we were not shipping any water on deck the sea could not be called rough, but for a man swimming it was far too rough. I did not see how a man unsupported by a lifebelt could long survive.

Assuming the worst I decided to sail back a full seven miles, which in theory would take us to the ship's position at 06.15, the time at which the accident had probably occurred. After that we could start searching back across our track. I say "in theory" because it could be only the roughest guess-work. How much leeway would she make? Would it be the same that she had made on the opposite tack? Would the speeds be the same? Even an error of a half-point would in the course of 7 miles bring us to a position that differed by nearly one mile.

And in the conditions prevailing, the white horses and the increasing glare of the sun on the water, we should be lucky to spot a man's head even three or four hundred yards away. When so much depended, or might depend, upon the course we steered, upon our making a lucky guess, my feelings as I sat watching the compass may be easily imagined.

By 10.00, when we had run our distance and sighted nothing, we handed the sails, started the engine, and began to motor back across our track, ranging about a half-mile either side of it. A sound enough plan if we were approximately in the right place, otherwise perfectly futile. Nor could one suppress the terrible feeling that we might have already sailed past David, that he had watched *Mischief*'s familiar mast go by and that we had failed to spot him. The crew continued their watch from up the shrouds where they remained throughout that most dismal day, one of them in turn coming down for a bite of food. Standing on the ratlines, hanging on to the shrouds hour after hour, taxed both strength and determination. With no sails to steady her *Mischief* rolled and pitched heartily and the higher a man is above the deck the more violently is he flung about. For the first two or three hours hope buoyed us up but as the weary day dragged on we became increasingly despondent; until at last the lengthening hours since the first news of the disaster finally extinguished hope. A small school of dolphins chose this day of all days to accompany *Mischief*, leaping out of the water and turning somersaults with a gay abandon that contrasted bitterly with our despairing gloom.

At 18.30, the sun about to set, I decided that no more could be done. Setting main and staysail, we hoisted a riding light and hove to for the night, unwilling to leave the scene of the tragedy and uncertain of what course to steer. Were we to continue to South America or turn for home? It seemed best to sleep on it. In the morning I could ask the crew what they wanted to do. Apart from all its other sad aspects, the loss of David Shaw was a wellnigh fatal blow to my hopes and expectations. As mate, as a competent navigator, a reliable, likeable man with whom I could get on, a man whose training imbued him with a sense of loyalty to the ship in which he served, his loss was irreparable. None of the others had the knowledge, the experience, or the force of character needed to take his place. With no one now who could take charge of the ship in my absence, Smith Island at any rate was out of the question. Had I known what might happen, as by then I should have guessed, I need not have waited to consult the crew before turning for home.

This accident, so obscure, so unexpected, and so unnecessary, hit us hard. For the first day or two one could not realize that it had actually happened, that there was not some mistake, and that David was not merely absent from the cabin on watch and would presently come below. An accident calls for some explanation and it is the more disturbing when no reasonable explanation is forthcoming. We discussed it at length that night and on subsequent occasions without any useful result. David had kept the meteorological logbook and 06.00 was one of the times when observations were made. When taking the sea temperature he had what I thought the bad habit of leaning out under the guard rail to lower the thermometer into the sea, instead of drawing a bucketful of seawater. As *Mischief*'s freeboard amidships is less than 3 feet this was easy to do. That he might have been doing this and had leant out too far occurred to me at once, but when we found both thermometers on board in their usual place this possibility had to be ruled out.

Again, the vang, its lower end clove-hitched round the outer end of the boom, sometimes comes adrift and has to be recaptured, usually by a man leaning out over the rail with a boathook. I have had occasion to do this and have then stood on the bulwarks at the counter (where, by the way, the guard rail ends) to refasten it round the boom. I have done this when no one else was on deck to see me fall in, or likely to come on deck for some time, which goes to show how careless or over-confident one can be. But, as we could see, the vang was fast nor could we find anything loose in the rigging or adrift on deck to account for David having lashed the tiller and left it. That it had been so securely lashed that *Mischief* had held her course for so long was another puzzle, though I knew that

David enjoyed playing with the tiller and so adjusting things that *Mischief* sailed herself. How fatally successful he had been! If the helmsman leaves the tiller to put something right on deck he would normally take a few turns round it with the tiller line and a couple of hitches. This would be good enough for the few minutes before the line worked loose, the tiller shifted, and the boat came up into the wind. Even when on the wind *Mischief* does not sail herself for long and I was astonished that on this occasion she had held her course for nearly two hours. If only David had not been so successful in lashing the tiller! She would soon have flown up into the wind, when the ensuing racket, the flapping of sails and banging of the boom, would inevitably have woken and brought me on deck to see what was happening. In which case we should have had more chance of saving David.

That night it rained heavily, a sure sign that we were still in the region of the south-west Monsoon and not yet near the south-east Trades. In fact our dodging about on the previous day and heaving to at night had probably lost us more ground to the north. In the morning, much to my surprise, not one of the crew expressed any desire to turn back, a desire to which I would have been ready, even glad, to accede. In fact I felt like turning back and had opinions been divided would have done so. But to insist upon turning back seemed unfair because it would have been easier for me than for them to give up the voyage and arrive home unexpectedly. True, my arrangements for a year's absence had been made, but had I returned I should not have had to start looking for a job, as they would, or in some cases for lodgings. Nor would it be for me, as it might be for them, the only chance of making a long voyage to strange lands.

So we decided to proceed, though I made it clear, or thought I had made it clear, that there could be no attempt to land on Smith Island. On the other hand we were a quite strong enough crew to take the boat to the South Shetlands, even though morale had been a little shaken. And for my part, without David to back me, there would be more work and worry.

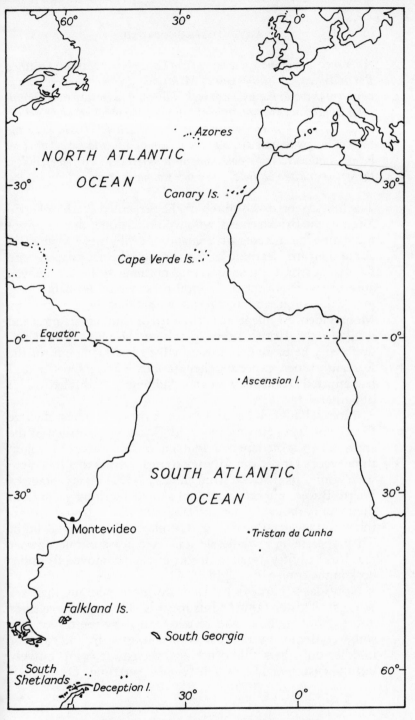

Back to the South: the unhappiest voyage

After sixty days, and 5,300 miles from Las Palmas, Mischief *reached Puerto Buceo, nine miles east of Montevideo. The crew were not yet apparently too unhappy, although Tilman had crossed swords with John Ireland over the question of eating up the previous night's curry for breakfast. Tilman believed that the traveller "should have the back of an ass to bear all, and the mouth of a hog to eat what is set before him". Ireland's objections were overruled. At Montevideo, there was much to be done; and much trouble to come.*

The first essential was to report the presumed death of David Shaw to the British consul who would no doubt find means of informing his parents in England. At all costs I wanted to avoid their first learning of this through the newspapers, and for that reason I intended saying nothing to the Uruguayan authorities. From them the local press would probably have got wind of it and the news would not be confined to Montevideo. Accidents to yachtsmen or climbers are meat and drink to the British press to whom the news would undoubtedly be passed. In the crew list I had made out for the Port authorities, expecting them to show some interest in us, I had omitted David Shaw's name. Subsequently this led to a bit of bother.

It took about half an hour to reach the city by bus, the fare then being 2½ pesos or about 6d. When we returned in the spring of 1967 the fare had doubled. In the course of the next three weeks I made this journey so many times that it became wearisome. Its distance from the city is one disadvantage of Puerto Buceo, but on no account should a visiting yacht lie in the main harbour. "There be land-rats and water-rats, land-thieves and water-thieves", and Montevideo abounds in both. They operate on a wholesale scale. We heard of one steamer that had had fifty 5-gallon drums of paint removed from her deck in the course of a night.

Nowadays journeys by land are more perilous than sea voyages. This bus ride had its hazards. The buses have three doors, front, middle, and rear, operated by the driver. On some you enter by the rear door and leave by the front or middle, on others this order is reversed. A comparatively bucolic customer like myself found it puzzling. On one oc-

asion, having put a hand inside the middle door, the wrong
ne, preparatory to entering, the door closed and the bus
10ved off. Had it been the left hand (we drive on the right in
Jruguay) I might have sprinted alongside to the next stop, but
7ith the right hand jammed in the door I was facing the wrong
7ay and had to start running backwards. Fortunately a passer-
y, who had less contempt for gringos than the bus driver,
ersuaded the driver to stop before he had gone far. It would
e charitable to think the driver had not seen me, but more
robable that he wished to teach the gringo to use the right
oor.

Now that we had arrived events moved quickly and trouble
ame thick and fast. Only later, when Tom and I were alone
ogether, the sole survivors of the crew of six which had left
ymington with such high hopes, did I learn what had been
rewing for some time. Had I known I might have been more
ircumspect. As the Swahili say: "Cross the river before you
:art reviling the crocodile's mother." John Ireland I expected
vould leave and his loss was no great matter: even if we got no
ne else the four of us could have managed. Apart from curry
or breakfast he had some complaints about our fitness for the
oyage. A bolt securing the gaff saddle to the gaff was worn,
1e sheet winches slipped, as, too, did the anchor winch. As a
1atter of personal interest I let the offending bolt remain and it
7as still there when we returned to Lymington. With a
111 crew sheet winches are a luxury on a cruising yacht; in any
ase, if it is blowing hard and the sheets need hardening the
oat can be run off or brought to the wind. The links of the
hain did not exactly fit the cogs of the anchor winch so that a
nk or two occasionally slipped back. Short of a new cable or a
ew winch, patience and a foot pressed hard on the chain are
1e remedy.

His real grievance was that we had no distress signals and
arried no life-raft. In my view every herring should hang by
s own tail. Anyone venturing into unfrequented and possibly
angerous waters does so with his eyes open, should be
villing to depend on his own exertions, and should neither
xpect nor ask for help. Nor would equipment of this sort be
f much use in Drake Passage where the chances of being

picked up are so slim as to be hardly worth considering. A
yacht is supposed to carry distress signals but is not over much
reliance placed upon them by owners of small craft? A man
with a boat that may be in many respects unseaworthy will
happily put to sea secure in the knowledge that at least he has
his distress flares. Yearly around our coasts so many calls are
made upon the various rescue organizations that by now the
average man should be ashamed to think of adding to their
number. The confidence that is placed, and successfully
placed, in being rescued fosters carelessness or even foolish-
ness, and condones ignorance. More care and thought might
be taken if there were a penalty for the firing of distress signals
say £25 a flare, the proceeds to be collected by the R.N.L.I.
the fine to be remitted only if proof were forthcoming that the
boat had started out in all respects seaworthy and had been in
real danger. The perils of the sea are less apparent than the
perils of climbing and have to be carefully assessed. In climbing the penalty for a mistake is obvious and is sometimes
exacted instantaneously, so that on the whole there are fewer
foolish climbers than foolish amateur sailors.

But to return to John Ireland with whom I now parted
company, feeling that he and I would not get on together however many life-rafts we carried. To my surprise and chagrin
Mike Edwards, with whom I thought I had got on tolerably
well, then announced that he would go too, and forthwith
they both packed their gear and went. If possible this show
down should have been postponed until we had reached the
South Shetlands where there would be neither the opportunity
nor the temptation to leave the ship. One regretted the unfortunate proximity of the Yacht Club where rooms could be had
comparatively cheaply, where there were all the attractions of
gracious living and convivial company. The defection of the
older men could not but affect young Roger who, though he
professed to be still game, was obviously in two minds about
it. He seemed to be waiting for an excuse to book a room at the
Yacht Club—if he had not already done so—and the opportunity soon came.

Tom and I discussed the idea of the two of us sailing to Cape
Town, shorter and easier than the voyage homewards. Tom

would get some climbing and a crew to take the boat home
would have been easily found. By then the season would have
been too far advanced for going south, and in any case, owing
to contrary winds, it would be impossible to sail to the South
Shetlands from Cape Town. For two men in *Mischief* it would
have been a hard voyage.

The onward march of progress has inevitably extinguished
a few trades and professions—chimney-sweeps for instance,
body-snatchers, crimps. At Montevideo I regretted that there
were no longer any crimps, men dedicated to making more
widely known the benefits of a seafaring life. Two or three
bodies delivered on board, drunk or doped, might have cost
money but would have saved time; they would have been as
useful as those we eventually got and might have been less of a
nuisance. In the absence of crimps, or of resorts like Smokey
Joe's or Big Nellie's, I had in the end to apply to the Sailor's
Home run by the Salvation Army.

The home did not cater only for sailors, all were welcome.
Most of the inmates were perhaps men who had had losses and
deserved them, modern examples of Falstaff's ragged company, "revolted tapsters and ostlers trade-fallen; the cankers of
a calm world and a long peace." The Home lay near the docks
and its cleanliness inside contrasted with the dirtiness of the
street outside, for the Major in charge, an Australian, saw to it
that his lodgers earned their keep. Montevideo, by the way,
struck me as having become a little unkempt. The standard of
living had gone down, too. One never saw what had been a
common thing on our visit in 1955, workmen sitting round a
fire on the pavement broiling 2-inch steaks for their lunch.

In a short time the Major found three men for me to
interview. They were anxious to get to Europe, to Germany
for preference, were willing to work their passage, and did not
shrink from the idea of going there by way of the South
Shetlands. One of them who had no trade, no skills, no
experience, and not a word of English, I thought better to
discard forthwith. The second Uruguayan was quite black,
looking like a more refined negro. The majority of Uru-
guayans are European in appearance and this chap, Carreo
Javiel, may have had his origin in Brazil. Mixed crews in small

boats, like mixed marriages, need thinking about. We are all
as God made us, some of us much worse, and no one can help
his colour. Racial integration is a subject much to the fore and I
felt sure that Tom, who hailed from Birmingham, would
assimilate or stomach a black crew as easily as I could. Besides
we could not afford to be choosy and this man Carreo had one
skill which we needed. He was a marine engineer, having
served as such in the Uruguayan navy, from which he had a
discharge book alleging him to be of good character. He was
intelligent and had a fair smattering of English. As it would
take a little time to get used to the idea of living with him at
close quarters, I deferred my decision. But Carreo was more
than anxious to come and determined not to be put off. For
several successive nights after supper we would be hailed by a
lanky figure on the breakwater requiring to be brought on
board. Having him on board for a cup of tea and a cigarette
was good practice for Tom and I in the matter of racial
integration. He certainly had a noticeable smell and no doubt
he thought the same of Tom and I and *Mischief*'s cabin. His
anxiety to please and his persistence wore down my instinctive
resistance. I agreed to take him—no pay, find his own gear
and a passage to Europe by way of the South Shetlands and
Cape Town. His geography may have been a bit scattered but
he must have understood our general direction and we impressed upon him that the climate would not be like that of
Montevideo. I could see that Carreo meant business and that
he would undoubtedly be with us on sailing day.

The last of the trio was a young German, Herbert Bittner,
aged about 30, fair, slim, nimble and active—physically the
makings of a sailor but, as we were to learn, totally lacking in
any sea-sense or the ability to acquire it. His life history was
obscure and his habit of romancing added to the obscurity.
Apparently he had been in Montevideo about six months and
in that short time had gained some notoriety. Many people
had heard of him or of the incident in which he had rather
mysteriously figured. According to his account he had been
found lying on the steps of a church, having been knocked on
the head and robbed, and instead of the aid and comfort which
he naturally had expected he had enjoyed a short spell in the

"calaboos". Some said he was a Jew, in South America on the track of Nazi war criminals, and that this knock on the head had been by way of a hint to lay off. About one period of his life there was less doubt. He had once been a racing cyclist and at the slightest provocation he would produce his most treasured possessions, a packet of press cuttings in which the great Bittner hit the headlines—pictures of him and his bike, Bittner and his silver cups, or Bittner being garlanded in Delhi. He was extremely plausible and self-confident—"no problema" was his favourite expression—and assured me that he had had some sea experience and could cook, the experience having been gained on a voyage to India in his father's yacht. Well, he may have had a father, but the yacht, I am sure, was as imaginary as his sea experience. He had, however, the great merit of cheerfulness, chattered a lot, and was amusing in small doses.

Mike Edwards, unexpectedly, rejoined the ship; and with this unpromising crew Tilman sailed south to Punta Arenas in the Magellan Strait. Apart from Herbert's failure in the galley—cabbage with custard was particularly unwelcome—and the increasing tension with Carreo, together with a near-grounding caused by "a given course becoming a fixed idea, something to be adhered to even if it meant taking the boat overland", the voyage was successful enough to make Tilman determine to continue. Picking up a young Canadian, Louis, as spare hand, Mischief *sailed for the South Shetlands.*

The further a man goes, the more reluctant he naturally becomes to turn back. As might have been expected, the thought of tamely giving up at this stage was unbearable, even when weighed against the bleak prospect of sailing south with a disgruntled and discordant crew. Only a mutiny on their part could have persuaded me to think differently and they had not yet reached that stage. Though the prime objective had long since been given up, a voyage to the South Shetlands could be regarded as a reconnaissance, either for myself or for some future party, and I had still some hope that Tom and I might do something on Livingston Island, provided we found a secure anchorage. Moreover only some 800 miles now separated us from our goal, albeit the greater part of those miles lay across the cold and reputedly stormy waters of Drake Passage.

We got our anchor at 8 a.m. and sailed away unnoticed. With the ebb tide still under us we carried on to the Second Narrows through which we passed escorted by a large school of Commerson's dolphins, a species peculiar to these waters, some 5 feet to 6 feet long and genuine piebalds. The grace and speed of these lithe creatures, clearly visible in the smooth, pale green water, held us fascinated and kept our cameras busy; but I strongly suspect that one of them snatched our left-hand rotator which disappeared about this time. For the rest of the voyage outwards and homewards we dispensed with a patent log, making the man on watch responsible for recording his estimate of what mileage the boat had sailed during his watch. The tide turned against us as we left the Narrows and we did not come to an anchor in Gregory Bay until after midnight. While sounding our way up to the anchorage Tom hove the lead without making it fast with the result that we lost the lead-line and its 7-lb. lead.

Next morning we passed the First Narrows and anchored again a few miles beyond where we remained for the rest of the day and the night waiting for a fair wind. Shortly after starting on the following day we sighted the R.R.S. *Shackleton* which altered course to close us, her deck crowded with bearded figures peering at us from behind cameras. Next day she passed us again bound south having made a quick turnround at Punta Arenas where she had called to land a sick man from one of the Antarctic bases. On neither occasion did they speak to us. One could not but feel that they regarded us with a faint air of disapproval.

The weather behaved in its usual erratic way, the wind hanging obstinately in the east, bringing with it a lot of rain and some fog. By the third day since leaving the Straits we had got only as far as Rio Grande where there is a large "*frigorifico*" and a wireless station. The Rio Grande marks the dividing line between the pampas country of the northern part of Tierra del Fuego, where the sheep-runs are, from the mountainous regions to the south. At last we got a breeze from the west, hoisted the twins and ran fast to the south-east. At 8 p.m. wind and sea having increased, we reefed the twins, and when I came on at midnight we were north of the entrance to Straits de la Maire.

Dangerous tide rips extend for many miles from both sides of the entrance to the straits, and when southbound it is necessary to enter at high water. I much wanted to pass through the straits but not only had we ill-timed our arrival; we should have to lower the twins, set the main, and steer south with a biggish sea on the beam. There are never any lack of reasons or excuses for inaction. I decided to leave well alone and to carry on eastwards along the north shore of Staten Island. In the morning we had glimpses of the lower slopes of this mountainous island, thickly clad in Antarctic beech, glimpses that were soon blotted out by cloud. According to some doubtful sights we were 10 miles east of the island when the wind dropped. The glass had fallen to 29 inches, so we set the trysail fully expecting a dirty night. Nothing came of this but next morning with the island still in sight, we lay tumbling in a horribly confused sea for many hours making no progress at all. The meeting of the current coming round Cape Horn with that through the various channels of Tierra del Fuego causes an unusually agitated sea off the coasts of Staten Island. As the *Pilot* warns: "There are very dangerous overfalls off the eastern extremity of the island when the wind is against the tidal stream; they have been reported to extend 18 miles from the island."

Given a knowledge of Spanish and the right frequency one could no doubt receive weather forecasts from the Rio Grande station. As we were not so equipped we were not liable to be frightened by any forecasts. The warnings of the barometer are at least silent but in a small boat, when the sails can be handed and all made snug in a few minutes, one sometimes wonders whether they too could not be dispensed with. Why disturb one's peace of mind by trying to peer into the immediate future? "Let us cease to consider what may never happen," said Dr Johnson, "and what when it shall happen will laugh at human speculation." It seemed to be the custom in these parts for the wind to fall light as the barometer fell, and only when the barometer rose did things begin to happen. On the 15th it fell to 28.6 inches, and that evening, when it had started to rise, the wind came in so hard that we set the trysail and double-reefed the staysail. Whereupon the wind began to moderate. It had become noticeably colder, the air temperature 36°F. and the sea 39°F., and we shifted into our winter woollens. We had minor worries besides the cold. First the cabin heater, which burns diesel oil, caught fire and had to be extinguished with the help of one of our appliances, and then the lavatory got blocked. I was glad to see that our marine engineer Carreo made no bones about tackling this.

I'm afraid that by now Carreo thoroughly disliked us all, with a special aversion for Mike Edwards whose blond hair and beard he may have found provocative. He seldom opened his mouth except to quarrel. In arranging the watches I took care to precede him so that I was the one to call him. When woken in the middle of the night he might be in a belligerent mood and he would be less likely to start a fight with me than with one of the others. Herbert had developed such a crop of boils that he could not work on deck and had to revert to the galley, but in spite of all remained remarkably cheerful. Since neither of these two had much in the way of warm clothing we all subscribed what we could spare towards their wardrobe. Tom, who so far had been most loyal, now turned sour. He claimed that had he known we were to attempt no landing on Smith Island he would not have left Punta Arenas. Ignorant of what the people at the British base on Deception Island were like, I promised that if we found a climber among them, as seemed likely, he could accompany Tom while I looked after the boat. I felt sure that a man would be allowed time off for such an enterprise.

On December 19th we had a good run of 90 miles under the twin staysails, an unusual rig for these waters, and by next day I reckoned we were about 90 miles north of Livingston Island. The wind increased that night so that at 2 a.m., when two small icebergs were sighted, we hove-to on account of the wind and the poor visibility. In this latitude, 62°S., it never became properly dark, only the two hours either side of midnight were a bit murky. Deception Island lies to the south-west of Livingston Island and the approach to it from the north is guarded by a chain of islands stretching for nearly two hundred miles from Smith Island in the west to King George Island in the east. The northern side of the chain abounds with islets, rocks, and breakers, and most of the islands are separated by comparatively narrow channels, so that the only safe and sensible approach for strangers like ourselves, is by the 20-mile wide Boyd Strait between Smith Island and Snow Island. It had become increasingly rare for us to get a reliable sight, especially noon sights for the all-important latitude. Either it would be cloudy, raining, snowing, or foggy, and on one occasion, having already had the sextant dowsed with spray, I found that the wind made my eyes water too much to take a sight. Not that one need complain about difficulties that must be expected and allowed for when by choice one visits such regions. As Byron said: "Comfort must not be expected by folk who go a-pleasuring."

Having been hove-to for most of the 21st, when by dead reckoning we were 25 miles north of Livingston Island, we let draw in the evening in fog, visibility less than half a mile. But by next morning we were again hove-to in a heavy sea and south-easterly gale, the weather too thick for us to see anything except two moderately large icebergs. By now we were more than a little uncertain of our position. Snow Island should have been only a few miles away and with the wind at south-east we were drifting safely away from it. In order to lessen the drift we tried out a parachute anchor I had brought for just such a contingency. On the voyage to Heard Island, such an anchor, a 29-foot diameter parachute on 5 fathoms of anchor chain, had held *Patanela*, a boat twice as heavy as *Mischief*, more or less stationary for an hour in a severe gale. Finally the fitting between the cable and the parachute had parted, but the parachute itself remained intact. The material of our present parachute must have been inferior or maybe it got foul of the cable. In five minutes we were hauling inboard its tattered remnants. Normally when hove-to one might expect to drift 25 to 30 miles in 24 hours, a distance well worth trying to save.

That it never became completely dark did something to lessen the anxiety that a stormy night naturally inspires. I had a chill and stood no watch and might have enjoyed the luxury of undisturbed sleep had it not been for the whining and howling of the wind. Only by plugging one's ears could the mournful and nerve-racking dirge played by the wind upon the rigging be shut out, and then one would be fearful of missing some more significant noise—a hail from the deck, the breaking of a skylight, or some worse disaster. Long before there is any reasonable hope of the gale abating one begins to time the intervals between the gusts, in the hope that if the lulls lengthen the wind is taking off. The glass remained high and steady throughout and each lull served only to make the next gust sound fiercer. The wind by itself is of less consequence than the sea it raises, except that its noise, like the noise of a bombardment, in time wears a man down. In the open sea waves have to build up to 20 feet or more before their breaking crests become dangerous to a small boat, however seaworthy, and if the wind blows hard enough for long enough this is bound to happen. Whether hove-to or running the chance of being hit by a breaking sea is always there, and though a bad helmsman can increase the chances, a good one cannot do much to lessen them. Not all seas run true, on a dark night a man cannot see, and a heavy boat like *Mischief* is not quick enough on the helm for a man to take avoiding action.

On the afternoon of the following day, when still hove-to, we had to lower the mainsail to repair a seam. When it is reefed right down the sail and the massive boom are not too difficult to control even in a hard blow. Even though the wind had blown steadily for 24 hours the sea had in it no real malice. The wind, even in gusts, had not risen above force 9 and since it was blowing from south-east the sea had no long fetch. Our steady drift away from the islands caused us some concern but it would have been far greater had we been drifting towards them. On the early morning of December 24th we let draw again and sailed slowly southwards in cold, wet fog. When the wind died we continued southwards under the engine until a fresh fall in the barometer frightened me into stopping to await clearer weather. For three days we had had no reliable sights and our rate of drift could only be guessed at. We might be in Boyd Strait, for all I knew, between Smith and Snow Islands, not a good place to be in if another gale started either from east or west. In fact, as the next day showed, we had enough sea-room.

On Christmas morning at 3 a.m. the fog rolled away, revealing to my surprised gaze an unbroken horizon, no land anywhere in sight. I put the visibility at about ten miles so that had we been near Smith or Snow Islands, as I thought, we should certainly have seen something. This clearing did not last long. A wind sprang up from north-east, bringing in its train sleet and rain, and with this fine quartering breeze we sailed southwards at 4 knots. If we missed the islands, we could hardly miss the Antarctic continent some sixty miles beyond. Long before breakfast I had to call all hands to change the main for the trysail, a call that they did not respond to with much alacrity; not for the first time I sensed how bloody-minded they were becoming. And, Christmas Day though it was, I felt out of humour, angry with myself more than with anyone for not knowing where we were. In the brief diary I kept, I notice that under the heading "Christmas Day" there is the query, "My worst?" It had a faint resemblance to Christmas Day 1955 when we were not exactly lost but in doubt about our next move. We were in a tent on the Calvo glacier, dining largely off pemmican, uncertain as to whether we should find any route ahead or be forced to retreat to the boat. It is not so much where you are that matters but whom you are with, and on that occasion I had two staunch companions.

Meantime snow began to fall and the cabin heater created another diversion for us. After Carreo had tried in vain to make it burn, Herbert had a go and was only too successful, setting the whole thing on fire. The extinguishers finally subdued it, but their fumes made the cabin untenable for some time. Thus we were all on deck, but it was Tom, I think, who first sighted land. Vaguely through the murk, not much more than a mile away, we saw a white blur with a dense black rock to one side of it. This most welcome and dramatic landfall we took at first to be Snow Island, which has off its western shore the 500-foot-high Castle Rock. But as we drew nearer our

"Castle Rock" became a part of the island, a part too steep to hold snow, and we realized that the broken glacier we looked at, and the steep snow slopes above, must be descending from high, cloud-hidden peaks. It could only be Smith Island, a magnificent landfall achieved entirely by accident. We closed the shore, if an ice-cliff lapped by the sea can be called a shore, and had to stand out again when the wind showed signs of failing. Before the weather closed in, as it did when the wind died, we had time to discern what looked like a cape to the north-east. We confidently hoped that this was Cape Smith at the northern extremity of the island, for the island is 20 miles long from north to south and we were on the wrong side, that is the west side of it. From some hidden store Herbert produced a bottle of beer and we had buns for tea, thus thriftily celebrating both Christmas Day and a successful landfall. Having started the engine we soon rounded what proved to be Cape Smith and set a course for Deception Island some sixty miles to the east. After supper, the fog having become dense, we stopped.

"There is something personal and compact about an island, no matter how desolate it may be." These words of Shackleton, which probably applied to Elephant Island where his party took refuge, seemed to me equally applicable to Smith Island. It is as compact as could be, no bays, inlets, or fjords, as desolate an island as any I have seen, and it had a grim enough personality even though some 5,000 feet of its more daunting aspect remained hidden. In the very short distance that we coasted along it, sheer ice cliffs, glacier tongues, rock cliffs, or boulders, forbade even the thought of a landing. Yet somewhere along that considerable coastline there must be some kind of a cove and a beach. To search for it from a small boat might take days and would involve the risk of being caught in a gale on the wrong side of the island; for it would not be easy, in view of its 20-mile length, to nip quickly round to the lee side. And having found a landing place there is the problem of the 6,900-foot Mount Foster which unfortunately we never saw. It would be too much to expect that the landing place would also be the most convenient spot from which to tackle the mountain. In mountaineering the means are more important than the end, so that one must hope that this rich prize does not fall to some party that has been landed conveniently adjacent to the mountain by helicopter.

DISCORD ON DECEPTION ISLAND

The sight of Smith Island on Christmas Day was the last moment of elation, for Tilman, on this difficult voyage. The British base on Deception Island did not welcome his crew; his own isolation became more obvious every day.

WE BROUGHT UP first in unexpectedly shoal water of only 2 fathoms. As this would not do we anchored again in 7 fathoms and immediately began to drag. Unlike the cliffs of Neptune's Bellows, the snow-covered ridge behind the base did not afford much of a barrier to the north-east wind which still blew with great force. The third time we let go, the anchor appeared to be holding so I went below to gather myself together before visiting the base. Meantime Tom and Louis already had the dinghy in the water and were in such haste to get ashore that they were about to push off. Unwilling to be preceded by two such uncouth heralds I hastened to join them. The voyagers who landed on islands inhabited by savages were at first often kindly treated; only later, reasoning perhaps from the uncivil behaviour of their visitors, did the natives turn hostile. So it was with the savages of Deception Island. A reception committee some half-dozen strong gave us a warm welcome, though the base leader himself was not there. As we walked towards the huts a short distance away I remembered to ask if among the dozen or so men at the base there were any climbers, and learnt that there were not. Had there been one he would not have been able to accompany us; no one was even allowed to visit *Mischief*.

We were on the point of entering the hut when, happening to look back, I saw *Mischief* moving rapidly away from the shore with no one on deck. Muttering some hasty apologies to our would-be hosts I turned and ran for the dinghy, to be followed presently by Tom whose seaman's instinct for the moment overcame his ill-will. Louis remained there. We were told later that he had had a bath and used up all their hot water, a fact which conceivably may have contributed to the blighting of our prospects. As Tom and I rowed off in haste to overtake *Mischief* before she fetched up on the opposite shore, our former acquaintance *Shackleton* turned the corner out of Neptune's Bellows. As soon as she had anchored and put a warp ashore her launch came over with an invitation from her captain to lie alongside her for the night, an offer we gladly accepted. They were a cheerful crowd, both the crew and the men bound for the various Antarctic bases, and treated us well. After a hot shower I had a drink with Captain Turnbull who told me that for the last four seasons he had been looking in vain for a possible landing place on Smith Island. He also told me that about three days before Christmas they had visited Port Foster and found it full of pack-ice. At that moment there was not a fragment of ice anywhere.

Port Foster is the Port of Entry for the South Shetlands and the base leader is also the resident magistrate. Accordingly I went ashore next day with the ship's papers and crew's passports. Christmas, or Boxing Day, had apparently exhausted the stock of goodwill at the base. I got no further than the outer office where I had a formal interview with the base leader who expressed surprise at our visit and some disgust for Louis and Herbert, for he, too, had been there the previous night for a bath. I mentioned that I would like to buy a small quantity of stores and learnt that it was unlikely that any could be spared. I was surprised at this and had no complaint to make but one could not help comparing the treatment strangers received at similarly remote foreign bases, where one had not even to ask for anything. At Kerguelen, for example, the French had loaded us with bread, butter, potatoes, enough chocolate to last the voyage home, jars of pâté, tins of fruit, all the petrol and paraffin we needed, and finally a barrel of red wine. At Pond Inlet the Royal Canadian Mounted Police post had so stocked us up that we left with more food on board than when the voyage began. At Tingmiarmiut in East Greenland, where seven Danes maintained a weather station, we were shown into their store and told to help ourselves. Such places are usually overstocked, for they keep a year's supply in hand in case of accidents to the relief ship. This may or may not have been the case at Deception Island, but we heard of, and later saw for ourselves, cases of tinned butter, dried eggs, dried milk, dried potatoes, etc. rotting away in one of the several disused oil tanks, once part of the whaling station. These tanks had been holed by the navy in the last war to prevent their possible use by German raiders.

Meantime we enjoyed brief popularity on board *Shackleton* where we had been invited to take our meals in the mess with the British Antarctic Survey party. We particularly welcomed this invitation because Carreo had dismantled the stove, strewing the cabin with bits of iron and soot. With the help of one of *Shackleton*'s engineers he was busy constructing it on a new principle. Though the effects of any action are plain enough, their causes are sometimes obscure; and there were two reasons currently offered for the sudden eclipse of our popularity—no more meals were to be served to *Mischief*'s crew, and a little later Captain Turnbull asked me to move *Mischief* elsewhere. One version was that the wardroom had been left without enough sausages for breakfast, the other that Tom had somehow fallen foul of the captain. Since our arrival I had seen little of Tom who had transferred himself to the seamen's mess where he had been the life and soul of the party. But he had been seen having a short talk with the captain and judging from Tom's own version of what had passed I was not altogether surprised at being asked to shove off. Before we parted company we filled our water tanks from *Shackleton*'s hose, thus saving a lot of trouble later. She was taking on water from a well on shore. There are several wells and it is said that each whaling ship had its own well.

We anchored once more off the base, this time using our 1-cwt. Fisherman type anchor instead of the 60-lb. CQR anchor which was no use in this bottom of ash and cinders. We also took a line ashore, made fast to a boiler, the debris of the whaling station. Having attended to this I once more sought out the base leader to give him a list of our modest requirements. He was busy with the construction of a small jetty but took time off to give me a lecture on the irresponsibility of sailing a small boat to the Antarctic. He looked like the earnest young head of Dr Whacko's Academy and I felt like a newly joined urchin, too dumbfounded to utter. I can only think that this far-flung Government official, monarch of all he surveyed—provided he ignored the two foreign bases—greatly resented private intruders upon his small domain.

Back on board Mike cleaned up the refuse habitually deposited in the galley by Herbert, and with the stove put together and burning the cabin had become almost inhabitable. Carreo's reconstruction was not a success. It burned dangerously fiercely and gave out volumes of filthy smoke. Rather than perish by fire at sea, or become as black as Eskimos cooking over a blubber fire, we preferred to be cold. Long before reaching South Georgia we gave up using it, and later on had the satisfaction one always finds in throwing things overboard. Louis had now developed boils and since the British base had no doctor, the three of them, Louis, Herbert and Carreo, walked to the Chilean base three miles away. A dry glacier of black ice, black with cinders, had to be crossed, so mountaineer Tom, who had long dissociated himself from any work on board, showed them the way. They did not go there entirely for their health. As I was told by Louis, whom I had come to regard as a seagoing bum with neither manners nor principles, all three hoped to arrange a passage to Punta Arenas. This hope was not fulfilled, though while we were there, a naval tug arrived and departed. Louis attributed his boils to a low diet, the same diet that Mike, Tom, and I had been living on for six months, free from either boils, scurvy, or any other disease. Louis was another example of an adventure-lover who wanted his adventure on a plate without the attendant discomforts or risks. Not only should we have had the latest drugs on board but also a radio transmitter, distress signals, etc.

We had no further contact with anyone at the base. One or two of them had rowed past in their boat, eyeing us curiously from a safe distance but never coming alongside, much less on board. They must have had their orders. I was therefore surprised when Dr Whacko himself brought off the promised stores—20 lb each of flour and sugar, 5 lb of tea and coffee, 30 gallons of diesel oil, 5 gallons of paraffin, and 1 gallon of methylated spirit. It is to his credit that he did not demand cash down, but in due course the bill came and was paid. This visit must have been prompted by curiosity or, perhaps, as may happen to anyone, he had been suddenly overcome with friendly feelings. It was a beastly morning with a cold north-east wind and snow, so when the boat had been unloaded we naturally asked him and his underling on board for a drink. The alacrity with which he accepted surprised us and gave us the warm, satisfying glow felt by those who turn the other cheek, a warmer glow than can be got by retaliating in kind, tempting though that is. Despite two snorts of whisky the conversation remained stilted, consisting mainly of questions on our part about their life at the base. One felt sorry for them, for it must be a damnably dull life on Deception Island with no prospect of travel as there is at some of the bases. One of their jobs, too, was the breeding of huskies to be used for sledge journeys at those bases. They climbed into their boat and we saw no more of Whacko and his academy.

Since Herbert and Louis were daily walking to the Chilean base to have their boils treated I decided to go there and remain until they were reported fit. On the last day of 1966, a fine day with a good sailing breeze, we sailed round, a better way of going there than by walking over a dry glacier. The Chilean base is on the same side of Port Foster at Pendulum Cove, the place where in 1829 Captain Foster, of H.M.S. *Chanticleer*, established his pendulum station and carried out experiments for determining the force of gravity. The cove has since silted up. Where there was once a considerable inlet there is now only a small cove and beyond the beach a freshwater lake. We anchored in 6 fathoms and put a warp ashore, the wind by now blowing offshore in very violent gusts. Tom and Mike, who heartily despised each other, had a fierce slanging match over the proper way to run out a warp.

The Chilean base is large, modern, and fitted with all conveniences, electric light, hot water, central heating. In summer there are over 100 men there and at the moment they were engaged in building a runway for a seaplane. The Commandant, an Air Force officer, who had already seen something of our quality in the shape of Louis, Carreo, and Herbert, did not welcome me effusively. Still he proved more hospitable than stern, path-of-duty Whacko, inviting us to have our meals in the men's messroom, and to ask for anything we needed.

We had not yet eaten a large, home-made Christmas pudding and New Year's Eve seemed the time to eat it. For twenty minutes I occupied myself in the galley making a rum sauce to help it down, and on returning to the cabin learnt that Mike and Louis had gone ashore to have a fight. This was better, of course, than staging it in the cabin, and their showing so much consideration left me astonished. Nevertheless it boded no good. This crew of mine should have shipped with Fanning, the sealing captain already mentioned. "It was always with me," he writes, "a cardinal duty to state, on shipping of crew, that it must be well understood by them, as a prominent part of our agreement, that all the quarrelling and swearing was to be done by myself and the work by them." Since they could not devour each other like Kilkenny cats, I rather hoped that Mike would win, but it was not to be. Louis was a bit of a pugilist as well as a bum, he read books on prize-fighting, and presently returned to announce, rather disappointedly, that a couple of punches had been enough for Mike who had refused to return on board with him. I found Mike, now with a fruity black eye, pacing the shore in bewildered fashion, and persuaded him to come back to the boat. Even before this it was clear that the crew hated each other, that we all hated Carreo, and that they were united only by their hatred for me. Except that Dr Johnson himself was by no means hated, our situation reminded me of life in what he had called his seraglio, three elderly, indigent females whom he charitably lodged in his house along with one Levett, an equally indigent, unqualified medical practitioner: "Mrs Williams hates everybody; Levett hates Mrs Desmoulins and does not love Mrs Williams; Mrs Desmoulins hates them both; Poll loves none of them."

New Year's Eve continued its eventful way. The crew, less Mike and I, were to go ashore for a party with the Chileans. While they were changing into their best rig Carreo, already half drunk, made determined efforts to push off by himself in the dinghy. The only way to checkmate him was to take the oars below. Having got rid of them Mike and I had to divide the night for anchor watches, the wind now blowing offshore with gale force. Towards midnight Tom brought off Herbert with news that could not wait, news confided to him secretly by a Chilean friend, that proved to be stupid enough to have been invented by Herbert—so puzzled was the Chilean doctor by Herbert's various ailments, that if we did not sail next day we would probably be put in quarantine for a month.

Leaving me to think this out they re-embarked, missed the warp by which they could have hauled themselves ashore, and were rapidly blown out of the cove, Tom rowing furiously but in vain. We lost sight of them about a cable's length away trying to round a point where they might find a lee. If they failed they would be blown two miles across the bay to somewhere near the Argentine base, that is if the dinghy did not fill and sink in the rough sea further out. I remembered they had no baler. In the morning, the wind still blowing hard, we could see no life on shore where the effects of the New Year's party had evidently been severe. Mike and I discussed the chance of the dinghy surviving a two-mile voyage across the wind-swept bay. I felt ashamed that we had made no effort to go after them, hard though it might have been with only the two of us on board and a wind that might have been too much for our engine to fight against. The suspense lasted until midday when, happening to go on deck, I caught sight of a figure wearing Herbert's unmistakable red balaclava. Later we saw him and Tom walking out beyond the point, where they had evidently got ashore, in order to retrieve the dinghy. In the afternoon all hands came off bringing some eggs and tomatoes as a peace-offering. No more was said or heard of the quarantine problem, had it ever existed outside Herbert's fertile imagination. "No problema", by the way, was still his favourite, overworked idiom, expressing his unbounded and singularly ill-founded optimism.

January 3rd was clear, calm, and sunny. Such days, I imagine, are far more common on the Antarctic mainland than on the off-lying islands. So fair a day could not be wasted so for the first and last time I put on some boots and climbed the

easy snow slope leading to the ridge, the rim of the old
volcano. Behind Pendulum Cove this attains to a height of
1,800 feet and is the highest point of the island. Below lay
Bransfield Strait, blue enough to have been taken for the
Straits of Gibraltar were it not for the numerous icebergs
sparkling in the sun. Across the water sixty miles away,
though in appearance no more than twenty, were the mountains of Graham Land. Smith Island was in cloud but to the
north and close at hand was Livingston Island, dazzling white
snow and ice from end to end and from sea to summit. At its
eastern end I could see Mount Bowles (3,314 feet), the peak I
had had in mind as a poor consolation when Smith Island had
to be written off. There is said to be a secure anchorage at
Livingston Island, though not very close to Mount Bowles,
but by this time I had no heart left for climbing and indeed felt
reluctant to leave the ship even for a day.

The others, except Carreo, had gone off for the day to visit
another penguin rookery at the north-east corner of the island.
When they had not returned by nightfall I felt uneasy about
them and annoyed, too, because Carreo and I had again to
share an anchor watch, the wind having come in strong from
south-west. It seemed more likely that they had spent the
night at the Argentine base than that any mischance had
befallen, so in the morning I went ashore to find out, the two
bases being in contact by radio. Sure enough they had been
there and at midday they turned up, very pleased with themselves, and went straight on shore for lunch. A small snow-
covered island is not the place for men to jump ship, otherwise
I doubt if *Mischief* would ever have left. But when I named the
next day, January 6th, as the day of our departure for South
Georgia en route to Cape Town, no objections were raised.
Herbert, accompanied by Tom, immediately set out for the
Argentine base where he said he must have a blood test. In
reply to my objections, he said that for him this was a matter of
life or death.

Carreo, who had spent the last 24 hours in his bunk, neither
eating nor drinking, then took his gear ashore. He was last
seen trudging slowly along the shore evidently bound for the
Argentine base, and late that evening, on their way back, Tom

and Herbert found him floundering in bewildered fashion in a snow drift and brought him back. On sailing day it took the Chileans a long time to convince him that he could not stay with them. Late in the evening they escorted him down to the beach with his kit and a large box of tinned food, his private sea stores. He had also acquired a crimson, peaked, American-style cap with a flap that came down over the back of his neck. In spite of this fine cap, which henceforth never left his head, he looked even more out of place in these arctic surroundings. Peary took his faithful negro, the stalwart Matthew Henson, to the North Pole, but our sub-tropical species did not flourish in high latitudes.

At 7 p.m., to my untold relief, we sailed. In Neptune's Bellows the wind failed and we drifted slowly past the great cliff now glowing golden red in the light of the setting sun. From the top two men from the British base watched us go. They did not wave. Perhaps Dr Whacko had told them not to.

Mischief then sailed for the island of South Georgia, in the hope of finding a passage home for Carreo (who refused to go east to Cape Town). More fights broke out there, and Tilman had to sail back to Montevideo to offload Carreo. There the whole crew left him, his money was stolen, and with another hastily gathered and ill-assorted company, he sailed back to Lymington. The voyage took a year and a day, and covered 21,000 miles. "Ships," the author quotes with some bitterness, "are all right, it's the men in 'em." It is worth recording that of all his difficult crew, he speaks most affectionately of Herbert. "I had come to regard him as part of Mischief; *a part not to be leaned on too heavily."*

In December 1967, as I wrote this chapter, Deception Island began to erupt violently. First reports spoke of a threat to the safety of the British base. My reaction was like that of Churchill's who, on hearing of the illness of a political opponent, remarked cheerfully, "Nothing trivial, I hope". The threat proved far from trivial. Both the British and, more regrettably, the Chilean base, had to be abandoned.

H.W.T.

VI

1968: The Loss of Mischief

Mischief *had served Tilman for fourteen years, and taken him 114,000 miles to the farthest corners of the earth. In 1968, off the coast of Jan Mayen Island, 300 miles from Greenland, she was wrecked. Tilman's landfall was off the South Cape of the Island, on 18th July. It was a bad ice year. The commandant of the Norwegian weather station suggested that he move the boat round to a bay close to the base; accordingly, on the 20th,* Mischief *set out on her last unlucky passage. Tilman's companions were Charles Marriott, Simon Beckett, Kenneth Winterschladen and Ian Duckworth.*

IN A FLAT calm we started motoring south until a wind sprang up from dead ahead. As we tacked down the coast the brilliance of the morning faded. Beerenberg's shining splendour was dimmed and finally extinguished and soon we were enveloped in the familiar wet fog. Upon making our final board to the east which I judged would lead well clear of Sjuskjaera, we again sighted those seven rocky fangs close aboard. Unable to weather them we went about and on the next tack cleared the rocks but had the breakers off South Cape too close for comfort. The wind failed and left us drifting, the breakers and some ice-floes close on the port hand. So we handed the sails, motored due east for half an hour, and lay to for the night, the fog still thick.

All this was the immediate prelude to a disaster for which I must take the blame: primarily for not getting far enough away from the coast, a coast off which there were outlying rocks and towards which the northerly set we had already experienced would certainly set us. I had the watch from midnight and in view of the fact that we were not moving or so I supposed, did not spend the whole time on deck but came up at frequent intervals. Ian had the next watch and like a fool I told him that he need not be on deck all the time but to come up frequently. Stupid enough orders! How frequent is frequently? Admittedly it was perishing cold and clammy on deck and one tries to make things as easy as possible for the crew, but there is only one place for the man on watch however safe the conditions may seem. Lying to a mile from a rocky shore in fog, visibility some 200 yards, we were by no means safe. Nevertheless what followed need not have done. Ian must have interpreted my imprecise orders liberally. Had he been on deck any time after three o'clock he must surely have heard or seen something to rouse concern. At 3.30 a.m. I woke to a horrible crash and it hardly needed Ian's hurried dash below to tell me we had hit a rock. On reaching the deck the first thing I saw was a rock pinnacle looming above us—I could almost have touched it with a boathook—and *Mischief* was aground on its plinth bumping heavily in the slight swell. I had lost no time in reaching the deck but the panic-stricken Ian had been even quicker to pull the cord of the life-raft without first launching it; and if that were not enough was even then hastily cutting the dinghy lashings. Had there been any rats on board they could not have been smarter about attempting to leave the ship. The great yellow balloon of the inflated life-raft now obstructed the starboard deck. Over the top of this I imparted to Ian a few first thoughts and told him to stop mucking about with the dinghy. The engine started at once and in a matter of minutes the boat slid off but not before the hull had taken some hard knocks.

She was making a lot of water but not more than the whale pump could handle if used briskly. The only plan seemed to be to beach the boat in the hope of being able to get at the damage. The bay we had been making for was not far off if we could find it, and I felt sure the Norwegians would give us all the help they could. The outlying rock on to which we had drifted, the only rock in the vicinity, lay about half a mile out from the shore; we must have drifted north some 3 miles at the rate of nearly half a knot. No land could be seen so we steered north-west to close it and the nearer we got the more infested with floes the water became until, when within a cable's length or less from the low rocky shore, we could scarcely find a way through. After some messing about I spotted the runway lights and knew we had overshot the bay. We turned back keeping as close inshore as possible in order not to miss it. In the clear water the rocky bottom showed close under our keel. The bay seemed to have even more ice in it than before, so we anchored off while I rowed ashore to give word of our plight. The Commandant agreed that ice or no ice it would be best to beach the boat there rather than at Kvalrossbukta where we would be too far away for them to give much help.

Threading our way between the floes we ran *Mischief* up on the little beach of black sand at the head of the bay. To my dismay we found that the rise and fall of the tide was a mere 3 feet, meaning that unless she was hauled much further up we would not be able to get at the keel or even the planks above the keel, where most of the damage must be. Only the forefoot would be clear of the water. The beach shelved steeply, too, so that there would always be 2 or 3 feet of water round her stern, the boat drawing 7 feet 6 inches. In order to haul her higher we began the heavy task of lightening her, removing the ballast, emptying the water tanks, and dropping the cable over the side.

We started on the ballast that afternoon and made little impression. Each pig, some weighing 100 lb., had to be hauled up the forehatch, carried across the deck, dumped over the side, and then carried up the beach above tidemark. Had we left them by the boat they would have soon dug themselves into the sand just as *Mischief* herself proceeded to do. Lying on her side at low water, the floorboards out, she had become untenable. About 50 yards inland and high above the beach was a small wooden hut with four bunks which we now occupied, carrying up bedding, food, Primus stove, and cooking gear.

Work began in earnest next day. The Commandant arranged for one of his men, an engineer and an excellent chap

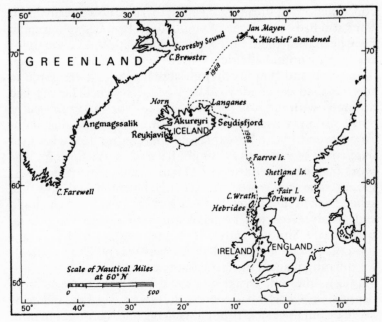

The loss of *Mischief*
(from *In Mischief's Wake*)

who spoke good English, to give a hand. In the bay they had a big float which they used for landing stores and this was now beached alongside *Mischief*. We rigged a tackle for hauling the ballast up the hatch whence it could be swung across the deck, lowered on to the float and stacked there. Except for a few pigs that could not be reached we soon had about 4 tons out. Ian, a strong lad, now in an extremely morose mood, nevertheless did the hardest work down below, starting out the pigs and carrying them to the foot of the hatch. Charles was *hors de combat* but the other two worked with a will, Simon and I manning the tackle while Ken stacked them on the float.

On the next day a bulldozer did its best to haul the boat higher and gained but a few feet. I then rigged a stout line to the masthead by which the bulldozer could haul her down, careening fashion. We got her well over but perhaps I was too concerned about breaking the mast to heave down really hard. For I still had every hope of sailing to Iceland where she could have been hauled out on a slipway and made tight enough for the voyage home. Charles, I knew, would stand by the ship, while Ken and Simon, though apprehensive, were game to try. Ian had other ideas. The day we beached her he had arranged with the base for a passage to Norway in *Brandal*, a small sealing vessel chartered to bring stores and due about August 2nd. Had he expressed any regret for what had happened, or sympathy, I might have felt sorry for him. The work on the ballast finished, he sat in the hut, a silent picture of gloom. The only words we exchanged were several days later when I asked him to fetch water and received a convincingly rude reply. Nor did he have much to say to the others, particularly Simon, with whom, as nominal owner of the life-raft, that incident rankled. As there was no CO_2 available for inflating it again the raft was of no use.

Life in the hut, therefore, could hardly have been more depressing. Charles had soon withdrawn to the base where he lay in bed in their sick-room having his meals brought to him. Visitors from the base, to whom we could at least offer a drink, sometimes dropped in in the evening to give us the news or to commiserate. As well as the staff there were four young students out for the summer on an archaeological expedition, searching for traces of the seven Dutchmen who in 1633 were landed to observe through the winter the facilities for whale-fishing. They all died of scurvy, the last survivor, who died just before the return of the fishing fleet the following spring, having kept a diary recording their observations right up to the end. Having no worries other than the possible loss of a boat, it was with some shame that I found on coming to write this account that my brief diary of daily events had stopped the day after we landed.

When the engineer and I examined the port side we found no serious damage, no sprung or started planks, only a lot of spewed-out caulking. Underwater aft, where it could not be got at, a piece of the keel some 10 feet in length, and its iron shoe, had broken away. This in itself would not be a source of leaking but a keel bolt might have been moved or the garboard strake started. It was now too late to try to turn her round and haul out stern first, and what with the rudder, the shape of the heel, and the soft sand, it would have been hardly possible. Having covered the suspect parts with a huge tingle of tarred felt and copper we moved the bow round and hove her down on the opposite side. With the starboard side treated the same way I felt sure that the leaks had been reduced though by no means cured. When the tide was in she made far less water.

One of our most frequent visitors, a Mr Holvik, whom I called the Viking, was an enormously strong, red-bearded Norwegian, equally at home driving a giant bulldozer or painting a 200-foot high radio mast. He greatly admired *Mischief*, showing as much concern for her as I did. He propounded a plan to haul her right up out of reach of ice and winter gales on to solid ground near the hut, where in their spare time he could work on her. In the following summer I would return and together we would sail her back to Norway. Much as I admired the Viking—I could well imagine him in a longboat with Erik the Red—I doubted whether even he and his bulldozers could haul *Mischief* that far out. Between beach and hut the ground rose steeply and was the sort of sand that overflows into one's boots. With a cradle for the boat and skids or rollers I suppose it might have been done: the builders of Stonehenge, for example, would have thought nothing of it. One main snag was the attitude of the Commandant who discouraged the idea, rightly so from his point of view, for he foresaw, as I did, that the Viking's plan would inevitably mean borrowing from the base plant, material, and probably time.

Shortly after our arrival ice had moved in and completely filled the bay. Had this happened a day sooner there would have been no chance of beaching *Mischief* there. The ice helped in one way by completely damping down any swell; no waves, hardly a wavelet, broke on the beach. Having done what could be done we began preparations for refloating her. We put back the ballast, all but a ton which I decided to leave out thinking she would be that much easier to refloat. By the time that had been done most of the ice in the bay had gone out except for a line of heavy floes right inshore and probably aground, while outside the bay no ice could be seen. The fact that no waves had been breaking on the beach, owing to the presence of the ice, had lulled us into a false sense of security. Only my engineer friend realised that the boat might now be in peril and urged me to get her off quickly. At the moment though, an unbroken line of floes prevented this. As the result of most of the ice having gone waves now began to break on the beach. Either that night or the next—I had lost count of the days—we had some wind and when I went down to the beach in the morning I found about 5 feet of the bowsprit broken off lying in the water in a tangle of wire. The float had been shifted from alongside, but not far enough, and even the web of mooring warps we had laid out had not prevented the boat surging about and hitting the float with the bowsprit. We had reefed the bowsprit by hauling it inboard but not completely so.

Sailing to Iceland without a bowsprit would be slow work. Instead I arranged through the Commandant for *Brandal* to give us a tow to Norway. They agreed to this and also to bring out a small, portable motor pump to ensure our controlling the leak while on passage. By July 27th only the line of massive floes fringing the beach still prevented us from getting afloat and ever since the rest of the ice had gone out *Mischief* had been bumping on the sand. As well as doing her no good it distressed me to watch. Floating her off would mean living on board and keeping the pump going until *Brandal* arrived when, perhaps, the motor pump would give us a spell, but the engineer and I both thought we should try. By means of a wire led from the stern to a block slung from some nearby rocks and thence to a bulldozer we tried hauling her stern back into the water. After we had gained a few feet she stuck immovably, that much nearer to the floes through which, anyway, there seemed little hope of forcing a way.

Next day, a Sunday, the Commandant came down armed with dynamite sticks and detonators to see what could be done. A big floe threateningly close to *Mischief*'s rudder succumbed to this treatment, splitting into two after a few sticks of dynamite had exploded alongside. A bigger floe only a yard or so from the port side proved too tough and massive, and I feared that repeated explosions so close to the boat might harm her more than the ice. Having done what he could the Commandant departed.

Towards mid-day the wind blowing into the bay had increased to nearly a gale. The waves rolling in set the floes to rocking up and down and lurching forward, and *Mischief* began to bump even more heavily on the sand. The crew had for some days since lost interest but I rallied them for a last effort to shift her by means of a warp to the anchor winch and the engine. With the wind behind it the water was now deep enough under the stern for the propeller to bite. Their efforts lacked conviction. Ian in particular showing more concern for what would happen when she floated than for the consequences of letting her remain. I thought that with the water so high, a couple of bulldozers might do the trick, and that she might just squeeze through a gap by the big floe. With that in mind I ran to the base as fast as I could and found hardly a soul there, certainly no one with power to act. By the time I got back the big floe that had been close aboard, urged forward by the rising sea, had battered a hole in the hull just below the engine water intake, and started several of the adjacent planks. That evening, in despair, I wrote her off. She was one third full of water, so we took ashore anything of value below, books, charts, instruments.

The Viking came along next morning, refusing to admit that all was lost, more convinced than ever that his plan was the best, and determined to have a go at hauling her out whatever the Commandant might think. Clutching at straws I agreed and persuaded the crew to start taking out the ballast once more. The gale had pushed her higher up the beach and most of the water had drained out. Late that evening the Viking brought down a big bulldozer with which he succeeded in moving her about 2 yards. The soft sand and the steep ascent, where the real tug-of-war began, were still yards away. Even then at high tide she still lay among the breakers, the wind continued to blow, and the waves rolling in lifted and dropped her heavily on the sand. She was a heartbreaking sight.

The Viking's plan was tacitly abandoned. Either failure had subdued him or the Commandant had put his foot down.

Instead, on July 30th, he came down to patch the fresh damage, the Commandant being equally bent on seeing *Mischief* safely away under tow. After a drive round the base stores to collect material, the Viking and I set to work to put on a tingle. But with another gale on August 1st the breakers tore off our rudder. This, I feared, might put paid to towing, but the skipper of *Brandal*, with whom the base was now in touch by radio telephone, reckoned they could still tow. *Brandal* arrived on August 2nd according to schedule, having first fetched up well north of the island in spite of radio beacons, radar, and Loran. The same morning the sea tore off the big patch or tingle. Upon which the Viking and I together sought out the Commandant, hoping that after this last blow he might be persuaded to fall in with the Viking's plan. Obviously for success, the use of men, material, and machines would be required. They were very busy, a lot of work having to be done in what remained of the short summer season, as well as the routine work of the base. The Commandant was therefore right to refuse and to limit his assistance—already generous— to getting *Mischief* afloat and ready for towing. This proved to be no easy task.

Accordingly the Viking and I put on another patch. He had built a stage from which to work slung over the side, and with waves continually sweeping the stage it proved a wet job. The base had a big whaler with a powerful engine which they used for ferrying, and that evening I went out in her to *Brandal* anchored well outside the bay. The skipper spoke no English and seemed to me a little fuddled; the mate, young and confident, spoke very good English. At the suggestion of the Commandant they agreed to put on board *Mischief* an electric pump to be supplied with power by a cable from *Brandal*, to reinforce the little petrol-driven pump that they had brought which was already installed in our cockpit. I could not see this running more or less continuously for three or four days, nor were I or any of the crew capable of giving it the necessary nursing. I had to sign a guarantee against the loss of the electric pump, the implication being that *Mischief* was not expected to last the journey and that we might have to leave her in a hurry. The tow was to be on a "no cure no pay" basis; I urged the

Left: Tilman on *Mischief*

Below: Mid-Atlantic calm

Photo: W. G. Lee

With David Shaw. Tilman "took to him at once – red-haired,
sturdy, quiet and self-reliant". Shaw was later lost overboard
in mid-Atlantic

North side of "Neptune's Bellows", Deception Island,
South Shetlands

The new island of Surtsey erupting from the sea

Looking back to Bylot, after the rescue by an Eskimo
motorboat. The haze explains why Tilman's signal fire was
invisible to *Mischief*'s crew

The final days of *Mischief*, beached at Jan Mayen
Island and battered by ice

Sea Breeze trapped in the ice

Hacking out an ice bollard to moor the boat to a berg

Haircut at sea

Baroque

Right: Freemansund,
Spitzbergen: hoisting
stones aboard *Baroque*,
for ballast, after the
grounding

Below: Beached ice-floes

Sea Breeze

mate to take it easy and he assured me that *Brandal* was no flyer. The Commandant did everything he could to ensure success and our safety, bespoke for us one of *Brandal*'s life-rafts and arranged for a walkie-talkie set and a field telephone as well to keep the two ships in touch.

Overnight we rove a 3-inch wire through the big block slung on the nearby rocks, and passed a 6-inch nylon warp twice round *Mischief*'s hull. At 7 a.m. on August 4th, a fortnight to the day since we had first put her ashore in this ill-omened bay, the Norwegians rallied in force to get her off. Since we were not going to sail we had not attempted to restow the ballast—I doubt if the crew would have consented—but abandoned it on the beach. Light as she was, hauling her off took the united powers of two bulldozers, and the whaler pulling from seawards. Either she had dug herself in or the sand had piled her, because at first she refused to budge. So the bigger bulldozer, a real monster in the capable hands of the Viking, dropped its scoop into the sand and using the sand as a cushion advanced on *Mischief* to push her bodily sideways. Having so to speak broken her out they then harnessed the two bulldozers in tandem on to the wire, the whaler took the strain, and *Mischief* slid slowly into deep water. All the ice that had at first hindered us and that had been her undoing, had been swept away by the gales of the last few days. Simon and I were on board and the petrol pump going. It needed to be for she leaked like a basket.

Having secured to a long warp astern of *Brandal* we remained there tossing about in a moderately rough sea until late that afternoon. We found that we could just keep the water at bay by running the pump for five minutes and resting it for five minutes. Meantime the float made several trips out to *Brandal* and finally took off seven men from the base and the rest of our crew. The young archaeologists and my engineer friend were among those going home. Charles, whom I had not seen for the last few days, was to travel in *Brandal*, while Ken and Ian were to help in *Mischief*. Since we were to be in company, Ian had agreed to come. He had in fact reconsidered his earlier decision when we were still hoping to sail away, but only under certain rigid conditions. As with two unfriendly powers when relations have been severed, his ultimatum was handed to me by a third party. I still have the scrap of paper stating his terms:

1. There must be a transmitter on board.
2. Adequate life-saving gear including another life-raft.
3. A forty-eight hour trial run in the vicinity of Jan Mayen.
4. Direct return to England.

On the whole I thought that the chance of *Mischief*'s survival and the morale of the crew would be better without him on board.

After the float had made its last journey to *Brandal* it came alongside bringing Ken and Ian (who was promptly seasick), the mate and a sailor to make up the towing line, as well as their electric pump, a life-raft, and the walkie-talkie set and telephone. For the tow they used a nylon warp shackled to 10 fathoms of our anchor chain on which they hung three big tyres to act as a spring. The remaining 35 fathoms of our chain with the 1-cwt. anchor attached we led to the stern to drop over when the tow started. This served in place of a rudder to keep her from yawing about. The heavy electric cable, to supply current from *Brandal* to the pump, they had merely dropped loose in the sea. Its own weight imposed a heavy strain, no current ever passed, and immediately the tow began they told us it had broken. Had it been hitched to the towing line or to another line, as it could have been, *Mischief* might have survived. It meant that the little petrol pump must function for three days without fail and I did not think it would.

At 8 p.m. that evening the tow started. For the vicinity of Jan Mayen the conditions were good: no fog, no gale, and a moderate sea. An hour later Simon and I, who had been at it all day, went to lie down, leaving Ken and Ian to carry on pumping for the next four hours. With a lot of water sloshing about inside sleep was hardly possible; I brewed some tea and we made do with hard tack. I must have dozed because just before midnight Ken woke me to say the pump had given up; the motor ran but it was not pumping. The crew were ready enough to quit and I confess that the skipper and owner, with so much more at stake, had no longer the will to persevere, a fortnight of toil, trouble, and anxiety having worn me down. Communication with *Brandal* was not easy either with the walkie-talkie or the telephone but she had already got the message. She lay to about a cable away and we were told to bring off only our personal gear. In a final round-up in the dark cabin, already a third full of water, I dropped a note-case and all my remaining money. After scrabbling about vainly in the water for a few minutes I gave up and joined the others on deck where they had already launched the life-raft. Since *Mischief* was not insured this "trifling sum of misery new added to the foot of the account" hardly counted. The premiums demanded for the sort of voyages *Mischief* undertook were always so high that it had never been worth while to insure her.

Thinking that water might ruin it, before leaving we hoisted the heavy electric pump up through the skylight, having quite a tussle. When the other three had stowed themselves in the life-raft I climbed over *Mischief*'s rail for the last time and joined them. Paddling over to *Brandal* we went on board while three of her crew took the raft back to salvage the two pumps. These met with scant ceremony. The electric pump, that we had so thoughtfully tried to keep dry, was thrown overboard on the end of a line and hauled through the sea to *Brandal*. She was soon under way while I remained on deck in the fading light watching *Mischief*, still floating defiantly, until she was out of sight.

As I have said, ice conditions in 1968 around Jan Mayen were bad. Apart from human failings ice had been the main cause of *Mischief*'s loss or that had certainly prevented her from being saved. For me it was the loss of more than a yacht. I felt like one who had first betrayed and then deserted a stricken friend; a friend with whom for the past fourteen years I had spent more time at sea than on land, and who, when not at sea, had seldom been out of my thoughts. Moreover, I could not but think that by my mistakes and by the failure of one of those who were there to serve her we had broken faith; that the disaster or sequence of disasters need not have happened; and that more might have been done to save her. I shall never forget her.

> The world was all before her, where to choose
> Her place of rest, and Providence her guide.

VII

1969–1972: Sea Breeze

ALTHOUGH SOMETHING OF an addicted pipe-smoker I never find any difficulty in abstaining if no tobacco is available. In the absence of a boat there should have been an equal chance of giving up sailing. The craving, however, was still there and within a few days of returning home I found myself scanning the advertisements in the yachting papers and writing to various agencies.

The loss of *Mischief* had been fully reported in the Norwegian press but only one or two English papers had noticed it in a very brief paragraph. Few people could have known of it. I was therefore suprised when at Lymington, within a month of returning home, I got what seemed to be the answer to my hopes in the form of a telegram: "Regret loss of *Mischief* can I offer you *Sea Breeze*. Oakeley." On looking her up in *Lloyds Yacht Register* I found that *Sea Breeze* was a Bristol Channel pilot cutter belonging to Sir Atholl Oakeley. Built at Porthleven in 1899 she was certainly a bit long in the tooth, but no more so, in fact a year less, than her prospective owner. For that was how I already began to see myself; the fact that she was of the same breed as *Mischief* investing her immediately with all the qualities I desired. No wonder Barnum believed that a sucker is born every minute.

He bought her; put the necessary work in hand, and assembled a crew. Leaving the Solent, "a fine view of the Isle of Wight between two of the water-line planks", caused a return to Lymington for re-caulking. Off Swansea, the topmast came down; at Appledore, two crew left. Finally, with John Murray, Ken Morgan, Colin Kavenan, and a

retired bank manager, Brian Potter, as cook, Sea Breeze sailed north
Her objective was Scoresby Sound, on the east coast of Greenland
where Mischief *had been bound the year before. However, it was no*
a very happy ship; and off the Greenland coast, within forty miles o
the target, Tilman suffered what he refers to as "A Polite Mutiny".

A POLITE MUTINY OFF THE
GREENLAND COAST

WE WERE STILL making too much water, 600 strokes of the
pump every watch to clear the bilge, until John had another go
at the stern gland when the number of strokes required fell to
100. Until then he had been gloomy but after being sick as a
result of crawling under the counter he brightened up a lot
That night after a supper of macaroni, hash, peas, and a sad but
nevertheless satisfying duff we crossed the Arctic circle.

It began to get cold, the air temperature 41°F. and the sea
down to 38°F., high time for long woolly pants and vests
Combined with the fog it had a discouraging effect upon a far
from eager crew and the refusal of the stove to burn properly
did not mend matters. Ken decided that the right-angle bend
must be eliminated, and together with John set to work as
though their lives depended on it. They effected a great improvement though the cowl had still to be carefully trimmed
according to the wind. Renewed mutterings came from John
who until our arrival in Iceland had struck me as entirely
reliable, the last man to want to quit, and one of the best mates
I had had. How much longer did I propose bumbling about the
Arctic in thick fog with a weak crew, no communication with
anybody, no variety in the food, and himself unfit? For supper
that night, a melancholy feast, we had sausages, cabbage, and a
prime treacle duff.

On the morning of the 6th, after some heavy rain, a
northerly wind sprang up. Obeying the rules, for once the fog
became less dense and our horizon widened. Unfortunately
the sun remained obstinately hidden and no sights could be
obtained. We sailed fast for most of the day and at 6 p.m.
when I took the sea temperature for entry in the meteoro-

logical log, it had fallen to 32°F. The hint that ice could not be far off was confirmed a little later when we sighted a small berg. More scattered floes appeared, the flotsam and jetsam of the main pack, and at 7 p.m. we hove to. The sighting of ice caused John concern though, as I pointed out, anyone who embarks on a voyage to the Arctic would expect to see something of the sort sooner or later.

I should have been happier myself had we known where we were. For four days we had had no sights and this meeting with the ice showed that the coast could not be far away. Our respite from fog did not last long. But the next day, for a change, the sun shone brightly while the fog returned as thick as ever—a shallow fog with blue sky overhead. To have a sun and no horizon is far more maddening than to have no sun at all. In desperation I brought the sun down on to the back of a fulmar sitting on the water a 100 yards from the ship and directly under the sun. After making due allowance for height of eye, height of fulmar, etc., the sight when worked out put us well up on the Greenland ice-cap.

August 8th is a day I always remember. It was our black day in 1970 just as it had been Hindenberg's black day in 1918, on which the unit I was happy to be with played an active part. With a light easterly breeze we had sailed quietly all night until the morning when the wind backed north and began to freshen. As the fog slowly thinned we sighted first pack-ice to the east. Then suddenly, like the raising of a curtain, the fog dissolved and we were gazing with astonishment at a wild, mountainous coastline stretching far into the distance on either hand. After having been more or less blindfold for so long it seemed to me more like a revelation than a landfall. Directly opposite were two big glaciers, evidently descending from the ice-cap, for the mountains in the vicinity carried remarkably little snow. A cluster of jagged pinnacles far to the south stood out black against the morning sky.

What a time one could have, I thought, poking about in those numerous, largely unknown fjords if one could only reach them, forgetting that if it were not for the ever-present ice they would not have remained so long unknown. To the north-east the coast seemed to terminate in a cape 20 to 25 miles away. A hasty sight taken from an assumed position 15 miles from the coast gave me a clue and comparing the lie of the land with the chart I took this cape to be Cape Brewster at the southern entrance to Scoresby Sound. Instead of an un-broken mass the pack-ice seemed to lie in scattered fields and my hopes began to rise. Sailing north in increasing wind we soon came up with one of these fields and turned in towards the coast in the hope of finding a lead.

Rain now accompanied the rising wind. Intent on seizing the chance that our first fog-free day had given us, thinking the barograph had risen whereas in fact it had begun to fall, I did not pay much heed to these warnings. As Lecky says: "A falling barometer with a northerly wind conveys a warning that cannot be disregarded with impunity." Upon meeting more ice we followed its edge to the north-west but were always confronted by more ice ahead. By this time, late afternoon, the wind looked like increasing to a gale and the rain fairly pelted down; but the sea remained perfectly smooth thanks to the protecting fields of ice that almost surrounded us. Under the engine, I thought, the ice might well be navigable. The question was whether to try it here or to go out to sea clear of the ice and make the latitude of Scoresby Sound before attempting to reach the coast. The last would probably be the better course, but meantime we could heave to where we were in calm water and wait for the wind to abate. Between the widely scattered fields there would be room to keep well away from any ice.

John would have none of it. Like Brer Rabbit, in the language of Uncle Remus, he seemed to imagine that "every minnit wuz gwineter be de nex". In order to pacify him we began sailing east in search of open water. While running along the edge of some ice that seemed to stretch interminably southwards, looking for a break, and getting tired of losing so much ground to the south, I took the boat in close and realised that the ice was no field but a thin line of floes. We sailed through without difficulty and the roughness of the sea beyond showed that there was no ice to the north. Whereupon we hove to on the starboard tack to ride out the night. A dirty night it proved and I soon realised we had hove to on the wrong tack when the boat, by fore-reaching, brought us back within sight of the ice. We went about and lay to on the port tack heading east.

The rain stopped before morning but the wind continued to blow with some fury throughout the day. As I listened vainly for any lulls that might herald a lessening of the wind I felt that this unlucky gale would be the breaking point for a half-demoralised crew. Instead of getting somewhere we were fast losing ground to the south. By evening the wind had eased enough for us to let draw and start making north again towards Scoresby Sound. At least that was my proposal but the crew, the mate their spokesman, thought otherwise—demurred strongly and refused to do anything of the kind. Brian, of course, was as keen as I was to persevere but felt that his inexperience and his position as cook did not allow him an equal say. There we were in a stout ship, plenty of food and water, suffering a few inconveniences but certainly no hardships, and only some 40 miles from our objective at just the right time of year.

Brian, John, and I argued, standing for some odd reason round the foot of the mast below. I knew it would be no use. I am not eloquent and it would have needed the fiery eloquence of a Drake or a Garibaldi to stiffen John's spine. Even the suggestion that if Scoresby Sound were ruled out we could go south to Angmagssalik, thus at least landing in Greenland, met with no favour. John reckoned that he had stretched himself to the limit for my sake, that he had reached the end of his tether, and that any delay might have serious effects upon his health. Cassandra Ken concurred and thought that if we were to go on, the chances of any of us even surviving were no better than fifty-fifty. Colin, with slightly less conviction, agreed. To give up when so near, in an able boat with ample supplies, was hard to stomach, but with an unwilling crew there was nothing to be done. "Home, and don't spare the horses," was the cry.

Once before I had had the melancholy experience of sailing homewards with a disillusioned crew. On this occasion the passage would be much shorter, so short that it should not be difficult to maintain harmony, to be polite instead of resentful.

It proved not to be so short, and Brian did not feel it incumbent upon him to conceal his disgust at our ignominious flight and the man mainly responsible. For the first ten days we were almost as fogbound as we had been on the way out. For the sake of the record, not by way of complaint, I see from the logbook that between August 4th and 18th we had fog every day except on the critical 8th, when it rained. In the Greenland Sea fog is to be expected and like any other vexations and hazards of the sea must be borne with what cheerfulness one can muster.

TRAPPED IN THE ICE

In 1970, with a strong crew of Colin Putt, Iain Dillon, Bob Comlay and Andrew Harwich, Sea Breeze *sailed north again; not to Scoresby Sound—the ice was particularly bad—but to south-west Greenland, and an encounter with pack-ice.*

CLOSE NORTH-WEST OF Torsukatak Sound there is a group of no less than 150 skerries, a feature, I had thought, by which the Sound would be far more readily identified than by any beacon. Early on the morning of July 5th the sight of a number of black objects convinced me that my reckoning was out and that we had most opportunely and by accident stumbled on these skerries. Calling Iain, I put the boat about and steered to pass round their western edge. On this drizzly morning, even from quite close, it took us a long time to decide that the black things were in fact icebergs, and the improving light left no room for doubt.

For most of the day we held on north-west through widely scattered floes, gybed once to escape from a cul-de-sac, and towards evening were again forced out to the west. After losing the little we had gained towards the east, and still surrounded by scattered floes, we hove to for the night. Curry and duff as usual, for it was Sunday night. Since our near encounter with the ship we had seen no heavy ice. I began to hope that the scattered floes we were among marked the northernmost drift of the Storis and that even if we could not fetch Arsuk, then Frederikshaab, the next port up the coast, would be easily attainable. As we learnt later, Frederikshaab was at this time closed to all shipping by ice. Fog held us up next morning until noon when a wan sun and a vague horizon allowed me to take a sight for latitude. It put us in Lat. 61° 30′ N., halfway between Arsuk and Frederikshaab, which was probably correct. We gained some more miles towards the land through gradually lessening ice until dense fog obliged us once more to stop. With the air temperature 35° F. and the sea only 31° we needed a lot of clothes.

"A long and trying day" is how my diary describes July 7th. In a small, unstrengthened vessel it is mere prudence not to enter close pack unless one knows that there is open water beyond and how far beyond. If the floes increase and the open water between them becomes less it is folly to persevere and common sense to turn back. These solemn truths were not learnt that day, they were merely heavily underlined. I knew them before, and for that reason the anxious hours that now followed were the more galling. In a flat calm we started motoring north-east through open pack that soon threatened to become worse. Instead of turning back we headed more to the north on the facile assumption that we were near the northern limit of the drift. In a short time there was no longer a question of steering a course, we had to take whatever lead offered, and many of these so-called leads led to nothing but trouble. When we got stuck, which was far too often, it might take a quarter of an hour or more to free ourselves. With her small, offset propeller, *Sea Breeze* needs a lot of room in which to turn. For manoeuvring in ice one wants a boat that will spin round in her own length.

Bob and Iain spent the day in turns high up the shrouds conning the boat, spying out the leads, and looking for signs of open water. They could not see far, visibility being about 300 yards. As the day wore on I had uneasy visions of spending the night and even being crushed in this icy wilderness, cheek by jowl with some of the ugliest ice I had seen, jagged, mis-shapen, old polar floes 10 to 20 feet high, and, what was worse, always on the move, the leads closing and opening with bewildering speed. Like men in a maze, lost to all sense of time and direction, we sought only to escape. Having probed in various directions, we now ignored all leads except those that trended south, the way by which we had entered our maze, and at last towards evening, to our great joy, the ice began to relent and we reached a large polynia (space of open water surrounded by ice). There we hove to while we supped appropriately off pasta and prunes. The fog then lifted and we sighted land a long way off. Much heartened we pushed on through fairly open water until at 1 a.m. we stopped for cocoa and rum and some much needed rest. When hove to, even in the largest polynias, there were always some floes about; the man on watch had to watch our drift, and on drawing near to a floe had to judge whether we would drift safely by or whether he must let draw and sail clear.

Andrew took my watch and I turned in thankful to have won clear and pretty certain that I knew where we were. During that brief glimpse of the land I was sure I had seen the Frederikshaab glacier away to the north-east. I had seen it before on an earlier voyage from well out to sea, and it is the only glacier on this part of the coast. This 10-mile wide glacier flowing down from the ice-cap some 35 miles beyond Frederikshaab makes an unmistakable landmark. No bergs can calve from this glacier for it ends on a flat which dries. The glacier showed up clearly enough in the morning when we hoisted sail and set off hopefully to the south-east in the direction of Frederikshaab. As the floes increased again we resorted to the engine. For sailing, the floes must be pretty wide apart, five-tenths ice cover at the most. Given room and a fair wind the floes can be dodged easily enough under sail, but if the wind is fresh the boat may be going too fast to stop in time should a mistake have been made and a collision appear imminent. For that reason fore and aft rig is less handy than a squaresail which when backed stops the boat short. A few Victorian yachtsmen who were rich enough to have large paid crews had a liking for northern waters. One of them, Leigh Smith, who has a Spitzbergen cape named after him, eventually lost his yacht *Eira* in the ice off Franz Josef Land in 1881. Another, James Lamont, whose hobby was killing walrus, used to sail his 142-ton schooner to Spitzbergen and then transfer to a much handier 30-ton sloop with a squaresail, having discovered that his fore-and-aft schooner was unsuited to ice navigation.

When the engine had to be stopped for a minor repair we tried the experiment of mooring to a floe in order to stop the boat drifting, the wind being very fresh. Selecting a good big floe with a clean-cut edge and no projecting tongues—nothing like those craggy miniature icebergs of the previous day— ideally with a little indented bay like a small dock, we would put our stem gently against the ice while two of the crew jumped from the bowsprit with ice-axes and mooring ropes. The floe needed to have some hummocks that with ice-axes we could quickly fashion into bollards, for in an otherwise well-found ship we lacked ice-anchors. That our first floe had not been well chosen we realised when a large piece broke off. We moored to another where we decided to stay for a while, the wind having freshened to a good force 6, and blowing, of course, straight from Frederikshaab. We were low on fuel and could not afford to waste any by punching into a strong head wind. With so much ice still about we realised that we depended largely on our engine.

The floe to which we moored, as well as all the ice in the vicinity, was constantly in motion. Consequently we soon found ourselves hemmed in. At midnight we managed to escape and moored to yet another floe. Twice more we repeated the performance until on the afternoon of the 9th, when we felt we were secure for some time, attached as we were to a really well chosen floe with a mile or more of open water to leeward. Not a bit of it. Within an hour ice began streaming into the polynia and this time we were not smart enough in casting off surrounded by several miles of tight-packed floes of all shapes and sizes intermingled with some vast icebergs. The floe we had picked on was a beauty, nearly 100 yards in length, the one half flat as a lawn, and on the side we were moored amply provided with hummocks that afforded bollards for head-ropes, stern-ropes, breast-ropes, springs, the lot. They came in mighty handy when we had to warp the boat forward or back to avoid some threatening neighbour. Through pressure and rafting these old polar floes are thick, unlike the sea-ice that results from one winter's freeze, which would not be more than 5 feet thick—the sort of ice in which the old whalers and sealers were able with ice-saws to cut themselves a safe dock. In the clear water one could follow the emerald green face of our floe down for 20 feet and there would probably be as much again below that.

During the five days of our imprisonment we kept normal watches except when at night, if the ice was restless, we kept double watches. The two men might well find themselves sweating while they fended off floes with our spiked poles or trudged about on the ice shifting mooring lines. On first realising that we were well and truly beset Colin had suggested having some survival gear ready on deck or on the floe in case the boat got nipped and we had to abandon her. We would, I thought, have good warning when any pressure started, and I doubt if we ever were in danger of being nipped, the few yards of open water that generally surrounded our floe affording that much "give". Nor was there ever any tossing about of the ice which would soon have knocked holes in *Sea Breeze*, for the many miles of ice that lay between us and the open sea perfectly damped any swell or motion. We lay as quiet as in a dock. Nevertheless we were by no means free from anxiety, especially at first before we had become inured and reconciled to our strange position. Even with several northern voyages behind me I had no experience of this sort of thing. Perhaps I had had more sense then. In Baffin Bay, in Lancaster Sound, off Baffin Island, or on the east coast of Greenland, we had seldom become entangled with ice and never for long. On the east coast of Greenland we had once been in heavy pack and had suffered for it, but it had been only for some fifteen hours and then we were under safe escort. The crew, for whom all this was novel and who had hardly bargained for being beset, remained quite undismayed and in excellent spirits. What, I wondered, would the crew of the previous year have made of it?

We needed to be always on the alert, fending off or warping out of danger, the situation changing almost from hour to hour. It was surprising how floes, covering perhaps half an acre, could be persuaded to move away a little by steady shoving. We were not vigilant enough. A small floe drifted under the counter and by jamming the rudder hard over broke our beautiful carved, wooden tiller, the pride of the ship. We had a spare iron tiller which we now got ready but for safety's sake did not fit until our escape from the ice. Icebergs were the greatest menace. The pack, and *Sea Breeze* with it, was moving steadily north-west with the current at the rate of about 1 knot. The bergs, drawing several hundred more feet, were unaffected or perhaps felt a counter-current, so that we had the impression that they were moving in the opposite direction at a similar speed, brushing aside everything in their path and causing all the ice within a quarter mile of them to jostle and gyrate. Here, then, was some danger of pressure. Any berg to the north of us we watched apprehensively, striving to determine its course and whether or not this would prove to be a collision course. Happily, none of them passed within a quarter of a mile, and great was our relief when they had drawn abeam and then safely astern. One monster, some 200 yards long and 50 yards wide, resembled an aircraft carrier steaming majestically by, complete with flight-deck, bridge, and funnel.

By July 10th we were well north of the Frederikshaab glacier and abeam of some skerries 2 or 3 miles off to which I took a bearing. In two hours' time the bearing had altered 90 degrees which, if our distance off was correct, gave us a speed of 1 knot. Besides this coastal navigation I also tried some celestial navigation, though with a horizon of ice the results had to be used with caution. I took a meridian sight from up the shrouds in order to cancel out the height of the ice on the horizon. It put us in Lat. 62° 53′ N. opposite Fiskenaesset, or 80 miles north-west of Frederikshaab. We were certainly getting on, though not in the right direction. The day being windless I took another sight of the sun reflected in a little pool of perfectly still water alongside, halving the angle so found. It agreed approximately with the first sight. Later, on our way to Arsuk, on a foggy day with a bright sun overhead, we tried the same dodge using a tin of oil on deck, with results so erratic as to be useless.

Some of us used to take a daily walk, pacing our ice lawn

back and forth twenty times to accomplish a mile. There was a
good pool of melt-water lying on the floe from which we
replenished our tanks, the water being perfectly fresh. The
Arctic Pilot gives the reason:

> The enclosed brine in frozen sea water is itself seldom
> frozen; it tends to sink through the surrounding crystal
> network on account of its density being greater than that of
> the ice. With the summer rise of temperature the process is
> more rapid, and level ice, as the young ice of this age should
> be called, may lose almost all its salt content. If there is
> hummocking the progress is again speeded up and a single
> summer is enough for the ice to become fresh. No taste of
> salt can be detected by taste and ice of this nature is a source
> of the purest possible drinking water.

The weather was as usual mixed—fog, rain, drizzle, even
one flawless day of unbroken sunshine when an aeroplane and
a helicopter flew low over the ice. No doubt they were taking
advantage of the weather to fly an ice patrol and we sincerely
hoped we had not been spotted, later to be involuntarily
rescued. It might be thought that had any of us had the wit to
understand a little Danish we might have benefited, or at least
kept out of danger, by listening to the ice reports broadcast
daily by Godthaab radio and local stations. To make use of
such information we would, of course, have to know where
we were, but apart from that there is always the time lag and
the rapid changes that take place in the ice picture. And, as we
have seen, the infrequency of weather clear enough for ice
patrols to be flown must affect the accuracy of the reports.

By July 13th, another foggy day, we could detect signs of a
loosening of the ice. Later, when the fog thinned, we could see
a lot of open water inshore of us. Next morning, to avoid the
pressing attentions of a neighbouring floe, we carried out what
proved to be our last warping manoeuvre. The fog then
cleared, disclosing nothing but scattered floes to the eastward,
and after a hasty lunch we cast off from our faithful friend.
After motoring to get clear we set all plain sail and sped
north-eastwards in more or less open water.

A passing fishing boat ignored us, but presently we sighted a small coaster coming our way. Having about reached the navigator's nadir of having to ask a passing ship where he is, we hove to and hoisted our ensign, whereupon, after circling round, he came alongside and we passed him our lines. The crew were Greenlanders, deaf and dumb so far as we were concerned, but the skipper, a young Dane, spoke good English. He was delighted to see us, delighted, that is, to see so strange a sight as a boat under sail in those waters. In the wheelhouse I had a good look at his large-scale chart. Faeringehavn was our nearest port, 20 miles distant, north by east magnetic, and no ice. Our five-day drift in the pack of just about 100 miles had carried us off my large-scale charts. I had brought no charts for north of Frederikshaab, never thinking we should find ourselves even that far north. Having inspected *Sea Breeze* and passed over a case of Carlsberg—refusing any gift in return—the Dane went on his way to Fiskenaesset. That night, instead of enjoying the bright lights of Faeringehavn, we were once more hove to in fog and a bitter north-west wind dodging stray ice floes. Pasta and stewed apples.

WRECK OF *SEA BREEZE*

In 1971 Tilman tried again for Scoresby Sound and, despite a good crew, was kept from it by ice. On the way, at Reykjavik, he was amused to meet a visitor from a cruise ship who asked where they were bound and, on hearing "Greenland", commented: "Ah, following in Tilman's footsteps!"

In 1972 the objective was Ellesmere Island, at the extreme north of Baffin Bay. After a delay with a broken boom, they made instead for East Greenland and yet another try at Scoresby Sound. Brian McClanagan, Mike Clare, Brian Potter and Richard Capstick sailed with him; Capstick was unhappy, and left at Reykjavik. "Brian," remarks Tilman, "had suspected him almost from the start on the rather flimsy grounds that he refused to eat sardine spines and wore a yachting cap. I felt that a man with the unseamanlike habit of wearing gloves at night in summer in the Atlantic would not prosper on a voyage of this kind." In Iceland, Dougal Forsyth, a sixteen-year-old schoolboy, joined from England; and Sea Breeze *set off for Jan Mayen Island.*

ON 18TH JULY, the day after Dougal's arrival, we sailed for Jan Mayen. Besides filling up time, or rather allowing time, as we hoped, for the ice off Scoresby Sound to clear, I expected to meet there a Danish friend, a member of a Danish expedition to the island. In a letter to me before his departure for Jan Mayen, where he was to be in charge of the commissariat, he had asked about the making of chapatties on a Primus stove. Chapatties are merely a dough of flour and water beaten between the palms of the hands until wafer thin and slapped on to a hot plate for a minute or two. Thinness is all important otherwise the outside is burnt black before the inside is cooked. Eaten hot, with butter oozing out, they are food for the gods as any traveller in the Himalaya would agree. On an expedition the beginner might find a bottle available as a rolling pin and even something that might serve as a board if the party is not travelling austerely; but the professional would scorn such aids and so should the aspiring amateur. All the skill and half the fun lies in achieving a paper-thin round of dough—not shaped like a map of Scotland—about the size of a plate, before it falls to pieces or wraps itself round one's wrist. Cooking it on a Primus is not easy as the heat is too fierce; over hot ashes is best. So much for chapatties.

We had no trouble with ice off Horn this year. Had similar conditions prevailed in 1968 *Mischief* might be still afloat. Wishing to make our number to the Norwegians we headed for the small bay close to their base near the south-east end of the island, the bay of evil memory where *Mischief* had been so battered by the ice. It lies 4 miles up the east coast from Sorkapp and is a poor anchorage wide open to all winds from north-east round to south.

As Mike and I rowed ashore a small party gathered on the beach of black sand ready to give a hand hauling the dinghy clear of the surf. The English-speaking member of the reception committee shook hands with the remark: "Mr Tilman, I presume." He had been at the base in 1968 and upon seeing another yellow-hulled cutter in the bay had put two and two together and concluded that it was that man again.

The time had now arrived for us to try our luck. Three hundred miles to the west lay Scoresby Sound and in a matter of a few days we should meet with success or failure. Although up here in summer the winds are generally light they most often have an easterly component and would be in our favour. Having last year's experience vividly in mind, when ice stopped us 60 miles out from the coast, I was prepared for the worst, but as we sailed on in bright, cloudless weather with not a vestige of ice in sight my hopes revived. Would it be a case of third time lucky?

Sailing along quietly one can hardly say we ran on with bated breath but that was how I felt as the hours went by and still no ice appeared ahead. At last on 3rd August when only some 10 miles off the entrance to the Sound we began meeting floes. They were well scattered and having found a suitable

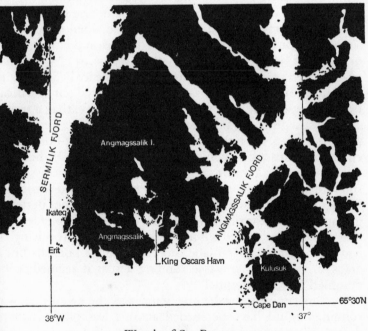

Wreck of *Sea Breeze*
(from *Ice With Everything*)

one—large, flat, straight-sided—we moored to it and passed a
peaceful night. We had learnt the mooring technique in 1970
on the west coast where we had spent many days moored to
floes. Besides the charm of novelty, if one wants to stay put for
the night it saves the trouble of jilling about or heaving-to and
drifting. Next morning, and not without strong hopes, we
started motoring through scattered floes towards the Sound.
For four hours or so, going slowly, we had no serious trouble
and we must have been within a few miles of the settlement at
C. Tobin on the northern side before the leads gradually
became harder to find, narrower, and sometimes ending in a
cul-de-sac. The view from the masthead offered little comfort
and regretfully I gave the word for retreat. It was high time.
The day clouded over and a freshening wind from the east had
set up enough swell to start the floes rocking up and down in a
way that made contact with them something to be avoided,
while the business of mooring to one became difficult if not
hazardous. If we were to spend the night among floes, mooring was preferable to heaving-to, because when hove-to we
should be constantly drifting down on floes and having to let
draw to get clear.

As we retraced our steps eastwards and the ice became more
open none of the floes we passed quite answered our specifica-
tion—a respectable size, somewhat bigger, say, than a tennis
court, a straight sheer side against which to put our stern while
the mooring party jumped ashore, and a few ice bollards or
embryo humps which could be quickly fashioned into bollards
with an ice-axe. While manoeuvring close to one to assess its
suitability our stern sustained a sufficiently hard knock to
further cool my waning interest in mooring to a floe. Better to
get out to sea clear of the ice. In the course of implementing
this decision we passed a floe that looked more promising. It
had no bollards ready made or even embryo bollards but a
crack or miniature crevasse running across it seemed to be
designed to hold a grapnel.

By this time the freshening wind and the swell that was
running would have persuaded anyone less pig-headed to
desist. We approached up wind and while I put her stem
against a short stretch of clean-cut, steep-to ice Mike leapt off

he bowsprit with the grapnel. By the time Mike had fixed the
grapnel the wind had blown the boat's head to one side so that
hort of running off and making a fresh approach head to wind
t was impossible to put her stem back against the steep-to
dge. To save time and to make sure of recovering Mike I ran
er forefoot up the sloping shelf of ice immediately ahead
vhile Mike, an athletic chap, waded down the shelf, leapt for
he bowsprit end, and swung himself up. We backed off the
helf readily enough then lay to the warp and grapnel. We soon
ealised that we had wasted our time. The floe was not massive
nough to lie immovable. More floes drifted down, joggled
igainst it, and started it spinning slowly round until after a
couple of uneasy hours the grapnel pulled out of the crack.
Recovering both warp and grapnel intact we went out to sea
or the night.

For the next few days we jilled about in the offing, greatly
ncouraged by the rapid disappearance of all the ice outside the
Sound. From C. Tobin, off which we lay, for 17 miles south to
C. Brewster the sea was clear of ice while the Sound itself
emained chock-a-block with ice, mixed with great icebergs.

For want of better our only plan at the moment was to wait
ind see whether the ice would move out of the Sound. Just as
patience is a virtue easily fatigued by exercise, so waiting about
it sea in a small boat is a tiring game to play. One thought of
he blockading ships in Nelson's day lying off some French or
Spanish port for months on end in fair weather or foul. But
hey were under orders and not on a pleasure cruise, and they
vere buoyed up, too, by the prospect of imminent action or of
prizes to be taken. Some islands a few miles north of C. Tobin
offered a chance of finding an anchorage but having gone there
ve found the ice lying thick jammed between the islands and
he coast. Our hopes were similarly dashed when we inspected
i bay just outside the Sound close to C. Tobin where there
vere a few Greenlander houses. There, a belt of shore-fast ice
extended out for several hundred yards, and this was the more
rustrating because we could now see the wireless masts of the
settlement sticking up from behind the cape only a few miles
iway.

The engine in *Sea Breeze* was a two-cylinder Kermath

"Hercules", an American engine, installed in 1958. Apart from
a reluctance to start from cold it had given no trouble since I
had had the boat. In these cold waters we made a point of
starting it every two or three days, and if it had not been in use
would run it for an hour to keep the batteries charged. On 8th
August, a black day in the annals of *Sea Breeze*, it made a queer
noise when started and on being stopped refused to start again.
I remembered 8th August because on that day in 1969, with C.
Brewster in sight, the crew had refused to go on. (Incidentally
8th August was what Hindenberg called the German army's
"black day" on account of the successful British attack at
Amiens in 1918 when I happened to be serving as a subaltern in
"I" troop R.H.A.) Various were the suggestions made but no
one among the crew could diagnose the fault, much less cure
it. Colin Putt, the maestro in these matters, believes the
trouble to have been a broken valve spring and had he been
with us perhaps the engine could have been run on one
cylinder.

Later that day, various remedies having been tried in vain,
we reluctantly concluded that the engine had "had it". From
then on we were a sailing ship in the strict sense of the word
and a more prudent man might have taken this as a hint that it
was time to quit the coast of Greenland where, without an
engine, or even with one, it is easy for a small boat to find itself
in trouble. No waters are foolproof and Arctic waters are less
so than any. Before the days of engines ships that plied their
trade in the Arctic were built for the job and usually cruised in
company so that if one was holed or nipped in the ice help was
at hand. Anyhow, we would gain nothing now by waiting; ice
conditions in the Sound might become easier but they would
not become easy enough for us to manoeuvre in without an
engine. Before starting for home we needed water and stores,
and instead of some Iceland port I thought we might get them
at Angmagssalik, thus giving the crew the slight satisfaction of
having set foot in Greenland. The entrance to Angmagssalik is
narrow but quite wide enough to sail through if unencum-
bered by ice, and I reckoned that by the time we got there, say
about 20th August, there would be little of that left.

On the night of 19th August, when only some thirty to

forty miles east of C. Dan, we encountered a hard north-easterly gale, quite the hardest blow of the voyage and one which went on for twenty-four hours. We had sea-room enough, for at C. Dan the coast falls away to the west, and we needed it as we drifted away to the south-west, hove-to and with only some six feet of the luff hoisted. On the morning of the 21st, the gale being then spent, we had land in sight to the north, but a heavy bank of fog lay over the sea, only the mountains showing above it, and it was impossible to identify anything. In the distance there was a ship evidently making for Angmagssalik and presently a Norwegian whaler appeared out of the fog and closed with us for a gam. He had been sheltering in Angmagssalik during the gale and was now on the way out to sea seeking.

One of the crew spoke a little English but we had difficulty in making ourselves understood. We told them of our engine trouble and finally managed to get from them what we wanted which was the course and distance to Angmagssalik—15 miles north-west. They then sheered off into the fog but presently we heard his engines again and once more he ranged alongside. They said they had spoken to Angmagssalik radio station and had been told in return that we would be helped in. We had not asked for a tow nor did I think it likely, in spite of what the Norwegians said, that anyone at Angmagssalik would bother their heads about us. On the other hand I felt pretty confident that if we did meet a local vessel near the entrance a tow would be forthcoming if we needed one—especially if the local vessel happened to be *Ejnar Mikelsen*, for example, whose skipper was an old friend. Later on we were to hear what the reaction had been to this friendly effort on our behalf by the Norwegian whaler.

The fog slowly dispersed and by evening we had closed the land a few miles south of Angmagssalik, a narrow belt of ice-floes ahead and beyond that open water and a rocky shore. The wind was light and what little there was unfavourable and I had half made up my mind to spend the night at sea. However, when an opening appeared in the thin line of floes ahead I decided to sail through and try to find an anchorage for the night in Sermilik fjord which lay temptingly wide and open to the south-west, a fateful decision that was to have consequences. This was an error of judgement. Sermilik is one of the fjords that has at its head a large glacier descending from the inland ice so that there is a constant supply of ice lurking somewhere in the fjord. Still there was little enough in sight at the moment and even if we failed to find an anchorage we were not likely to come to harm, the weather apparently settled and the glass still rising after the recent gale. Having sailed through the belt of floes without hitting any of them very hard and having reached open water, I felt satisfied. After more than three weeks at sea it would be pleasant to be at anchor in a Greenland fjord even though it was not in Scoresby Sound.

The wind became fluky and finally died when we were still a mile or more from the shore. We tried towing with the dinghy without success, nor were we so well equipped with oars and planks as on the previous voyage. A couple of long sweeps would have done the business. The glass had been rising smartly and was now high, the more unexpected therefore was the fierce onset of wind that came in suddenly from the north just as darkness fell, the herald of a dirty night. The first blast laid her over until the lee deck was half under water. The boat shot ahead, rapidly closing the dimly seen shore. She had way enough on, I reckoned, to take her in, and the rate we were going and the fear that we might hit something induced me to get the sails off in a hurry. I had misjudged the distance and we could get no bottom with the lead.

By this time the wind or the tide had brought quantities of ice down the fjord. Increasing numbers of floes were spinning by, so many that the thought of rehoisting and trying to sail among them in the dark with that strength of wind was too daunting. In fact all hands had their work cut out fending off the floes. The dinghy was still lying astern and we had no hands to spare to hoist it on board. For the next two or three hours we drifted slowly across the mouth of the fjord until some rock skerries loomed out of the darkness to leeward. In an effort to sail clear we got the stays'l up and we might have succeeded had not a floe got under the lee bow and stopped her. Her heel caught on a ledge and she spun round to be pinned by wind and waves against the rock, the cranse iron at the bowsprit end striking sparks from the rock face as she plunged in the surge. Dropping the stays'l we shoved desperately and vainly to get her off. She was hard and fast and taking a terrible hammering as she rose and fell on the ledge. Fearing she would soon break up or slip off the ledge into deep water I told the crew to take what gear they could and to abandon ship by jumping for the rock.

Waves swept the ledge on which she lay but from the ledge dry land was within easy reach. A sack of hastily collected food was first thrown ashore followed by Mike who took with him a line which he anchored to a boulder. Young Dougal then tied himself on and got ashore safely, though the line would have been better secured on board to use as a handrail. Without waiting for Mike to coil and throw back the rope Brian, the cook, clambered over the side and jumped for the ledge. A wave caught him and washed him back almost under the boat before the next wave took him shorewards to be grabbed by Mike and hauled to safety wet through from head to foot. The wind, the breaking waves, and the crashing noise made by the boat as she pounded prevented any communication with those on shore who still had both ends of the line. The lead line being the only rope handy young Brian tied himself to that and jumped while I held him. This left me with the weighted end and thinking, rather stupidly, that 7 lb. of lead round the waist might be a hindrance if it came to swimming I had to go below for a knife to cut the lead off. Normally I wear a knife on my belt and to be without one then was unseamanlike, as indeed was much of our behaviour that night.

Total darkness reigned below. Nor could I find a torch. But after first being thrown violently to the floor with a crash that made me think the deck had caved in I found my knife, regained the deck, and presently joined the others, wet only from the waist down. I am ashamed to confess that from our first striking, while all this was happening, it never even occurred to me to collect such essential and easily portable things as diary, log book, films, money, or sextant, all of which could have been stuffed in a rucksack and got ashore. As Dr Johnson well says:

. . . how often a man that has pleased himself at home with his own resolution, will, in the hour of darkness and fatigue, be content to leave behind everything but himself.

We moved a few yards inland to seek shelter under a low rock wall from the wind and from the rain that had now set in. I found I could not walk without support, the ground seeming to go up and down as it sometimes does on first landing after a rough passage. On taking stock our position seemed to be grimmer than it need have been. We were all wet, some wetter than others. All had sleeping bags but precious little else. Mike had done best by bringing a very light bivouac tent. I had a tin of tobacco, a dry box of matches, but no pipe. Brian, who had not spent the night on deck like the rest of us, had no oilskins and wore carpet slippers instead of gumboots. On the other hand he had a wet and useless camera. No one had brought any food and the sack that had been first thrown ashore had been washed away.

It was then about 1 a.m. and after a couple of hours of fitful dozing, at the first hint of dawn, some of us got up and went down to the wreck. By then I had recovered my balance. Only the top of the mast showed above water. She had evidently filled and slipped off the ledge, but whether this had happened soon after our leaving or later we could not tell. Even had there been time it would have been difficult and indeed perilous to go back on board to retrieve anything. Jumping down and getting ashore was one thing, but it would have been quite another to maintain a footing on the wave-swept ledge near enough to the boat to grab something and climb up her heaving side.

At full light we moved up to the top of our rock islet which was, I suppose, some seventy or eighty feet high and nearly a hundred yards across. On the chart it is called Erit. There we pitched the bivouac tent and Brian and Dougal, who were wettest and coldest, were put inside. We other three explored every nook and cranny of the rock, finding it rich in nothing but pools of rain-water. At least we should not die of thirst. Returning to the scene of the wreck we searched vainly for flotsam, or even for the jetsam we had thrown overboard—the sack of food. I examined closely a narrow crack full of brash ice. Among the ice was a piece of white board from the after hatch and, Heaven be praised, a pipe, one of several that I had on board. That was all that came ashore.

After this lucky find, there being no interlude for breakfast, Mike, young Brian, and I spent the morning pacing up and down, scanning the sea (empty except for ice), and speculating on our future. The nearest shore of the fjord was about 2 miles away. Brian's suggestion for paddling across on an ice floe seemed fraught with difficulties, not least the lack of paddles. Out of sight and a few miles up the fjord there was, as I knew, a small settlement, Ikateq, and no doubt there would be communication by boat between this and Angmagssalik. How frequently or infrequently was the question; and supposing a vessel of some kind did pass, would we be seen? We had no flares and no means of making smoke except by burning the tent or somebody's gumboots. Once a week, I thought, might be a reasonable guess, and we ought to be able to keep alive for that long. Perhaps if the sun had been shining and our clothes getting drier instead of wetter, for it was still raining, the prospect of a week or so without food might have been less daunting. Some might consider fasting no hardship, indeed beneficial. As Mr Pecksniff said: "If everyone were warm and well-fed we should lose the satisfaction of admiring the fortitude with which others bear cold and hunger."

After lunch—one gets into the habit of so apportioning the day—or, say, two o'clock we tried squeezing three into the tent where it was warmer than outside but no drier. Young Brian took the first spell and an hour later I began crawling in for my turn. At that moment Mike let out a yell, "A boat". There had already been one false alarm and I expected this too would turn out to be an ice floe. But there was no mistake. Close to the north shore and bound up the fjord was one of the small, local boats with the familiar red hull. At that distance, on a dull, drizzling afternoon, I doubted if they would spot us. All five of us gathered on the highest point of the rock and began waving our sleeping bags. Some even started shouting, futile enough considering the distance and the fact that her Greenlander crew would be sensibly and drily ensconced in their wheelhouse.

To our dismay she held steadily on course and we thought bitterly how stupid they must be to fail to notice five men standing on top of an uninhabited skerry. Or perhaps they mistook the flapping figures for those grotesque and frightening, mythological creatures depicted in Eskimo carvings, known as *tubilaks*, and had wisely decided to give Erit a wide berth. We had about given up hope when the boat slowed and turned in our direction. They had seen us all right as one might have known they would. No Greenlander worth his salt could fail to see us. Besides being keen-eyed they have an abiding interest in seals or anything shootable and while on passage, however routine it may be, are always on the alert and keeping a good look-out.

The crew of three set about the rescue in a seamanlike way. While the boat lay-to they launched a capacious dinghy which two of them brought close in to the rock stern-to, taking us all off in turn without mishap. Below in the cuddy they had an oil stove roaring away and relays of hot coffee were soon produced. Meantime the boat continued up the fjord to Ikateq where there were forty drums of oil—the winter fuel supply— to be landed. The crew of *Sea Breeze* lent a willing hand, young Brian in the hold slinging the drums, Dougal on the derrick guy, with Mike and Brian on the beach man-handling the landed drums. I was thankful when Brian and the last drum emerged from the hold, for the wire sling was so badly stranded that the most careless stevedore would have condemned it at sight.

Halfway to Angmagssalik we were met and taken on board a far superior vessel, one used by the doctor for visits to outlying settlements. On board were the doctor himself and the head of the Angmagssalik police force. We disappointed the doctor in that we needed no treatment but we were able to reassure the policeman who was a worried man. News travels too fast nowadays.

At the moment there are few if any amateur sailors likely to profit by it, but for me the lesson of this sad story is not to mess about in Greenland fjords without an engine, especially when they are full of ice. For all that I feel we were victims of an unlucky chain of circumstance—the calm that prevented us from finding an anchorage, followed shortly by a wind of such force that we could not sail safely among the ice brought down by the wind, but for which we would have come to no harm. *Sea Breeze* had made four voyages north and each voyage had seen some small improvement introduced. At the end I felt as proud and confident of her as I had of *Mischief* and thought her to be as able a boat as on the day of her launching in 1899. The fact that she had on her last voyage a new boom and a new mainsail was merely another trifling sum of misery added to the account. Certainly a staggering enough blow for me and only the fact that we had not sailed the seas so long nor had so many adventures together made her loss a little less heart-rending than that of *Mischief*. For fourteen years *Mischief* and I had sailed together and at the end I had to watch helpless while she lay on the beach, so battered by sea and ice that she did not long survive when finally got under tow.

Concerning regrettable incidents, and this ranks as such, Sir Winston Churchill's advice was never to look back, look to the future. Such advice is easier to give than to take, but in a case like mine it would help if I had another boat.

I will not say that the idea of giving up, calling it a day had not occurred to me, but I regarded this as the prompting of Belial who "with words clothed in reason's garb, counselled ignoble ease". We hear sad stories of men retiring after a life of toil and trouble who instead of enjoying their well-earned ease and freedom from care find it so insupportable that they soon fall into a decline. No doubt a friend, evidently a classical scholar, had this in mind when he sent me the following snippet of ancient wisdom: "The man who would be fully employed should procure a ship or a woman, for no two things produce more trouble" (Plautus 254–184 B.C.). The year ended on a happier note with a promise of full employment and a stock of trouble. *Baroque*, a Pilot cutter of 1902 vintage, was for sale, and needless to say I bought her.

VIII

1973–1977: *Baroque*

Despite his complaints about her troublesome pole mast and unsightly doghouse, Tilman and Baroque *dealt well together. In 1973, aged seventy-five, he sailed her to West Greenland, a shakedown cruise of 5,700 miles; in 1974 he broke the Greenland habit to head north for Spitzbergen, 600 miles from the North Pole. The aim was to circumnavigate the large island of Vestspitzbergen and to climb the low (13,000 ft) mountains.* Baroque's *crew were Paul Reinsch, Alan Stockdale, Andrew Craig-Bennett and David White. They made a remarkable non-stop passage of some 1,600 miles to Bear Island, just 200 miles south of Spitzbergen.*

CIRCUMNAVIGATION OF SPITZBERGEN

THOSE TWIN TOPICS food and seasickness must, I'm afraid, loom large in the early stages of any voyage. Paul was our chief sufferer. For many days even a moderately rough sea laid him out, so many that I became concerned, fearful that he might prove to be another chronic case for whom use and wont is no cure. For more than a fortnight he ate little enough and looked accordingly wan and spectre-like. However once the corner had been turned he reacted strongly, almost startlingly, making up for past omissions and speedily overhauling or out-eating Andrew who until then had been our chief cormorant. The contest between these two was stubborn. Andrew did not surrender the crown easily but the writing was on the wall when Paul assumed what hitherto had been Andrew's prerogative, taking care of anything left over and scraping the bottoms of the pans. Neither of them went as far as Sherpas do, holding the plate up to the face and licking it, or if mugs were being used, as for pemmican soup or tea and tsumpa, then polishing out the mug with the forefinger and licking that. We had with us some copies of *The Times* which had accumulated at Lymington where I had not had the leisure for battling with the Crossword puzzles. Doing them now, seeking inspiration from the adjacent Personal Column, my eye lit on a curious notice. I showed it to Paul and Andrew and stuck it in the log-book in case they wanted to follow it up when they got back: "Anorexia Nervosa, Compulsive fasting, stuffing. Box No. . . ."

On the 3rd, the wind fresh and free, we passed the Galloper light vessel. Becalmed once more on the following day, not far from the Dogger Bank, we caught two nice cod on the bottom in 20 fms., and later two mackerel also from deep down. Fish and chips for supper followed by a duff of Andrew's making, for David was still feeling his way, and frequently stumbling, among the foothills of cookery, far from the gastronomic heights.

If the navigator is asked by one of the crew where the ship is, he feels obliged to commit himself or at least hazard a guess. On the other hand, if he is not asked and he thinks he knows where he is, he should not let pride tempt him into announcing to a suitably awe-struck crew what sea-mark or cape they will presently sight and where, or, as in this instance, what they will not sight. But every ass loves to hear himself bray. I thought we were too far east to sight Smith's Knoll light vessel and rashly imparted this unimportant piece of knowledge to the crew. No one unkindly reminded me of this. It was humiliation enough to read later the log-book entry to the effect that we had left that particular light vessel close to port at 4 a.m. Soon after breakfast we sighted a Shell-Esso gas platform and were in fact carried rather too close to it by a strong tide. A helicopter landed on it as we passed. For the Dogger area where we now were a gale warning had been put out. About Force 6 was all the wind we had and enough, too, for Paul and Alan to succumb and for David to experience some mishaps in the galley. In the prevailing conditions, he did well to produce sausage and mash for supper, even if the sausages had to be scraped off the floor. Like onions, no ship should be without Tabasco Sauce. It gives a relish to the plainest fare and is probably a powerful germicide.

On the whole by the end of our first week at sea, in spite of Paul's persistent sickness and frequent bad news from the galley, I felt reasonably satisfied. We were well up the North Sea, about 150 miles east of Dundee and a like distance from the southern coast of Norway. The boat was drier as, of course, she should have been after recaulking and with a newly painted deck; but in any seaway she made quite a bit of water and there were still enough drips from the deckhead to be annoying. Plastic sheeting and drawing pins were again in demand. One reason for contentment lay in the crew who were cheerful, hard-working, and apparently enjoying themselves. In this last respect I was mistaken. A week had been enough for young David who now asked to be put ashore, life at sea falling short of his expectations and the prospect of months more of it quite insupportable. Request not granted. Quite apart from the replacement problem, probably insoluble, we could not afford to waste days beating to some port in Scotland, still less did I want to visit the complicated Norwegian coast of which I had charts only for the most northerly part. In a small crew the presence of one unhappy, unwilling member may well cause trouble. Happily I had no need to worry about that. The other three had the success of the voyage at heart as much as I had, that and the safety of the ship were all that mattered to them.

In Lat. 57° N., Long. 03° E., about ninety miles off the Norwegian coast, we sighted an enormous concrete island, a miniature town crowned by a chimney that almost rivalled that of Fawley, belching a flame of natural gas. Whatever one may think of the consequences of North Sea oil, some good, some possibly dire, or of the curious conviction of the Scots or their loud-mouthed spokesmen, that they not only put the stuff there in the first place, but rediscovered it, provided the money and the know-how to sink the wells and bring it ashore, the sight of these man-made islands are astonishing testimonies to the enterprise and technical skill of twentieth-

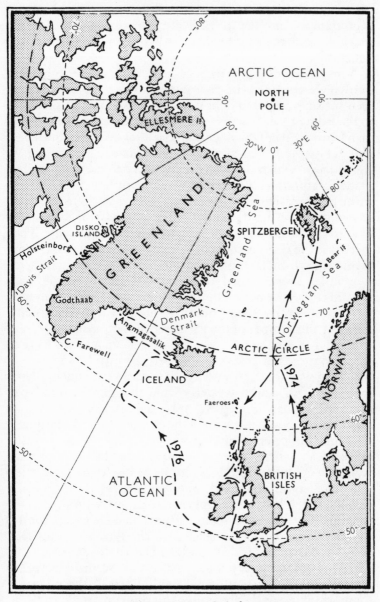

The voyage to Spitzbergen
(from *Triumph and Tribulation*)

century man, led, to be honest, by Americans. The North Sea is no tranquil lake and the skill and seamanship needed to site precisely and then build these structures is almost beyond belief.

A man describing a passage such as this through well-known waters, unless he can paint in words the ever-changing scene of sea and sky in faint imitation of a Conrad, is reduced to recording trivial events such as the making up of a Norwegian courtesy flag which we had forgotten to bring. Sufficient red, white, and blue bunting were obtained by cutting up signal flags (which we were never likely to use) and we had made careful note of the right way to combine these colours from the occasional Norwegian vessel that passed with its ensign flying. After doing the rough groundwork I handed it over to Paul who was a much better hand with a needle. Then there was the curious encounter with the German tanker from Hamburg which having passed ahead of us westbound, when two miles away turned round and steamed straight back towards us. As he passed for the second time I hailed him with the loudspeaker—"Are you all right?"—a question usually asked by the steamer of the yacht. We got no answer.

In N. Lat. 65 the fine weather packed up and we were to enjoy no more until close to Spitzbergen. Bear Is. and the seas for a long way south are noted for overcast skies and fog. After carrying a fresh south-westerly wind all night, by midday of the 21st we had logged 84 miles and I reckoned that by tea-time we should be north of the Arctic Circle. Accordingly we began our celebrations in time by having a slug of whisky in our tea. Shortly after a hail from on deck gave us the welcome news that Father Neptune, or his Arctic representative, had come on board, apparently over the bows. By coincidence I had just made some baggy wrinkle for the topping lifts to save the mainsail from chafe and except for this round the waist he was naked, but the flippers on his feet, goggles, crown and trident, and a red beard, together made up a striking ensemble. He concluded a short, seamanlike speech of welcome by presenting me with a scroll, the necessary passport giving us the freedom of his domain. In return I gave him what the French call "un grand coup de whisky", for in spite of being native to those parts he was obviously feeling cold. Andrew took charge of the subsequent banquet which comprised risotto Bolognese, alleviated by prunes and baked custard.

Before reaching Bear Is. we had some roughish weather. On three occasions in the last week of June we were either hove-to or lying-a-try, that is to say lying broadside on with no sails set. All this wind came from an easterly quarter so that by the 29th we had been set down nearly a hundred miles west of the island, so far that I was tempted to give it up and carry on for Spitzbergen in spite of water problems. Happily the easterlies subsided, the sea fell calm, and as we began making up lost ground the problem of finding Bear Is. began to loom large. Nowadays the navigator has to know only his own position, his objective's position being definitely fixed; but before the days of chronometers and Admiralty charts the navigator must have had as much or more doubt about the position of the island or cape he hoped to make as he had about the position of his ship, a consideration that makes the voyages of those days even more a cause for astonishment and admiration. Owing to the prevailing overcast our last noon sight for latitude had been two days before, and on the evening of the 30th a single snap sight from a fleeting glimpse of sun had put us 20 miles west of our dead reckoning position. With no certainty about our latitude this sight might well be far out.

Early on the morning of 1st July we handed the sails, there being no wind to speak of, and after breakfast started the engine and kept it going ruthlessly in the spirit of "Pike's Peak or bust". Assuming that our latitude was correct I determined to get into what I hoped would be the same longitude as Bear Is. and then steer north, trusting largely to Providence and to a lesser extent to birds. As the *Pilot* observes:

> At this time of year (summer) the island swarms with guillemots, and the flocks of these birds and the direction of their flight are of great use to vessels attempting to make Bjornoya in thick weather.

Which was exactly our position, for throughout the day we were pestered by drifting banks of fog. I spent hours on deck on the slight chance of the sun appearing and the still slighter chance that when it did the horizon immediately below would be clear. It did appear once for about ten seconds, long enough to take a sight, had not the horizon been indistinguishable, leaden-hued sky merging into leaden-hued sea, with no telling where one began or the other ended.

The guillemots had certainly increased in numbers—we felt we were getting warm—but were flying in all directions searching for food rather than Bear Is. Indeed in the prevailing calm conditions and no hours of darkness why should they bother to go home to roost. We would watch a flock set out purposefully as if it had to get there before closing time only to see it alight about half a mile away, merely changing its feeding ground. In one of Neville Shute's best stories, *Trustee from the Toolroom*, there is a character who successfully navigates his small boat from San Francisco to Hawaii by watching aeroplanes and birds. The vapour trails of planes are, I should think, better guides than birds; one could certainly sail from New York, say, and arrive at Shannon by following them.

In order to have supper in peace we stopped the engine. We had finished our sausage and mash and were contemplating a noble duff, David by now having mastered the art, when from on deck came the cry of "Land". Sure enough, its top just showing over a bank of fog, there could be seen the hard, black outline of a high rock. It was Stappen, the 610 ft. high stack lying off the south end of Bear Island, some five miles away and broad on the port bow. Whether attributable to luck rather than skill, a landfall such as this gives the small boat sailor unbounded pleasure. The doubt, the long suspense, and then the satisfaction and thrill of seeing this slender, black pinnacle floating above the fog, the island itself still completely hidden. For me it compensated for some hideous mistakes of the past and even took some of the sting out of the Smith's Knoll episode. Among some memorable landfalls it reminded me of our first sighting of Heard Is. in the Southern Ocean when from 40 miles away the snow-capped summit of Big Ben (9,005 ft.) appeared framed in a patch of blue in the middle of a great cumulus cloud high above the sea.

Circumnavigation of Spitzbergen
(from *Triumph and Tribulation*)

Turning eastwards along the north coast we soon spotted the radio masts and buildings of the weather station. An "open bay" is the official description of Nordhamm and when we closed it at midnight, so little shelter did it seem to offer that I thought the word "bay" might as well have been omitted. We anchored in 4 fms. with an ugly looking rock reef some fifty yards astern. A weather station is on duty all round the clock. As we came in they were busy launching a boat and presently six guests crammed into the cabin to be entertained with cocoa and rum.

From Bear Island they made north to Vestspitzbergen and the administrative capital, Longyearbyen. On the way Tilman had the rare satisfaction of taking a meridian sun sight at midnight. Engine trouble developed, however.

Paul had been wrestling with the engine ever since we arrived and had to confess himself baffled. Hence the calling in of the mechanic who after spending eight hours on the job could only suggest that we might need a new injector pump. Since the part would have to be ordered from Norway and brought out this did not help very much. Nevertheless, for his eight hours' work the Company, having their shareholders to consider, billed me for £52. This exorbitant sum shook me and outraged Paul's frugal Yorkshire instincts so much that he immediately set to work again on the engine, discovered at last that the timing was at fault, and soon had it running perfectly. Although we had got nothing for our money the bill had to be paid in full, the Company insisting on the cash and not caring who got the credit. Meantime, at the end of our second day here David was missing. He had gone ashore for what was to be two hours and had not returned.

On the whole it had been a trying day but I see from my diary that Andrew and I sat up till midnight playing chess. Before leaving we had been unable to find a sea-going chess set—one in which the pieces will stay on a moving board—so Andrew set to work with his penknife and by this time had finished a set of hand-carved pieces complete with pegs at the base to fit into the handsome board that Alan made. The chessmen finished, Andrew had tried his hand at ships in bottles, while Paul, not to be outdone, started carving seals and polar bears.

At midnight we all turned in and for the first and last time set no anchor watch in the belief that we were securely anchored. It was a disturbed night. At 1 a.m. David announced his arrival on the beach and having been brought off fell into the water while climbing on board. Alan, roused by the commotion, went to help Paul who was having trouble fishing out David, for it is no easy matter hauling up a more or less inanimate body. I was on deck myself at 3 a.m. when all seemed well, but half an hour later there was a bump and we found ourselves alongside a small vessel anchored much further out. Veering all the cable we had we dropped clear astern of her and then found that our cable was foul of her anchor. The two men on board whose sleep we had disturbed proved to be remarkably good-natured. Instead of venting a torrent of Norwegian Billingsgate they calmly made their appreciation, as the military say, got their anchor up, freed our cable, and anchored themselves again further away from the enemy.

David's long search for an escape from *Baroque* or an alternative means of getting home had failed, as inevitably it must in a place like Longyearbyen, especially if the searcher is without money. Consequently he was in a morose, unhappy mood, and most unwilling to face the inevitable. He had not yet attained to Lord Curzon's lofty philosophy: "It is inevitable, therefore it can be approved". But once we had left Longyearbyen, when with a little wishful thinking one could say that we were homeward-bound, he pulled himself together, cast care aside, and worked in the galley with zest and great success, running it more or less like clockwork with fewer and fewer calls upon Andrew to do some winding. Meantime he had something to occupy his mind in the matter of getting his clothes dried which he managed by having them steamed at the power station.

Paul, with the engine now going to his satisfaction, took a day off to go fossicking among the old mine workings. Industrial archaeology, he called it, and together with Alan triumphantly brought back some old miner's lamps which they lovingly cleaned and polished. All was grist to their mill. Besides lamps they had a pair of boots—miner's boots presumably—reindeer horns, and the skull of an Arctic fox, or maybe a domestic dog. As mementoes of Svalbard, for they had started collecting them at Bear Island, bones were highly prized by all the crew, bones of whales, seals, bears, and, of course, reindeer horns. Later on, at more than one anchorage, where there were the graves of old-time whaling men and trappers, I admired their restraint in not digging up a skeleton or two for their collection. These relics were not really welcome in the cabin, so we had a large box for them on deck.

We waited until 12th July in order to collect some expected mail and early that morning the cruise ship *Regina Magna* came in. Hundreds of tourists, Europeans, or at any rate middle-Europeans, disembarked to proceed by bus and taxi to the Post Office and the shop. A few of the hardier types preferred to walk and these became the prey of some enterprising Norwegian boys who had set up a stall by the roadside for the sale of fossils. Vestspitzbergen is rich in fossils.

Among the stores that we had bought were 24 loaves of white bread and it was the nature of this bread that really determined our next port of call. According to Sir Fopling Flutter, "Beyond Hyde Park all is desert"; beyond Longyearbyen, too, all is, so to speak, desert, it is the last place where anything can be bought. If we failed in our circumnavigation we should, of course, have to return by the west coast, but if we succeeded I intended going directly home (after a call at Hopen) and this implied starting from Longyearbyen with stores, including bread, for two months. The only kind of bread that would keep that long without going mouldy is black bread, readily obtainable in Greenland, for instance, under the name of "rugbrod". It has the additional advantage of becoming harder with age so that as time goes on the crew eat less and less. None of this could be had at Longyearbyen but I readily assumed that Russians would eat nothing else, despising anything so cissy as white bread. The Russian mining town of Barentsburg was therefore to be our next stop.

The Russians lease two mines at Isfjord, one at Pyramiden at

the head of the fjord and another at Barentsburg in Greenfjord
on the same side of Isfjord as Longyearbyen and close to the
entrance. Compared with most coal mines those in Vestspitzbergen are easy to work. The seams lie high up on the hillside
so that instead of deep shafts having to be sunk they can be
reached by adits driven in at the same level; moreover the
mines are close to the sea and the coal goes direct from the
mine to the ship's hold—in the case of Longyearbyen by a
cable conveyor 2½ miles in length. Finally owing to the frozen
soil there are no water problems and little need for pit props.

Thanks to a fresh northerly breeze, by supper time we were
off the Greenfjord entrance where we gybed and sailed in.
Inside the wind died away, thus frustrating our hope of
astonishing the natives by approaching the town under sail.
Why the fjord was named Green Harbour by Poole in 1610 is
not immediately obvious, unless it was because there are no
glaciers in sight. Three ships lay at anchor waiting to load and
one lay alongside a small jetty having coal poured into her in
rather slow time. Unlike Longyearbyen the town is compact,
all the buildings, badly in need of paint, huddled together a
few hundred feet above the jetty. Three helicopters were
parked nearby. Having cruised up and down and found no
obvious anchorage for small craft we decided to anchor off a
little bit of beach just ahead of the vessel coaling. By then (10
p.m.) a crowd of curious sightseers had gathered on the beach,
many of them armed with cameras. Close in the water shoaled
abruptly to 3 fms. Going hard astern had no effect—we should
have remembered—so that we slid gently to rest on the mud
almost eyeball to eyeball with the nearest Russian.

One could almost have waded, but I rowed ashore and
presently got into conversation with one of the reception
party. Conversation, implying two-way traffic, is hardly the
word. While my new-found friend volleyed away in fluent
German, the only words in that language that I could summon
up were "schwarzbrod" and "funfzehn". Apparently he got
the message. It was too late then, but early next morning we
should have our fifteen loaves of black bread. Meantime a
kindly bystander, catching at least part of the message, rushed
off and returned with four white loaves for which he firmly

refused the proffered cigarettes.

Back on board we had a visitor, a young Norwegian working for a Norwegian company who were laying a pipe-line across Greenfjord to augment Barentsburg's water supply. He messed with the Russians and found it distressing—beans for the most part and liberal quantities of poor quality margarine with everything. Instead of beer, which was not to be had, they got a ration of two bottles of vodka a month, and should we happen to have on board a copy of *Playboy* we could swop it for three bottles of vodka. He confirmed what one would suspect, namely that Russia is not so destitute of coal deposits that they have to be eked out with Spitzbergen coal, and that the leasing of the mines there is more for the sake of maintaining a foothold.

Early next morning before anyone was about I went ashore again for a quick look round. The only way of getting from sea level to the town above, apart from the coal chute, seemed to be by way of a long flight of wooden steps. This possibly accounted for the mass of material piled anyhow on the beach almost down to tidemark—iron pipes by the mile, steel joists, cement, timber, drums of cable, coils of wire. Except for the absence of warlike stores it might have been a badly organised war-time beach-head. Halfway up the steps was a mammoth greenhouse crammed with plants which I could not identify from outside. The door was locked. In this they were one-up on Longyearbyen though the produce from a single green-house would not go far among the thousand or more inhabitants of Barentsburg.

When the whistle blew and work started our beach re-mained singularly empty. No one came near it. Copies of *Playboy* would have found no takers, trade and barter had ceased, the Iron Curtain lowered and the Cold War resumed. Word must have gone around that fraternising with yacht-owning, capitalist lackeys must cease. All cameras had been put away or confiscated. Hours passed and no one came near the beach or so much as looked at us. We had already kedged ourselves off the mud, so when noon came and found us still, as it were, in quarantine, we got our anchor and sailed for the north. So much for Russian black bread.

Breadless, they sailed on around Vestspitzbergen, climbed, and saw their first polar bears. The circumnavigation was a complete success, nearly marred by a spectacular grounding in the narrow channel of Freemansund, between two of the eastern islands of the group, Edgeoya and Barentsoya. For a while it seemed as if Tilman was to lose his third boat.

The breeze having died we were again under engine when at 4 a.m. I took over the watch from Alan. What followed is not easy to explain and still less easy to excuse. Perhaps, having spent the last three days mostly on deck and enjoyed only disturbed nights, I was not as bright as I should have been. Zeiloyane, the two islets mentioned above, were in sight ahead and with the west-going ebb under us we were rapidly approaching them. We had already discovered that west of C. Heuglin along the north coast of Edge Is. the water was shoal and we intended passing north of the Zeiloyane islets. I had my eyes fixed on one but the northernmost looked to me like a spit of land projecting from the coast of Barents Is. What with the engine and the tide which, as we neared the islets seemed to gather speed for its rush through the channel, we must have been making 7 or 8 knots over the ground. Before I had really hoisted in what was happening we were heading between the two islets which are a mile or so apart. To attempt to pass between unknown islets however wide apart they may be is always a hazardous proceeding. A shoal extended the whole way between the two and the rate we were going ensured our being carried right up on the back of it before we ground to a stop.

If the crew thought the old man had taken leave of his senses, as they must have done, they studiously refrained from comment. As soon as the tide slackened a bit we ran out a kedge astern bringing the warp forward to the winch. The engine, as we knew, had no power in reverse and the winch alone failed to budge her. Circumstances had combined to make things as difficult as they could be. Although the ebb had been running for an hour or more we must have gone on at or near the highest level of water; it was three days after full moon so that the tides were taking off. The differences between high and low water proved to be only around 2 ft. which in one way was a good thing because the boat remained more or less upright. What happens, I think, is that when the ebb starts running west the water piles up in the narrow, twenty-two mile long strait and thus continues to rise or at any rate maintains its level at the eastern end when it should be falling. Something similar occurs at the eastern end of the Magellan Straits where the water is pent up in the First and Second Narrows with the result that the west-going and east-going streams continue running in the channel for three hours after high and low water by the shore. There, too, as we found in Freemansund, the duration of slack water is barely noticeable.

Our next move was to take out half the ballast and jettison it over the side. We had no choice. The nearest islet was half-a-mile away and in the absence of any appreciable slack water there was no question of rowing a heavily-laden dinghy that far. In spite of a strong westerly wind blowing out of the strait—a wind that blew incessantly for the next few days—the sea remained calm and the boat motionless. There was thus no fear of the boat damaging herself by pounding, but we had something else to worry about. When the west-going stream started again it brought with it numerous ice-floes, large and small. The big ones grounded on the edge of the shoal about fifty yards away where they furnished a kind of protective barrier. There were, however, gaps in the barrier through which any piece of ice that drew less than 6 ft. or 7 ft. of water found its way, and by driving past the boat at a rate of several knots threatened disaster to either our rudder or our propeller. Bits of ice moving at that rate, even if they weighed only half a ton or so, could neither be stopped nor diverted with boat-hooks. Watching a small floe apparently on a collision course we could only hold our breath and hope. Twice the rudder sustained a savage blow. Nor were we much better off when the tide turned, when those that had already passed came back with the flood.

No one doubted that we should get her off in time—at least no doubts were expressed—but I felt that we had only to stay there long enough for the worst to happen. Damage to the rudder would be bad enough but if the propeller were damaged the chances of getting off would be much reduced; for by now it was clear that we must get her facing the way she had come so that the engine could be used to advantage. We were a sitting target for these floes, dependent entirely upon luck. We could not afford to be aground three days as *Mischief* had been on her first voyage in '54 when she stuck on a reef in a Patagonia fjord. In the course of three days 3 tons of ballast were ferried ashore and she floated off. In the meantime drifting ice of far smaller dimensions than the Freemansund floes stripped the propeller blades and bent the shaft. Happily on that occasion, by being away on the ice-cap at the time, I was not only free from blame but also escaped the strains and stresses resulting from the stranding of a vessel, especially for the owner.

In the afternoon, near high water, we made several attempts to pull her head round, for until we could get her pointing the way she had come and so make full use of the engine we should never get off. Having got us into this mess I at least should have had skilly for supper, instead we finished up with one of David's increasingly majestic duffs. Care weighing heavy upon me, I could only toy with this, notwithstanding the advice of that strong-minded gastronome Dr Oppimian—"Whatever happens in this world, never let it spoil your dinner." No doubt the reverend doctor had never assisted at a stranding, a stranding that might well become a shipwreck if a piece of ice with *Baroque*'s name on it hit her in a vital spot. The crew having disposed of the duff we turned with renewed vigour to taking out the remainder of the ballast and emptying all the water tanks but for a few gallons for immediate use. The crew worked like heroes, Paul groping away in the bilge prizing out the slimy chunks of pig-iron—some weighing 80 to 90 lbs.—from the filthy bed where for years they had lain undisturbed. In no time all were once more coated from head to foot in black, oily sludge. Besides all the ballast and most of the water, we threw overboard an old flax mainsail that we had been carrying as a spare. It dated from the days of *Mischief* and when wet, as the sails stowed on a rack in the peak always were, it must have weighed about four hundredweight. Normally I get a lot of harmless pleasure from throwing overboard superfluous gear. The mainsail might be included in that category, but certainly not the ballast.

We had already lost a kedge and now Andrew went off in the dinghy with the big Fisherman type anchor hanging over the stern ready to drop in the selected spot. This anchor weighed about 1 cwt. and we were reconciled to losing that, too, for if she came off we were not going to risk going aground again while making an effort to retrieve it. The boat was now a lot lighter and in the course of the night by heaving away on the firmly embedded big anchor, little by little we brought her head round until at last she pointed in the right direction. The westerly wind still blew vigorously out of the strait. It seemed to be an almost permanent local feature and later when we were trying to make headway through the strait we had good reason to curse it. As they say in Africa, cross the river before you start reviling the crocodile's mother, and at this juncture, twenty-four hours after the first stranding, we wanted a west wind, the more the better. So with the whole mainsail and staysail set and drawing, the flood tide making, the engine flat out, the kedge warp quivering under the strain of the winch, and a subdued cheer from the crew, she began to move.

The big anchor had played its part, and having got in all the warp we could before it grew wide on the beam we cut it, and a moment later came to a shuddering stop alongside a large floe grounded on the edge of the shoal. We lost no time in playing our last card, another small kedge anchor of only about 25 lbs. weight. Surprisingly enough this diminutive anchor took good hold, and as we winched in on it—the sails, the engine, and the tide all working hard to assist—the boat reluctantly bumped her way off. We were too anxious to be clear of this baleful shoal to bother with the little anchor. This, too, became a sacrifice together with two other anchors, all the ballast, and the old mainsail. Our only remaining anchor was the 60 lbs. CQR which we normally used.

Giving the northernmost Zeiloyane islet the widest possible berth we headed for Freemansund, the ebb tide by then having begun to run. But even with the tide under us we made little progress against the westerly wind, so we sheered off to the north to anchor off the south-east corner of Barents Is. where we obtained a bit of a lee. In this short sail, while the absence of any ballast did not seem to make the boat unduly tender, the complaints that came from the rudder could hardly be ignored. After the two blows it had sustained from the ice, the fact that it was still there and still steering the ship was more surprising than the play one felt in the tiller and the occasional groans from under the counter.

When we sailed out next morning and were clear of the shelter of Barents Is. we faced the same west wind. Nevertheless we managed to make good some five miles inside the strait before the turn of the tide obliged us to make for the north shore where behind a little cape we found less wind and less current. Half a mile to the east the high ice front of the Freeman glacier projected well into the water. From this floes frequently broke off though few of them found their way into our shallow bay. Before beginning the long haul homewards we needed ballast and water and I had intended to look for these at some anchorage in Storfjord where one might expect to be free from the strong winds and currents of Freemansund. On going ashore that evening, however, I found a small trickle of water that if dammed up we could collect, as well as an assortment of reasonably sized stones. Like the plums in a poor man's duff they were not that plentiful and would need gathering, but we might go further and fare worse so I decided to stock up here. The plain that extended inland looked as barren as the beach, yet on it I counted eighteen reindeer busily grazing. Like yaks, they seem to subsist or even thrive on a diet of gravel slightly flavoured with moss.

The evil day had at last come when, our bread finished, we had to go on to biscuit, and since the supply of that was not abundant we agreed on a remarkably small daily ration. After a large dose of stiff porridge most of us went without breakfast allotment, saving it for lunch when it could be used to convey to the mouth cheese, sardine or peanut butter, all more interesting than marmalade. We were lying a good 400 yards out and when deciding to fill up here with ballast and water I had assumed we could bring the boat much closer to the beach. Andrew went off in the dinghy to take soundings and when he found the water started to shoal almost under the bows I regretted my decision and had half a mind to push on. However, we blew up the inflatable dinghy and set to work with that and the pram dinghy, our working hours being limited by the duration of the ebb tide. The west wind, we found, almost sufficed to offset the effect of the west-going stream. When the flood ran, with the wind behind it, work had to stop.

Since the amount of stone that could be got into the space occupied by the jettisoned pig-iron, which we estimated to be nearly 3 tons, would not weigh nearly so much, we made additional space for ballast by emptying the food lockers under the bunks on either side of the cabin, stowing more in the main food locker forward which by now was half empty. Even when stones had been shoved into every available hole and corner the pessimists reckoned that we should not be carrying more than 2 tons. Others put it as high as 2½ tons, while Andrew, despising guesswork, invoked the aid of Archimedes and his well-known Principles. Weighing on our spring balance a piece of iron and a piece of stone, he then measured the volume of water that each displaced and in due course, all calculations made and checked, announced smugly that our stone ballast would weigh exactly a quarter of the original pig-iron, or rather less than a ton. So much for what Goethe called the charnel house of science. Nothing has an uglier look than reason when it is not on our side and we hastened to tell Andrew what he could do with Archimedes and his bath-water.

For most of the next day the wind proved too strong for the tide and it was not until after supper that ferrying began again. By midnight, when only one load of stones and two of water were needed to complete the job, a brief puff of wind discouraged the crew. I was set on getting away on the morning tide and the crew, seeing my disappointment, fell to again. By 2 a.m. we were getting the dinghies on board for the last time. Ever since the stranding they had cheerfully given all they had in back-breaking, wet, and grimy toil to retrieve a bad situation. Accordingly, on the morning of 10th August, the west wind much less than usual, we completed the passage of Freemansund, homeward bound at last.

The voyage home, with improvised ballast, passed safely; but it was for Tilman an unhappy homecoming. In the Lymington river, he was told the news that his sister Adeline, with whom he had shared a home for most of his life, had died.

THE LAST VOYAGE NORTH

The Spitzbergen stones taken on as emergency ballast were soon claimed by souvenir-hunters from the quay at Lymington; one of them was fitted with an inscribed brass plate and presented to Tilman by the Lymington Town Sailing Club. Despite the blow of his sister's death, and his advanced age—seventy-seven—he decided not to give up the Arctic yet.

BY THE AUTUMN of 1974 circumstances had changed for the worse. I had now to face living entirely alone like a Himalayan ascetic in his mountain cave—a spacious cave, I admit, far too spacious for one man. Instead of making it easier, this made it harder to get away either for long or short periods, what with the dogs who shared master's cave and other considerations. Increasing feebleness would oblige me to swallow the anchor some day and that day was not far off. Dwindling resources, too, along with inflated bills plus 25% VAT. Like Tallulah Bankhead, in similar hard times, one began to wonder where the next magnum was coming from. In this weak frame of mind I even questioned the making of another voyage, to regard *Baroque*'s circumnavigation of Spitzbergen as a fitting occasion, a memorable last act, upon which to ring down the curtain. Wisdom certainly pointed that way but whenever there has been a choice between wisdom and what many might regard as folly I have usually chosen the latter. Strenuousness, we are told, is the immortal path, sloth is the way of death. Well aware of this truth I left the question for the moment, with a slight bias in favour of action.

In 1975, therefore, he sailed for Greenland again and, despite breaking the boom, reached home successfully with the mainsail set loose-footed. In 1976 the goal was Ellesmere Island, in the far north of

Baffin Bay. His crew consisted of two friends, Richard and Jim, a retired businessman, David Burrows , and a Scot named Hamish who left at Falmouth, "capsizing the dinghy alongside and falling into the drink. For the first and last time on the voyage, the crew enjoyed a wholehearted laugh". His replacement was Mike Holland, of Chichester.

As a general routine David worked most of the day, either on the engine, or tracking down leaks and stopping them, or many small jobs that were of benefit to the ship; Richard and Jim read voraciously or held long private conferences, while Mike mostly slept. The winds were mostly from the wrong direction and in the first week out from Falmouth we had made good a pitiful 240 miles. In the second week we did better, logging just under 400 miles, for by then we were beyond the influence of the anti-cyclonic weather that prevailed over the British Isles for most of a memorable summer. Iceland, on the other hand, had a very poor summer, while in the North Atlantic the month of June which is usually fairly quiet proved to be pretty boisterous. Besides a frightening bang like that from a 15-inch gun as Concorde passed overhead there were other disconcerting incidents. Because I had the mains'l down for stitching, we were motoring when Jim discovered that the port side fuel tank had again shifted and was dripping oil on to the hot exhaust pipe. The tank had to be emptied before we could get it upright and secured for a full due. A moderate gale on the 8th June broke a pane in the galley skylight and an immoderate gale the following night made her leak so much that we handed the sails and lay-a-hull. The drips from the deckhead over my bunk obliged me to rig plastic gutters under two of the beams; but strangely enough Richard's bunk, almost directly under the fore-hatch, remained driest of all.

A flat calm on the 10th induced us to make use of the engine when we discovered the batteries were flat. Jim attributed this to salt water though in the doghouse where the batteries live there had so far been nothing more serious than drips. David immediately set about converting the anchor winch handle into a starting handle and at that time there may have been just enough left in the batteries for this plan to succeed. Meantime with no engine and no compass light we were still a lot better off than earlier Greenland-bound voyagers. "Hellish dark and smells of cheese," was James Pigg's report on the night's weather, having when drunk looked into a cupboard instead of out of a window. So it was that night except for the smell and the darkness was accentuated by a featureless layer of cloud that blended sea and sky together indistinguishably. Without a compass steering was difficult and within five minutes of taking over from me David executed a Chinese gybe, so I went back and stayed on until it began to get light. In such conditions one needs to discard hoods, hats, and towels round the neck in order to steer by feeling the wind.

Saturday 12th June might be called Black Saturday in that it put paid to any hope of our reaching Ellesmere Is. After heavy squalls of wind and rain the previous evening the sky had cleared but the wind remained fresh. With three rolls in the mains'l we were heading north, the best we could do, and at the awkward hour of 5 a.m. a seam in the mains'l started to go. By the time enough hands had mustered to get the sail down some twenty feet of seam had gone as well as some bad tears crosswise. This was a serious blow for I could see little chance of repairing the sail at sea. It is far too big to have below for stitching and this could be done on deck only in more or less windless weather. These horizontal seams were a nuisance. A tear of an inch or so soon became an ell, and after the last voyage I had made a mental note to have narrow strips sewn every few feet vertically from head to foot. For me mental notes are not enough with the result that nothing had been done. On this occasion, after the sail had been repaired in rather amateurish fashion by a Reykjavik sailmaker, I added some cross strips myself. On land, bolting the stable door after the horse's departure is a well-known exercise; at sea it takes the form of handing a sail after it is ripped. With the wind backing and the glass falling, as they were, prudence should have suggested setting the trys'l instead of reefing the mains'l. The trouble is that roller reefing is too easy so that instead of changing sails one is inclined merely to put in more rolls.

This was only the start of Black Saturday. We set the trys'l, and after breakfast it began to blow in earnest, the barometer having fallen to 992 mbs. At two o'clock when we were doing 5 knots and making a lot of water, not to mention the odd spout through the skylight, we handed the trys'l and pressed on under the jib. Two hours later this had to come down for the sea had built up and waves were beginning to break with the usual menacing roars. Lying-a-hull with no sails set the vessel lies broadside on to wind and sea. Whether this is better or worse than heaving-to, when with a minimum of sail set she takes wind and sea on the weather bow, is a moot point. In either case the drift to leeward is the same, from 20 to 30 miles a day in a full gale. If lying-a-hull, there are no sails to blow out and there may be less strain on the rudder, on the other hand, if broadside on, a boat is more vulnerable than when lying bow on, especially if like *Baroque* she has a lofty and fragile dog-house. We had not been lying-a-hull long before a wave broke alongside and bashed in the starboard side of this erection, flooding the chartroom (for that is what is inside) with all the charts, navigational books, log books, sextant, chronometer watch, not to mention the batteries which on this occasion really did have a salt water bath. David got to work boarding up the hole and for good measure put boards over the port side as well. Meantime I got her before the wind and we ran under bare poles, a stratagem that did not escape the notice of Poseidon, ruler of the waves, for one of these promptly broke over the counter, cracking a bit more of the doghouse, filling the cockpit, and in its retreat nearly dragging the skipper through the life-rails.

To keep her before the wind with no sail set was not easy and when darkness fell we once more lay-a-hull. It blew hard until morning when the wind veered north-west and dropped to a steady Force 6 at which it remained all day. Richard retired from his watch at 2 a.m. to remain all day in his bunk suffering as he said from "exposure". Except for David, the crew seemed to be a little shaken by this gale. As I surveyed the scene on deck Mike took me aback by remarking that he assumed we should now be returning home, and no doubt he was equally astonished by my reply. He then said he would quit at the first opportunity and all three were decided we should go to Reykjavik for repairs, then about 500 miles to the north. Cape Farewell, for which the wind might be less favourable, was about 600 and from there to Godthaab another 400 miles. The lack of mains'l and engine, and the impossibility of finding at Godthaab a replacement for Mike, inclined me at first to agree; though over-riding these arguments should have been the fact that going to Reykjavik implied giving up Ellesmere Is. My own private thoughts about Mike were that if we got to Godthaab, the fact that we were still afloat and the high cost of getting away from there as compared with Reykjavik, might induce him to change his mind.

For the next three days the weather continued boisterous, though with winds mainly from west we were able to lay the course for Iceland. The serving of the eye-splice of the forestay round the mast had come off and to my annoyance chafed through the jib halyard, an almost new terylene rope. With no jib our speed fell off dismally and several days elapsed before we could get Jim aloft in his climbing harness with a top rope to reeve a new halyard. David made and discarded several versions of a starting handle for the engine and when his Mark V version, from which he expected success, failed like the others, he gave it up as a bad job.

The wind then began blowing from the direction of Iceland right in our teeth and when this had gone on for two days I altered course for C. Farewell hoping that by now the others would have recovered their nerve and see reason. We were then on the same latitude about 500 miles away and the wind was fair. Jim, who had become spokesman for the malcontents, at once protested, calling it an "undemocratic" decision, and at the sailor's Soviet he presently convened David and I found ourselves in a minority. Had I had any eloquence now was the time for an appeal to their better natures or even to their self-respect, but I felt mere disgust and no doubt allowed it to show. For me the voyage had now no aim and I could not feel much regard for those who had so tamely abandoned its objective. They were not the ill-conditioned lot that I had suffered from in '68 on *Mischief*'s last southern voyage—I felt no likelihood of being pushed overboard or knocked on the head—they merely lacked the requisite zeal. Giving up Elles-mere Is. also meant my failing to keep a promise of calling at Igdlorssuit, where we had been on *Baroque*'s first voyage, in order to bring back a Zodiac left there by a friend of mine, Professor Drever, who had recently died. To press on with an unwilling crew, who apparently expected the next gale to sink us, would be an ill task for which I had neither will nor strength. It is easy to criticise. When reviling it is not necessary to prepare a preliminary draft, but it occurs to me that for the state of affairs we had then reached I should have reviled myself. In the army one learnt that there were no bad regi-ments, battalions, batteries, there were only bad officers, and in the present case the skipper who had recruited his crew in the first place and who then failed to jolly them along and to infect them with some notion of high endeavour, was himself to blame. That said there is the truism about silk purses and sow's ears, and the fact that you can't hang soft cheese on iron hooks.

They made Reykjavik for repairs (and there, incidentally, had to move over for Tim Severin's remarkable hide boat Brendan*); Mike left and a replacement, another Hamish, arrived. To salvage some-thing of the voyage, Tilman resolved to cross to Angmagssalik on the East Greenland coast. It was not a lucky decision. On the crossing, the staysail split and had to be sewed; Tilman, untypically, felt unwell and had to spend time in his bunk, in three sweaters; finally they took uneasy refuge in King Oskar's Havn, up Angmagssalik fjord, and on trying to leave,* Baroque *struck a rock ledge and met near-disaster.*

We got too near the side. In Greenland fjords it is usually safe to go within spitting distance of a rock shore but not on this occasion. We should have gone astern, instead we came firmly to rest on a rock on a falling tide. As she floated easily enough at high water that evening I might have laughed the incident off as a minor mistake; what followed this mistake was disastrous and no laughing matter at all. Having wasted some time trying vainly to kedge off I picked up the first handy coil of rope, shackled it to the throat halyard block and sent Richard ashore to anchor it. We were close to the oil installation where some concrete posts came in useful as strong points. I had thought of using this coil of rope for the mainsheet and when I tried putting in an eye-splice had found the strands so tightly laid up that I gave it best. It proved to be nylon with apparently unlimited stretch. By the time I had grasped this and begun to unreeve the peak halyards for use as a masthead line *Baroque* had listed to 45° and was beyond recovery. The nylon line went on stretching until she finished up on her beam ends, the deck vertical. Meantime David had been trying to lighten her, sending ashore the heavy anchor and cable, draining the water tanks, and even lifting the floor-boards with a view to getting out the ballast—all to no purpose.

By afternoon we had four lines from mast to shore, a tackle on each, together with a very capable Greenlander who came along to encourage and assist. With David and I tailing behind he did most of the work as we gained a few inches on each line in turn in an effort to get the boat upright before the rising tide flooded her. I never saw the rest of the crew who must have gone shopping. At the extreme angle the boat lay over, the lines had little lifting power and needless to say the tide won, rising inexorably inch by inch, until long before we had her even half upright she was completely full of water. Little enough that was of use or value had been got out—all the food, except that in tins, was destroyed, clocks, barometer, binoculars, camera, film, radio, clothes, sleeping bags, and worst of all the engine and batteries, all soaked in a mixture of diesel oil and sea water. A number of Danes and Greenlanders had gathered on the rocks to watch. One of the Greenlanders took the opportunity to pocket a thousand or so of David's cigarettes lying among the small pile of stuff that had been salvaged. When detected by David and forced to disgorge the bystanders merely laughed, evidently more in sympathy with the culprit than with his victim. Among the Danes was the man in charge of the oil installation who offered at a price, a high one, to pump out the boat. They ran a power line down, put a pump on board, and within an hour had all the water out.

By then she had floated off so I got them to tow her to the buoy. We then began ferrying the salvaged stuff on board in the dinghy. I stood by until the last load had gone and it was about 10 p.m. before I got back on board.

What a homecoming! Anything floatable had floated so that debris lay about everywhere, a film of oil covered everything, the floorboards were up, and both pumps were at work. While lying on her beam ends a plank had been started. David slightly lessened the copious flow by cutting up a rag and stuffing bits in, but the pumps had to be kept going all night. A hut at the oil installation had kindly been put at our disposal and we took it in turns to row over and doss down for a couple of hours in a warm, dry room. Early in the morning I got hold of Martin who came off and speedily stopped the leak with his sawdust trick. A bucketful of sawdust with a long pole attached to the handle is capsized alongside bottom up, thrust smartly down to the vicinity of the leak where, by joggling the pole, the sawdust escapes and is sucked into the leak. A refinement is to have a box with a sliding lid, actuated by a line, fixed to the pole. When the box is in position the lid is drawn and the sawdust released. I arranged with Martin that after the week-end we would beach *Baroque* so that he could put tingles over the leak.

David and Jim had drained the engine and cleaned it out but the electrical parts needed professional attention. Through the hospital doctor, whom I knew, I got in touch with a Dane who ran a taxi and plant-hire business who sent two of his mechanics on board that evening. They soon had the cylinder off and took the batteries, dynamo, and starter motor to their workshop. From the doctor, by the way, we received other kindnesses including gifts of whale meat and arctic char and the use of his house to dry out our gear. Our beaching arrangements looked like being in jeopardy when the local hospital ship limped in with propeller trouble. The beach, which is reasonably smooth, is very small and the hospital ship obviously had first claim; in the end, however, Martin, who is in charge of all repair work, got us in together. The acting skipper of the hospital ship paid me a visit along with his cook, also acting, who turned out to be an Englishman, a very dark

one. The skipper's real motive was to buy spirits and I had to
tell him I would rather he drank them on board, which he did
with a will. Greenlanders can buy alcohol only in the form of
beer (Carlsberg or Tuborg lager) and the sale of that is stopped
on Fridays in the hope that the wives will be able to grab
enough of their man's wages for housekeeping. The skipper
looked forward to retiring early in order to devote all his time
to the business or pastime of seal-hunting to which he was
addicted. His English was nearly as good as that of the cook
and both became increasingly voluble. Not surprisingly, from
this rum session only one item of seal lore remains clear,
namely that the blue-back skin is the best, followed by that of
the ring seal.

Except for David the crew had now taken to sleeping
ashore. The boat seemed the more wholesome for it though I
realised that it would be difficult to sail without them. They
turned up on the Monday and at high water we rowed the boat
with our sweeps on to the beach in the wake of the hospital
ship. The rise and fall of the tide is from 8 to 10 ft. and in the
absence of any wall to lean against we rigged lines to keep her
upright. By late evening Martin had finished his tingles of felt
covered with aluminium sheet and we kedged off as soon as
she floated. Instead of the calm conditions of the morning
there were violent gusts of wind and what with this and the
numerous small craft yawing wildly at their moorings we had
to anchor before we were in deep enough water. By midnight,
with another three hours of ebb to go, she was on the bottom.
With the sweeps and a big baulk of timber David and I rigged
legs and also took a long line from the mast ashore. Half of this
long line turned out to be the same damned line that had
literally let us down before, but the boat was still upright and
every ten minutes or so we took in the slack by hauling on the
throat halyards. The legs appeared to be taking most of the
weight so when the mast line became block on block we let it
go in order to shorten it, whereupon the lashing of the
midships leg parted and over she went with a bang. She was
nothing like right over and by pumping we kept the water
down until she began to lift when, having rigged another
masthead line, by heaving in on both we presently got her

upright. David and I spent the night on deck, the crew's contribution being pumping and saving their gear from the threatened inundation.

My relations with them were becoming strained and these came to a head the next afternoon. After our all-night performance I wanted some sleep and with Richard prowling about on deck in his climbing boots I found it difficult. My suggestion that he should either come below or jump over the side was not well received. All three hastened below to announce that they were quitting, that they were unhappy, and that the boat was not safe. What, I think, they really wanted was to oblige me to leave the boat at Angmagssalik and so make me responsible for getting them home. Rather than this I reckoned that David and I could take her to Reykjavik and hope to get some more crew there. Richard took his gear ashore. Hamish packed his but continued using the boat as a restaurant, while Jim, who had some sense of duty, declared that "he was ready to stick his neck out" but only as far as Reykjavik, and always provided the engine worked.

Owing to the exertions of the last few days I felt extremely weak and could only crawl around. We had once more to arrange for taking on water and fuel and before that could be done the fuel tanks needed draining off and a water pipe had to be repaired. When she was full of water the cabin water tank had come adrift and broken the outlet pipe. At this time *Tycho Brahe* came in. She had landed her geologists at Kulusuk, whence they would fly home, and she was now homeward bound empty. Her skipper, whom I did not meet, apparently advised or even invited *Baroque*'s crew to take passage with him. Richard was on board like a shot and that night, or rather at three in the morning, a voice by my bunk was heard intoning: "This is Hamish. I've come to tell you that I'm leaving."

In the morning (4th Sept.) we warped up to the quay astern of *Tycho Brahe* who was supposed to be leaving. Her skipper must have been of a cautious disposition for though she was a vessel built to shunt ice, and by then there was little enough left to shunt, he was waiting for a helicopter report on ice conditions. She finally got away, spurred on by *Brandal* which was again waiting to come in, with Richard and Hamish safely on board, Richard on deck busy with warps, Hamish out of sight below. Some moderately kind words are no doubt owing to Jim, who all along had been apprehensive, for resisting the terrible temptation offered by *Tycho Brahe*, especially as the engine had not yet been started and might well never start. That was settled the same evening when the two mechanics came and in a short time had it running as well as ever.

They reached Reykjavik, and there found two crew, Nicholas and John, willing to sail to England; setting sail in rough weather, Tilman found himself again less than well, and spent a day below decks.

Wind and rain continued all night and although the man on watch could shelter in the lee of the doghouse or inside I was thankful when David offered to take my watch. We lay-to all next day in the same disagreeable weather while I had the stays'l sent below and put in the morning stitching. Apart from that I lay at earth, missing meals, and thus remained ignorant of the consultations that were no doubt going on and unprepared for the impending "bombshell", the name that journalists have for the unexpected.

Though still in the same quarter, by morning the wind had moderated and I was feeling more like myself. It was time to start sailing. Whereupon Jim piped up with a demand that we return to Reykjavik and to my astonishment and dismay David, who hitherto had been a tower of strength, doing his utmost for the success of the voyage, backed him up. "Et tu Brute," was my inevitable thought as he gave his reasons—the boat leaking, a new suit of sails needed, the skipper on the point of collapse, and another depression imminent. Naturally our two landsmen took no part in the heated dispute that followed, and considering their indifference to the weather of the last two days they must have wondered what all the fuss was about, that the two whom they took to be hardened sailors, accustomed to gales, should want to turn back. With David's support we could have taken the unhappy Jim home willy-nilly, but with the two of them bent on going back there was nothing to be done.

Besides the folly of ever spending a day or half a day in one's bunk, this episode brought home to me another disadvantage that this particular bunk had in addition to its proximity to the galley and the heads, its poor light, and a certain amount of dampness, namely that of being apart from and out of touch with the crew; so that even if one, as it were, smelt a rat, one could not, to continue the metaphor, nip it in the bud. This forced return to Reykjavik had enough implications, I think, to preclude its being received with good grace. A winter in Iceland, hauled out for something like seven months, would not improve *Baroque*, and it put paid to any lingering hopes I may have had of a voyage the following year. While Reykjavik is well placed geographically for a northern voyage, fitting out and the buying of stores there would be prohibitively expensive, and to that would be added the cost of flying out a crew.

David's imminent depression turned into an anti-cyclone that for the next week embraced Iceland and the surrounding waters. We sailed back in benign weather, sweetness and light everywhere except in *Baroque*, and by the time we made fast alongside our too familiar crane I had the stays'l repaired. Next morning Stefan, surprised by our return, took me out to Jon Elevan's yard where I made arrangements for the boat's wintering. She could not be hauled out at once as Jon had to get his slipway ready and a cradle built. He had a respect for old wooden boats, felt as much concern for *Baroque* as I did, and I was confident she would be in good hands. On returning I found David alone, Jim having already taken his gear ashore. For some reason he had undergone a change of mind and heart. I had misunderstood him and jumped to conclusions; his sole concern had been for my health and he was quite willing to finish the voyage.

Anxious as ever to get the boat home I took this revised version at its face value. As the Arabs say, the camel driver has his thoughts and the camel he has his, so I set about the unpromising task of finding a replacement for Jim. Our last hope was now the Fishermen's Union many of whose members apparently took a holiday at this time of year, generally in

Majorca. *Baroque* could not compete with Majorca, for although for many Icelanders the sea is their livelihood we never found one who wanted to make it his playground.

On the Monday, therefore, we unbent the sails, unshipped the bowsprit, and unrove the running rigging, stripping her to a gantline as the saying goes. In the absence of anyone else able or willing the skipper, despite his recently alleged failing health, spent an hour or so aloft unshackling and sending down all the wire ropes, blocks, and strops. When the gear had been labelled Jon took it to his store. Nicholas and John were still on board to give us a hand, and apart from my own feelings over this mournful affair I felt that they had been badly let down. In due course, I hope *Baroque* will sail back to England and that will probably be my last voyage in her. As my birthday is in February it would be difficult to celebrate my eightieth north of the Arctic Circle, though I should have liked to have made a voyage in her in 1978 if only as a gesture of defiance. However, steeply rising costs and waning strength had already inclined me to call a halt, and now with the boat lying at Reykjavik, together with the frightening possibility that one might again be stuck with a similar crew, the decision is no longer in doubt. As Conrad's old seaman Singleton remarked: "Ships are all right, it's the men in them."

The verses below by Humbert Wolfe are by way of farewell to the few who have followed my varied fortunes. They appeal especially to me now because three great beech trees below the window where I write are still stripping themselves. In the last verse perhaps poetic licence will allow the use of "running close-hauled" though it grates on a seaman's ear. Just as it is proverbially impossible to blow and swallow at the same time, so is it to run and sail close-hauled.

> Listen! The wind is rising
> and the air is wild with leaves;
> we have had our summer evenings;
> now for October eves.
>
> The great beech trees lean forward,
> and strip like a diver, we

had better turn to the fire
and shut our mind to the sea

where the ships of youth are running
close-hauled on the edge of the wind,
with all adventure before them
and only the old behind.

The ships of youth did not leave H. W. Tilman behind, after all. In May and June 1977 he sailed Baroque *home to Lymington and arranged her sale. In August of the same year Simon Richardson, a valued crew on* Baroque's *first Greenland voyage, invited him to join an expedition to Smith Island in the South Shetlands in a converted steel tug,* En Avant. *Fired by a wish to spend his eightieth birthday in the Antarctic, Tilman joined as an ordinary crew member. "A very easy life," he wrote from Rio, "doing practically nothing beyond standing a watch."*

It was to be his last adventure. En Avant *sailed southbound from Rio on 1st November 1977. Neither she nor her crew have been heard of again.*

APPENDIX

Mischief: A Chronology

Bristol Channel Pilot Cutter built at Cardiff, 1906, by Thos. Baker, East Canal Wharf. *Length* 45 feet. *Beam* 13 feet. *Draught* 7 feet 6 inches. *Net tons* 13.78. T.M. 29 tons.

1906–1919	Working pilot boat owned by William Morgan or "Billy the Mischief"	
1920	Sold for £450 to Mr Unna who sailed her to Takoradi	
1927	First appears in the Yacht Register and had subsequently in 27 years ten different owners	
1954	Bought at Malta by Ernle Bradford who sailed her to Palma, Mallorca and sold her to her present owner, H. W. Tilman	
1954	Palma—Gibraltar—Oporto—Lymington	2,000 m.
1955–56	Las Palmas—Montevideo—Magellan Straits—Valparaiso—Callao-Panama —Bermuda—Lymington (*Mischief in Patagonia*, 1957)	20,000 m.
1957–58	Las Palmas—Bahia Blanca—C. Town —Durban—Beira—Comoro Is.— Aldabra—Aden—Port Said—Malta —Gibraltar—Lymington (*Mischief Goes South*, 1968)	21,000 m.

1959–60	Las Palmas—C. Town—Iles Crozet— Kerguelen—C. Town—St Helena— Lymington	20,000 m.
	(*Mischief Among the Penguins, 1961*)	
1961	West Greenland: Godthaab— Umanak Fjord—Godthaab— Lymington	7,500 m.
	(*Mischief in Greenland, 1964*)	
1962	West Greenland: Godthaab— Evighedsfjord—Holsteinborg— Exeter Sound (Baffin Is.)—Lymington	6,500 m.
	(*Mischief in Greenland, 1964*)	
1963	Baffin Bay: Godthaab—Godhaven— Upernivik—Lancaster Sound— Bylot Is.—Pond Inlet—Godthaab— Lymington	6,500 m.
	(*Mostly Mischief, 1966*)	

Surveyed Dec. 1963 and reported no longer fit for long voyages.

1964	East Greenland: Faroe Is.—Reykjavik —Angmagssalik—Lymington	3,700 m.
	(*Mostly Mischief, 1966*)	
1965	East Greenland: Reykjavik— Angmagssalik—Skjoldungen— Lymington	4,000 m.
	(*Mostly Mischief, 1966*)	
1966–67	Las Palmas—Montevideo—Punta Arenas—South Shetland Is.—South Georgia—Montevideo—Azores— Lymington	20,400 m.
	(*Mischief Goes South, 1968*)	

Two mountains and a cape have officially been named after her—Mont du Mischief, by the French, on Ile de la Possession, Iles Crozet; Cap Mischief, also by the French, on Ile de Kerguelen; Mount Mischief, by the Canadian Survey, Exeter Sound, Baffin Is. near to Mt Raleigh.

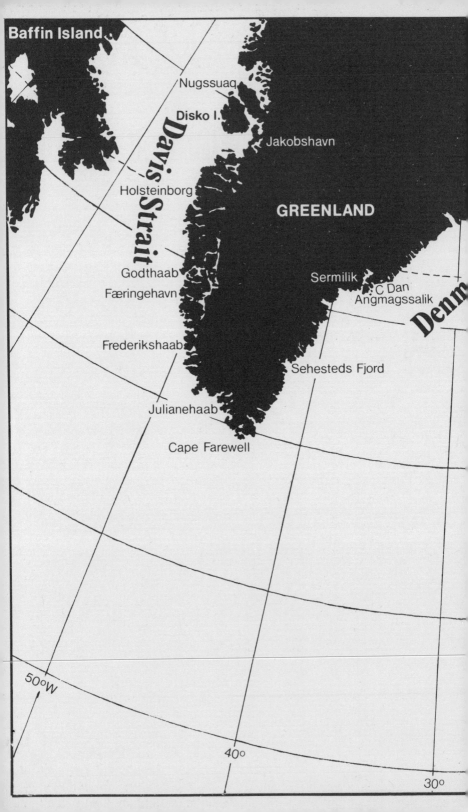